Image & Geolocation Intelligence: Reverse Searching and Mapping

Algoryth Ryker

In an era where digital footprints extend beyond text and interactions, images have become one of the most revealing sources of intelligence. Every photo tells a story, capturing not just a subject but also hidden details—geographic locations, time stamps, environmental clues, and even subtle metadata that can unlock critical information.

From identifying unknown locations in crime scene photos to verifying social media claims using satellite imagery, the field of Image and Geolocation OSINT (Open-Source Intelligence) is rapidly evolving. Investigators, journalists, cybersecurity experts, and researchers rely on these techniques to track missing persons, expose fraud, and even debunk misinformation campaigns.

This book provides a structured and practical guide to mastering Image & Geolocation OSINT. You'll learn how to reverse-search images, extract metadata, analyze photos for location clues, leverage GIS tools, and use advanced mapping techniques to uncover intelligence. Through real-world case studies, you'll see how professionals apply these methods in criminal investigations, corporate research, and fact-checking operations.

Whether you're a beginner looking to explore OSINT techniques or an experienced analyst aiming to refine your skills, this book will equip you with the knowledge and tools to extract meaningful insights from images and location data.

Chapter Breakdown

1. Basics of Image & Geolocation OSINT

- Understanding how images contribute to OSINT investigations.
- Hidden details within digital photos: metadata, context clues, and more.
- The structured OSINT workflow for image & location analysis.
- **Key challenges**: manipulated images, missing metadata, and misinformation.
- Ethical & legal concerns in tracking images and locations.

2. Reverse Image Searching: Techniques & Tools

- The science behind reverse image searches.
- How to use Google Lens, TinEye, Yandex, and other search engines.
- Advanced search operators for more precise matches.
- Finding image duplicates and tracking modified versions.
- **Case Study**: Identifying a fake social media profile using reverse image search.

3. EXIF Metadata & Digital Forensics

- Extracting EXIF metadata (camera details, timestamps, GPS coordinates).
- Tools for analyzing metadata: ExifTool, FotoForensics, and others.
- Identifying metadata tampering and missing location data.
- Cross-verifying metadata against other OSINT sources.
- **Case Study**: Finding a hidden location using image metadata.

4. Analyzing Photos for Clues: Shadows, Objects & Context

- How lighting and shadows can reveal time and direction.
- Identifying objects and recognizing patterns in images.
- Using depth, perspective, and landmarks to estimate locations.
- Spotting AI-generated and deepfake images.
- **Case Study**: Verifying the authenticity of an image through contextual analysis.

5. Social Media Image Tracking

- How social media platforms process and store images.
- Extracting hidden location clues from photos shared online.
- Tracking reposted images across multiple platforms.
- Identifying trends and viral images using OSINT tools.
- **Case Study**: Finding the original source of a viral image.

6. Identifying Landmarks & Locations in Photos

- Recognizing famous landmarks and their role in geolocation OSINT.
- Using AI-based tools for automatic landmark identification.
- Analyzing architectural and cultural markers in images.
- Cross-referencing photos with open datasets for geolocation.
- **Case Study**: Locating a person using background clues in a photo.

7. Satellite & Street View OSINT

- Leveraging satellite imagery for geolocation investigations.
- Using Google Earth, Bing Maps, and OpenStreetMap for analysis.
- Tracking location changes using historical imagery.
- The limitations of satellite data in OSINT investigations.
- **Case Study**: Confirming a suspect's location using satellite data.

8. Open-Source Mapping: Google Earth & GIS Tools

- Introduction to Geographic Information Systems (GIS) in OSINT.
- Advanced mapping techniques with Google Earth Pro.
- Extracting terrain data, coordinates, and real-world insights.
- Using open-source GIS platforms for in-depth analysis.
- **Case Study**: Mapping a subject's movement using GIS tools.

9. Tracking Live Events Through Geotagged Media

- Finding geotagged social media posts in real-time.
- Using crowdsourced images and videos for crisis monitoring.
- Verifying timestamp and location consistency in live content.
- Detecting misinformation and image manipulation.
- **Case Study**: Confirming a protest's location using geotagged media.

10. Video Analysis & Frame Extraction for OSINT

- Differences between image-based and video-based OSINT.
- Extracting key frames for enhanced investigation.
- Identifying objects, landmarks, and people in video footage.
- Analyzing environmental factors like weather and shadows.
- **Case Study**: Identifying a suspect from surveillance footage.

11. Case Study: Solving Crimes with Image OSINT

- Using image analysis to track criminals and missing persons.
- Real-world applications of image intelligence in crime-solving.
- Combining image OSINT with cyber and financial investigations.
- **Case Study**: Using OSINT techniques to crack a fraud case.

12. Ethical Considerations in Geolocation OSINT

- Legal challenges in using images and geolocation data.
- Understanding privacy concerns in OSINT investigations.
- The risks of false accusations and misinterpretation of data.
- The future of AI, deepfakes, and geolocation OSINT.
- **Case Study**: Examining the legal and ethical controversy of an OSINT investigation.

Final Thoughts

The power of Image & Geolocation OSINT lies in the ability to extract meaningful intelligence from publicly available visual data. Whether you are verifying social media claims, tracking down missing persons, or conducting cybercrime investigations, mastering these techniques is essential in today's digital age.

This book will take you from beginner to expert in analyzing images, extracting metadata, using reverse image search engines, and leveraging geolocation data for real-world intelligence gathering. With practical tools, case studies, and hands-on techniques, you'll be well-equipped to apply Image & Geolocation OSINT to various investigative scenarios.

Let's dive into the world of digital forensics, where every pixel holds a story waiting to be uncovered. 🚀

1. Basics of Image & Geolocation OSINT

In this chapter, we will delve into the foundational concepts of Image and Geolocation OSINT, exploring how images and geographic data are key to uncovering valuable intelligence. From analyzing satellite imagery to interpreting geotagged photos, we'll examine the critical techniques and tools used to reverse-search images, pinpoint locations, and extract insights from visual data. Understanding the basics of this field equips analysts with the skills necessary to make sense of the vast visual and locational information available online, enabling them to track events, uncover hidden patterns, and identify the context behind digital content in the modern intelligence landscape.

1.1 Understanding the Role of Images in OSINT Investigations

In the age of digital connectivity, images have become one of the most prevalent forms of communication and documentation. Whether through social media, news outlets, or personal photography, images capture moments, convey messages, and store significant data. For OSINT (Open Source Intelligence) analysts, the importance of images cannot be overstated. These visual artifacts can serve as valuable sources of intelligence, providing clues that might be hidden in plain sight. The analysis of images plays a central role in investigations, helping to validate claims, uncover hidden details, and trace events to their origins.

The Power of Images as Sources of Intelligence

Images are far more than mere visual representations; they are rich in context, offering data that can be parsed and analyzed for intelligence. For OSINT investigators, images provide key pieces of evidence that often tie together disparate elements of an investigation. A single photograph can contain a wealth of information—such as geolocation, time, and details about the environment—that can significantly contribute to uncovering the truth.

Take, for example, a situation where an image is posted on social media during a live event, such as a protest or a natural disaster. This image might show a group of people gathered in a specific location, with visible landmarks or street signs. The timestamp on the image could offer insights into the event's timeline. Even more telling, the metadata embedded within the image file, such as the camera used, location coordinates, and other details, can aid in verifying the image's authenticity. In such cases, images not only tell the story visually but also support the validation and analysis of other types of intelligence.

Types of Images Used in OSINT Investigations

There are several categories of images that OSINT analysts typically encounter during investigations, each offering unique forms of intelligence. Broadly speaking, these include:

Social Media Images

Social media platforms like Instagram, Twitter, Facebook, and TikTok are constantly flooded with images that can provide a wealth of real-time intelligence. These images, whether of people, places, or events, often contain geotags, timestamps, and other contextual clues that can be analyzed to understand where and when an image was captured. Social media images offer unique insights into global events, user behavior, and the spread of disinformation or rumors.

Satellite Imagery

Satellites provide high-resolution images of large geographic areas, which can be used to track changes in landscapes, infrastructure, or military activity. OSINT analysts can use satellite images to monitor the construction of new buildings, identify the movement of vehicles, or detect environmental changes. These images are invaluable for understanding geopolitical developments or monitoring areas of interest in real time.

News and Media Images

Images published by news outlets are often a key component of OSINT investigations, especially when analyzing events such as conflicts, elections, or natural disasters. Images from reputable news sources can provide critical visual evidence that corroborates reports, adding credibility to claims. OSINT analysts often cross-reference such images with other open-source data to verify facts and ensure accuracy.

Surveillance and Security Footage

Surveillance camera footage can play a critical role in criminal investigations or security-related OSINT analysis. These images often provide vital evidence, such as identifying suspects, tracing movements, or capturing important details about the surroundings.

Security camera footage can offer an unfiltered view of an event, providing context that might be missing from other types of media.

Geotagged Images

Geotagged images are those that contain GPS coordinates embedded in their metadata. These images are particularly valuable in OSINT investigations because they provide exact location data. A geotagged image can show where an event took place or even help track an individual's movements. For example, a photo posted on social media that is tagged with a specific location can provide an OSINT analyst with invaluable information about the geographic context of the event.

How OSINT Analysts Use Images for Investigations

Images in OSINT investigations are used for a variety of purposes, ranging from verification and validation to identifying patterns and connections. Below are some of the key ways in which OSINT analysts leverage images during their investigations:

Verification and Validation

One of the primary roles of images in OSINT is to verify claims. In the digital age, false or manipulated images can easily spread across the internet, and distinguishing between authentic and fake visuals is crucial. Analysts use reverse image search engines (such as Google Images or TinEye) to trace the origins of images, determine where else they have been posted, and assess their authenticity. By cross-referencing images with other sources, analysts can confirm whether an image truly represents the event it purports to document.

Geolocation

Images often contain embedded location information that can help identify where they were taken. This is especially important in open-source intelligence investigations focused on mapping events or tracking the movements of individuals or groups. Through techniques such as analyzing visual cues (landmarks, architecture, environmental features) and using satellite imagery, OSINT analysts can pinpoint the exact location of an image's origin. Geotagging metadata, when available, can also streamline this process by providing direct GPS coordinates.

Pattern Recognition and Analysis

When dealing with large quantities of images, pattern recognition plays a crucial role in OSINT investigations. By analyzing the content of multiple images over time, analysts can identify recurring themes or trends. For example, multiple images from different sources might show similar activity in the same location, pointing to the escalation of an event. Alternatively, an analyst may identify specific symbols or logos appearing in various photos, indicating links between different organizations or movements.

Contextual Analysis

Images provide context that can enhance understanding of a situation. Analysts might examine elements like the people in the image, the time of day, or the objects present in the scene to build a fuller picture of the event or environment depicted. Contextual analysis can also help verify the timing and sequence of events, as well as provide insights into the cultural, social, or political factors at play. For instance, a photo showing a protest in front of a government building can give analysts clues about the political situation in the region, helping them draw conclusions about the motivations behind the protest.

Event Mapping

Mapping events using images is another key use of visual intelligence. OSINT analysts can use images, particularly geotagged ones, to track real-time developments during dynamic situations, such as natural disasters or ongoing conflicts. This helps to provide situational awareness and identify emerging trends in a timely manner. For example, images from various sources showing the aftermath of an earthquake can be plotted on a map to assess the affected areas and aid in relief efforts.

Images are a central component of OSINT investigations. Their ability to capture specific moments in time, convey a wide array of contextual data, and reveal hidden details makes them indispensable tools for analysts. Whether through social media, satellite imagery, or security footage, images provide valuable insights into the who, what, where, when, and why of an event. By mastering the techniques of image analysis—such as verification, geolocation, and pattern recognition—OSINT analysts can extract actionable intelligence from visual data, ultimately enhancing the accuracy and depth of their investigations. The role of images in OSINT will continue to grow, becoming increasingly important as more data is generated in digital and physical spaces.

1.2 How Digital Photos Contain Hidden Information

Digital photographs are not just a collection of pixels; they are rich in information that can offer insights far beyond what is immediately visible to the eye. This hidden data can play a pivotal role in Open Source Intelligence (OSINT) investigations, allowing analysts to uncover critical details such as the time and location an image was taken, the device used to capture it, and even subtle clues about its authenticity. While many users are familiar with the concept of metadata, the deeper layers of information embedded in digital photos often remain overlooked. Understanding how to extract and analyze this hidden data is crucial for OSINT analysts who need to verify claims, track down individuals, or piece together the context surrounding an event.

The Basics of Digital Photos and Metadata

Every digital photo contains more than just the image itself. It includes various forms of metadata—data about data—that provides contextual information about the image. This metadata is embedded within the image file when it is created or modified, and it can contain a wealth of hidden details that are not visible in the photo itself. The most commonly known form of metadata in digital photos is EXIF (Exchangeable Image File Format), but other forms of metadata, such as IPTC (International Press Telecommunications Council) and XMP (Extensible Metadata Platform), can also be present.

The metadata embedded in a digital photo often includes:

Timestamp

A crucial piece of metadata, the timestamp records the exact date and time the image was taken. This can help investigators verify whether the photo aligns with other known events or provide insights into the timeline of an unfolding situation. However, it is important to note that timestamps can sometimes be manipulated or altered, so it is critical to cross-reference them with other data points.

Geolocation (GPS Coordinates)

Many modern cameras and smartphones embed GPS coordinates within the image's metadata when the photo is taken. These geotags provide the exact location of the photo at the time it was captured, down to a specific latitude and longitude. Geolocation data is especially valuable in OSINT investigations as it allows analysts to pinpoint the geographical location of an image and, in some cases, correlate it with other publicly available information, such as maps or satellite images.

Camera Information

EXIF metadata often contains information about the device used to capture the image, such as the camera model, brand, and even the specific settings used (e.g., aperture, ISO, shutter speed). This information can be useful for analysts in identifying whether an image appears to have been taken with a particular type of camera or device, which can be cross-referenced with other images or known sources. It can also help verify the authenticity of an image by determining if it was captured with a device consistent with the context of the image.

Image Editing Data

Another form of metadata that can be embedded in a digital photo is information about any editing or modification done to the image. This can include the software used to edit the image, the type of changes made (e.g., cropping, resizing, color adjustments), and whether any filters were applied. Detecting signs of editing can alert analysts to potential manipulation or disinformation, which is especially important when verifying the authenticity of images used in media or investigations.

The Role of EXIF Metadata in OSINT Investigations

EXIF data, as the most commonly used metadata format, plays a central role in OSINT investigations. By extracting and analyzing EXIF metadata, investigators can often unlock critical details about an image that are not immediately visible. Below, we explore some of the specific ways EXIF metadata is used in OSINT investigations:

Verifying Image Authenticity

One of the most important uses of EXIF data is in verifying the authenticity of an image. OSINT analysts can extract the metadata to determine whether an image has been edited, when it was taken, and where it was captured. For example, if an image purports to show a recent political protest in a particular city but the EXIF data reveals that the photo was taken several years ago or in a different location, it becomes clear that the image is not an accurate representation of the event in question.

Geolocation and Mapping

Geotagged images, which contain GPS coordinates within their EXIF data, are particularly valuable for analysts working with geographic information. By extracting these coordinates, investigators can map the location of an image and track the movements of individuals or groups across different locations. This can be especially useful in monitoring events like conflicts, protests, or natural disasters, where the geographic context is key to understanding the situation.

Building a Timeline

The timestamp included in EXIF metadata is another important tool for investigators. By analyzing the time that photos were taken, OSINT analysts can build timelines of events, connecting images with other sources of information to create a cohesive narrative. For instance, images posted on social media during a terrorist attack may have timestamps that help investigators understand the sequence of events, identify witnesses or suspects, and track the spread of information in real time.

Tracking Devices and Consistency

EXIF data also includes information about the device used to take the photo, which can be critical in determining whether an image is consistent with other available data. If the same device appears in multiple photos related to an investigation, it can help establish a connection between the images and individuals or groups. For example, a specific phone model might repeatedly appear in photos posted from a certain location, indicating that the device is frequently used by a particular individual.

Uncovering Edited or Fake Images

One of the most important aspects of EXIF analysis in OSINT is identifying edited or manipulated images. Digital forensics tools can analyze the EXIF metadata to detect signs of editing, such as changes in the software used, alteration of timestamps, or inconsistencies in image resolution. If an image is presented as unaltered, but the EXIF data shows editing software such as Photoshop was used, analysts can conclude that the image has been tampered with, which may cast doubt on its credibility.

Other Forms of Hidden Information in Digital Photos

In addition to EXIF metadata, digital photos may also contain hidden information in the form of steganography or additional embedded data formats. Steganography refers to the practice of hiding data within an image file, making it invisible to the naked eye. While steganography is often used for malicious purposes, it can also be used for legitimate data protection or communication. OSINT analysts may employ specialized software to detect hidden data in image files, revealing additional layers of information that could be relevant to an investigation.

Another important consideration is the potential for hidden clues within the visual content of the photo itself. For example, subtle reflections in windows, writing on walls, or background objects that can be identified through pattern recognition may provide additional intelligence. Analysts trained in image forensics can analyze these details to uncover clues that are not immediately visible in the foreground of the image.

Digital photos contain far more than meets the eye. With embedded metadata, such as EXIF data, GPS coordinates, and timestamps, these images offer a treasure trove of hidden information that can be critical for OSINT investigations. By learning how to extract, interpret, and analyze this hidden data, OSINT analysts can enhance the accuracy and depth of their investigations, ensuring they make informed decisions based on verified and contextualized evidence. Whether validating the authenticity of an image, pinpointing a location, or uncovering hidden messages, the ability to uncover hidden information within digital photos is an indispensable skill in the modern intelligence landscape.

1.3 The OSINT Workflow for Image & Geolocation Analysis

Conducting effective OSINT (Open Source Intelligence) investigations using images and geolocation data requires a structured workflow. A methodical approach ensures that analysts extract maximum intelligence while maintaining accuracy, verification, and ethical integrity. The OSINT workflow for image and geolocation analysis involves a series of critical steps, from data collection to verification and reporting. This chapter will break down the structured process used by analysts to uncover intelligence from images, determine their locations, and verify their authenticity.

Step 1: Data Collection – Acquiring Images and Location Data

The first step in any OSINT workflow is gathering relevant images and associated location data. This process can involve multiple sources, including:

1.1 Social Media Platforms

- Publicly available images on platforms such as Twitter, Facebook, Instagram, TikTok, and Telegram provide valuable intelligence.
- Many images include timestamps, user interactions, and even geotags that can be extracted for analysis.

- Reverse image search tools can help find reposted or edited versions of an image to track its origin.

1.2 News Websites and Blogs

- News organizations frequently publish images along with reports, which can provide useful context for investigations.
- Checking multiple news sources helps identify potential biases or inconsistencies in reporting.

1.3 Government and Open Data Sources

- Official sources such as satellite imagery repositories (e.g., NASA, ESA, USGS) and open mapping tools (e.g., OpenStreetMap) can provide high-quality imagery for verification.

1.4 Satellite and Street View Services

- Tools like Google Earth, Google Street View, Bing Maps, and Yandex Maps allow analysts to compare locations in images with real-world geographic features.
- Time-lapse satellite imagery can help track changes in locations over time.

1.5 EXIF Metadata Extraction

Images captured with digital devices often contain EXIF metadata, which can reveal:

- GPS coordinates
- Device model and settings
- Date and time of capture
- Software used to edit the image

Specialized tools such as ExifTool and Jeffrey's Image Metadata Viewer help extract this data.

After collecting images, the next step is ensuring they are analyzed systematically.

Step 2: Image Verification and Reverse Searching

A key component of OSINT investigations is verifying whether an image is authentic, manipulated, or misleading. Verification techniques include:

2.1 Reverse Image Search

Reverse image search engines help track down the origin of an image and detect whether it has been altered or repurposed.

Recommended tools include:

Google Reverse Image Search

TinEye

- Yandex Reverse Image Search (especially useful for identifying locations)

Bing Visual Search

2.2 Identifying Manipulated Images

- Some images may have been digitally altered or taken out of context to spread misinformation.
- Tools like Forensically and InVID help detect signs of manipulation, such as inconsistencies in shadows, lighting, and metadata.

2.3 Checking for Image Compression & Edits

- If an image has been compressed multiple times (as happens when it is repeatedly shared on social media), critical metadata may be lost.
- Analyzing pixel-level artifacts can reveal tampering.

Step 3: Geolocation Analysis – Pinpointing an Image's Origin

Once an image is verified, the next step is determining its geographic location. This requires a combination of tools and techniques:

3.1 Extracting GPS Coordinates from Metadata

- If the image contains EXIF metadata with GPS coordinates, the location can be plotted directly on a map.

3.2 Identifying Landmarks and Background Objects

- If GPS data is missing, analysts use visual clues such as buildings, street signs, terrain, and environmental features to match the image with real-world locations.
- Google Earth, Google Street View, and OpenStreetMap are useful for this process.

3.3 Cross-Referencing Satellite Imagery

- By comparing images with publicly available satellite maps, analysts can verify whether a location exists as depicted.
- Platforms like Sentinel Hub, NASA Worldview, and Zoom.earth provide historical and real-time satellite images.

3.4 Using Local Language and Signage for Context

- Analyzing text on signs, license plates, or storefronts in an image can provide regional and linguistic clues.
- Translating street signs or advertisements using Google Translate can help pinpoint a specific location.

3.5 Analyzing Shadows and Sun Positioning

- Sunlight direction and shadow angles can help determine the time of day and even verify whether the image aligns with claimed timestamps.
- Tools like SunCalc allow analysts to estimate an image's time and location based on shadows.

Step 4: Cross-Referencing with Other Data Sources

Once a location has been estimated, it's essential to verify findings using multiple sources to ensure accuracy.

4.1 Corroborating with Open-Source Databases

- Cross-checking locations with databases such as Wikimapia, Geonames, and other GIS (Geographic Information System) sources adds credibility.

4.2 Verifying with Eyewitness Reports and Social Media Trends

- Searching for local social media activity and user-generated content related to the image's location can provide supporting evidence.

- OSINT analysts often use Twitter Advanced Search, Reddit threads, and Telegram groups to gather real-time context.

4.3 Comparing Historical Data

- Time-series satellite images can help determine if a location has changed over time, such as construction of new buildings, changes in road networks, or environmental shifts.

Step 5: Reporting and Documentation

After conducting thorough analysis and verification, the findings must be compiled into a structured report.

5.1 Creating an OSINT Investigation Report

- Reports should be clear, structured, and include:
- Summary of findings (image verification results, geolocation details)
- Evidence sources (links, screenshots, metadata)
- Analysis methodology (tools and techniques used)
- Verification steps (reverse image searches, cross-referencing)

Final conclusions

5.2 Ethical Considerations

- OSINT analysts must ensure they adhere to ethical guidelines, respecting privacy laws and avoiding doxxing.
- Always verify information before dissemination to prevent spreading misinformation.

5.3 Presenting Evidence

- Visual evidence should be presented in a clear, organized format with annotations highlighting key findings.
- Mapping tools can be used to create geolocation overlays for better visualization.

The OSINT workflow for image and geolocation analysis is a structured, multi-step process that ensures accuracy, verification, and ethical integrity. By systematically collecting, analyzing, and cross-referencing images with open-source data, analysts can uncover vital intelligence and verify the authenticity of visual information. As digital imagery continues to play an increasing role in investigations, mastering this workflow is essential for anyone involved in OSINT, journalism, or security analysis.

1.4 Differences Between Reverse Searching, Metadata Extraction & Visual Analysis

When conducting OSINT investigations using images, analysts rely on three core methods to extract intelligence: reverse image searching, metadata extraction, and visual analysis. While these techniques complement each other, they serve distinct purposes and involve different tools and methodologies. Understanding the differences between them is crucial for effective image and geolocation intelligence gathering.

1. Reverse Image Searching: Finding the Source and Context of an Image

What is Reverse Image Searching?

Reverse image searching is a technique used to trace the origins of an image by finding visually similar or identical versions of it across the internet. It helps determine where an image has appeared before, whether it has been altered, and if it is being used in a misleading context.

Key Uses in OSINT:

- **Verifying image authenticity** – Checking if an image is being misrepresented (e.g., an old image being used as "breaking news").
- **Finding the earliest known appearance of an image** – Tracing where and when an image was first published.
- **Detecting manipulated or doctored images** – Comparing different versions of an image to spot modifications.
- **Tracking individuals, locations, or objects** – Identifying whether an image has been previously shared with context or additional details.

Tools for Reverse Image Searching:

- **Google Reverse Image Search** – A widely used tool for finding visually similar images across the web.

- **TinEye** – Focuses on identifying modifications and earliest-known versions of an image.
- **Yandex Reverse Image Search** – Particularly useful for locating faces, buildings, and objects in non-Western sources.
- **Bing Visual Search** – Offers image-based searches with related information.

Limitations of Reverse Image Searching:

- Cannot analyze images that are not already indexed on the internet.
- Does not work well with highly edited, cropped, or AI-generated images.
- Some images may appear on private or closed platforms (e.g., encrypted messaging apps) and may not be found.

2. Metadata Extraction: Uncovering Hidden Data in Images

What is Metadata Extraction?

Metadata extraction involves retrieving the embedded data within an image file. This metadata often includes technical details about how, when, and where the image was captured, along with information about the device used. The most common form of metadata in images is EXIF (Exchangeable Image File Format) data.

Key Uses in OSINT:

- **Extracting geolocation data** – If GPS coordinates are available, they can reveal where the image was taken.
- **Verifying timestamps** – Checking when an image was actually captured versus when it was posted online.
- **Identifying the camera or device** – Determining whether multiple images were taken with the same phone or camera.
- **Detecting photo editing** – Finding out if the image was modified using software like Photoshop.

Tools for Metadata Extraction:

- **ExifTool** – A powerful command-line tool for extracting and analyzing metadata.
- **Jeffrey's Image Metadata Viewer** – A web-based tool for quick metadata checks.
- **FotoForensics** – Includes metadata analysis along with forensic image analysis.
- **Metadata2Go** – Allows users to extract metadata from various file types.

Limitations of Metadata Extraction:

- Many social media platforms (e.g., Twitter, Facebook, Instagram) strip metadata from uploaded images.
- Metadata can be manually altered or removed to hide information.
- Some image formats (e.g., screenshots) do not retain original metadata.

3. Visual Analysis: Extracting Clues from the Image Content

What is Visual Analysis?

Visual analysis involves manually or algorithmically inspecting the content of an image to extract intelligence. Unlike reverse searching and metadata extraction, which rely on external databases or embedded data, visual analysis is about interpreting what is visible in the image itself.

Key Uses in OSINT:

- **Geolocation estimation** – Identifying landmarks, terrain, street signs, or weather patterns to determine where the image was taken.
- **Object and pattern recognition** – Identifying vehicles, clothing styles, license plates, or architectural styles that may provide contextual clues.
- **Analyzing shadows and lighting** – Estimating the time of day or checking whether the lighting is consistent with the claimed timestamp.
- **Language and text identification** – Deciphering street signs, billboards, and other text elements that can hint at a location.

Tools for Visual Analysis:

- **Google Earth & Street View** – Useful for matching buildings, roads, and landscapes.
- **SunCalc** – Helps analyze shadow angles to estimate time and location.
- **InVID WeVerify** – Provides frame-by-frame image analysis from videos.
- **Adobe Photoshop / GIMP** – Can be used to enhance and inspect images for inconsistencies.

Limitations of Visual Analysis:

- Requires a trained eye and experience to accurately interpret details.
- Some visual clues may be misleading or staged.

- Highly subjective compared to metadata analysis, which provides concrete data points.

Comparing the Three Techniques

Feature	Reverse Image Search	Metadata Extraction	Visual Analysis
Purpose	Find similar images & sources	Retrieve hidden image data	Analyze visible content for clues
Best for	Verifying authenticity, tracking reposts	Extracting timestamps, geolocation, device info	Identifying locations, objects, and inconsistencies
Key Tools	Google, TinEye, Yandex, Bing	ExifTool, Jeffrey's Viewer, FotoForensics	Google Earth, SunCalc, InVID
Limitations	Works only with indexed images	Metadata can be stripped or falsified	Requires human interpretation, can be misleading

How These Techniques Work Together in OSINT Investigations

A successful OSINT image analysis often combines all three techniques to ensure accuracy and completeness. Here's how they work together in a typical workflow:

Reverse Image Search First

- Determines if the image has appeared before and in what context.
- Helps find different versions of the image.

Extract Metadata for Technical Details

- If metadata is intact, it can reveal the image's origin, timestamp, and GPS location.
- Confirms whether the image was modified or captured on a specific device.

Perform Visual Analysis for Additional Clues

- If metadata is missing, landmarks, street signs, weather, and shadows can help verify the location.
- Text and symbols in the image may provide additional intelligence.

Example OSINT Investigation:

Imagine an image claiming to show a recent protest in Paris:

Reverse Image Search:

- The image appears in a news article from two years ago. This suggests it is being misrepresented as a recent event.

Metadata Extraction:

- If metadata is present, it may reveal the actual date and location of capture.
- If missing, it suggests the image was edited or downloaded from another source.

Visual Analysis:

- A street sign in the background appears in French, supporting the Paris claim.
- However, the weather in the image does not match the reported conditions on the alleged date.

Conclusion: The protest image is old and being falsely used as current news.

Reverse image searching, metadata extraction, and visual analysis are distinct but complementary techniques in OSINT investigations. While reverse searching helps find an image's origin, metadata extraction reveals hidden technical data, and visual analysis provides contextual clues. A skilled OSINT analyst must know when and how to use each method effectively, cross-referencing results to ensure accuracy and avoid misinformation.

1.5 Common Challenges in Image-Based Investigations

Image-based OSINT (Open Source Intelligence) investigations are powerful but come with numerous challenges that analysts must navigate. While images provide critical information for verifying events, geolocating incidents, and tracking individuals or objects, they also present obstacles such as missing metadata, image manipulation, disinformation, and legal concerns. This chapter explores the most common challenges faced in image-based investigations and how to mitigate them.

1. Image Manipulation and Misinformation

Challenge:

One of the biggest threats in OSINT investigations is image manipulation. Bad actors frequently edit, crop, or alter images to spread misinformation, deceive the public, or obscure key details. This can include:

- **Deepfakes** – AI-generated images that create realistic but entirely fake scenarios.
- **Photoshopped images** – Manually edited pictures that remove or add elements to mislead viewers.
- **Cropping and context removal** – Images presented without important surrounding details to alter their perceived meaning.

Mitigation Strategies:

- Use forensic analysis tools like FotoForensics, Forensically, or InVID WeVerify to detect inconsistencies in lighting, edges, and pixel structures.
- Perform reverse image searches (Google, Yandex, TinEye) to find the original, unedited versions of an image.
- Compare the image with videos, eyewitness accounts, or news sources to verify authenticity.

2. Stripped or Missing Metadata

Challenge:

Metadata, especially EXIF data, is critical in determining when and where an image was taken. However, most social media platforms strip metadata from uploaded images, and some users remove it manually to protect privacy or mislead investigators.

Mitigation Strategies:

- **Check the original source** – Download images from direct URLs or archives instead of social media reposts.
- **Use metadata extraction tools** (ExifTool, Jeffrey's Image Metadata Viewer) whenever possible.
- If metadata is missing, rely on visual analysis (landmarks, shadows, objects) and reverse searching to place the image in context.

3. Geolocation Difficulties

Challenge:

Determining where an image was taken is a core aspect of OSINT investigations, but various factors make geolocation difficult:

- **Lack of identifiable landmarks** (e.g., indoor photos, rural landscapes).
- **Image taken in multiple similar-looking locations** (e.g., generic cityscapes).
- Obstruction of key details like street signs or license plates.

Mitigation Strategies:

- Use Google Earth, Google Street View, Yandex Maps, and OpenStreetMap to compare terrain, buildings, and landmarks.
- Identify regional features such as vegetation, architectural styles, and road markings to narrow down possible locations.
- Utilize language clues (billboards, shop signs, newspapers) to determine the country or region.

4. Low-Quality or Blurry Images

Challenge:

Many images used in investigations are low resolution, heavily compressed, or blurry due to:

- Poor camera quality.
- Screenshots instead of original images.
- Loss of detail from repeated sharing and compression.

Mitigation Strategies:

- Use AI-powered image enhancement tools (Remini, Let's Enhance) to clarify details.
- Look for text, colors, or recognizable shapes instead of expecting a perfect match in geolocation searches.
- If text is present, use OCR (Optical Character Recognition) tools like Google Lens to extract readable words.

5. Reverse Image Search Limitations

Challenge:

Reverse image search engines are powerful, but they have limitations:

- They can only find images that are indexed online.
- AI-generated or heavily altered images may not match the original.
- Some search engines (Google) prioritize similar-looking results rather than exact matches.

Mitigation Strategies:

- Use multiple search engines (Google, Yandex, Bing, TinEye) as they index different images.
- Search for cropped or altered versions by manually editing the image (e.g., flipping, changing brightness) before searching.
- Perform a keyword-based search alongside image searching to find related contexts.

6. Identifying Individuals in Crowds or Poor Lighting

Challenge:

Images taken in crowds or poor lighting conditions make it difficult to identify individuals, as faces may be obscured, pixelated, or poorly lit.

Mitigation Strategies:

- Use facial recognition tools (if legally permissible) such as PimEyes or Azure Face API to analyze facial features.
- Compare clothing, accessories, tattoos, or unique features to match people across multiple images.
- If available, check multiple frames from a video instead of a single image to improve recognition.

7. Real-Time Tracking and Verification Challenges

Challenge:

During live events (e.g., protests, conflicts, disasters), verifying images in real-time is challenging due to:

- Rapid sharing of old or unrelated images.

- Lack of official verification sources.
- Difficulty in confirming timestamps and locations.

Mitigation Strategies:

- Use social media monitoring tools (TweetDeck, Crowdtangle) to track posts related to the event.
- Check time zone differences, weather, and lighting conditions to verify authenticity.
- Compare the image with live-streaming services, satellite maps, or eyewitness accounts.

8. Legal and Ethical Concerns

Challenge:

Using images in OSINT investigations raises ethical and legal concerns, including:

- Privacy violations – Unintentionally exposing personal data of individuals.
- Misinformation risks – Sharing unverified images that could mislead audiences.
- Legal restrictions – Some countries have strict data protection laws that limit image use.

Mitigation Strategies:

- Follow ethical OSINT guidelines (avoid doxxing, respect privacy laws).
- Verify information before publishing or sharing findings.
- Use blurred images or censored data when presenting sensitive information.

Image-based OSINT investigations are powerful but come with many challenges, from manipulated images and missing metadata to geolocation difficulties and ethical concerns. Analysts must be aware of these obstacles and use a multi-layered approach—combining reverse image searching, metadata analysis, visual clues, and verification techniques—to ensure accuracy. By understanding these challenges and implementing mitigation strategies, OSINT practitioners can extract reliable intelligence while maintaining ethical standards.

1.6 Ethical & Legal Considerations in Image & Location Tracking

Image and geolocation intelligence are powerful tools in OSINT investigations, but they come with significant ethical and legal responsibilities. While these techniques can help verify information, track individuals, and uncover hidden details, they also risk violating privacy, enabling surveillance abuse, and breaching data protection laws. OSINT practitioners must navigate a fine line between investigative work and ethical responsibility, ensuring that their actions remain lawful and morally sound.

This chapter explores key ethical dilemmas, privacy concerns, legal regulations, and best practices in the responsible use of image and location-based OSINT.

1. Ethical Challenges in Image & Geolocation OSINT

1.1 Privacy Concerns and the Risk of Doxxing

One of the most significant ethical concerns in OSINT investigations is privacy invasion. Using images to track individuals, identify locations, or reveal personal details without consent can lead to unintended harm, including:

- **Doxxing** – The malicious publication of private or identifying information about an individual.
- **Harassment or stalking** – Images can be used to track movements or expose home addresses.
- **Endangerment** – Uncovering a person's real-time location (e.g., a journalist in a conflict zone) can put them at risk.

◆ **Best Practices to Avoid Privacy Violations:**

✓☐ Never publish sensitive location data (home addresses, workplaces) of private individuals.
✓☐ Redact or blur identifiable features (faces, license plates) when sharing findings.
✓☐ Use geolocation tracking only when there is a justified investigative need (e.g., war crimes, human trafficking cases).

1.2 The Ethics of Live Tracking and Surveillance

Tracking individuals in real time using social media images, live-streamed events, or geotagged posts raises ethical concerns.

- Should OSINT practitioners track someone without their consent?
- Is it ethical to monitor protests or movements in politically sensitive areas?

◆ **Best Practices for Live Tracking:**

✓□ Use location tracking only in cases of public interest (e.g., disaster response, crime investigations).
✓□ Avoid actively exposing individuals who are not part of an investigation.
✓□ Consider the potential harm of publishing location-based findings before releasing them.

2. Legal Considerations in Image & Geolocation OSINT

2.1 Data Protection Laws & Regulations

Different regions have strict laws governing the collection, sharing, and use of personal data, including images and location information. Key regulations include:

General Data Protection Regulation (GDPR) (Europe)

- Protects personal data, including geolocation metadata and identifiable images.
- Requires explicit consent for collecting or processing personal location data.

California Consumer Privacy Act (CCPA) (USA)

- Grants individuals the right to know how their personal data is used.
- Includes geolocation tracking as protected personal information.

United Kingdom's Data Protection Act (DPA)

- Restricts the sharing of location data without legal justification.
- Imposes penalties for misuse of personal images.

Other Country-Specific Laws

Brazil's LGPD, Canada's PIPEDA, Australia's Privacy Act all regulate location tracking and personal data protection.

◆ How to Stay Legally Compliant:

✓☐ Always verify whether geolocation data collection is permitted under applicable laws.

✓☐ Do not store or share images containing personally identifiable information (PII) without proper justification.

✓☐ If working in a jurisdiction with strict privacy laws, consult legal experts before publishing findings.

2.2 Using Images & Location Data from Social Media

Many OSINT investigations rely on images and geolocation data extracted from social media platforms. However, each platform has its own terms of service (ToS) regarding data usage.

- **Facebook & Instagram** – Strictly prohibit scraping and automated data collection.
- **Twitter/X** – Allows public data collection but removes metadata from uploaded images.
- **TikTok & Snapchat** – Geotagging data is limited to user settings and permissions.

◆ Best Practices for Social Media-Based OSINT:

✓☐ Use manual analysis instead of automated scraping to avoid violating ToS.

✓☐ Ensure fair use of images by citing sources and avoiding unauthorized republishing.

✓☐ Do not misrepresent an individual's intent or location based on misleading image data.

2.3 The Legal Risks of Reverse Image Searching

Reverse image search tools (Google, Yandex, TinEye) are legal to use, but their application may breach privacy in some cases. Key risks include:

- **Unintended exposure** – Matching a personal image to an obscure source without consent.
- **Defamation & misidentification** – Misattributing an image to the wrong person or context.
- **Breaching site policies** – Some websites prohibit automated scraping or AI-assisted searching.

◆ How to Use Reverse Image Search Legally:

✓☐ Only search for images in public interest investigations (e.g., misinformation, crime verification).

✓☐ Do not share search results that expose private individuals without their consent.

✓☐ Use open-source intelligence techniques that comply with local laws.

3. Responsible OSINT: Balancing Ethics & Investigation Goals

3.1 When is Image & Geolocation Tracking Justified?

Ethical OSINT practitioners must constantly weigh the risks and benefits of their investigations. Justified use cases for geolocation OSINT include:

✓ **Verifying misinformation** – Identifying false claims using image analysis.

✓ **Tracking criminal activities** – Investigating human trafficking, war crimes, or missing persons.

✓ **Disaster response** – Locating affected areas in real-time.

Unethical or unjustified uses include:

✗ **Personal tracking without consent** – Using OSINT for harassment, stalking, or exposing individuals.

✗ **Doxxing** – Publishing addresses, workplaces, or other private information.

✗ **Manipulative investigations** – Using misleading analysis to push false narratives.

3.2 Best Practices for Ethical Image & Geolocation OSINT

✓☐ **Respect Privacy** – Avoid publishing sensitive images or data that could harm individuals.

✓☐ **Verify Before Sharing** – Cross-check findings using multiple sources.

✓☐ **Follow Platform Rules** – Comply with the terms of service of social media and mapping platforms.

✓☐ **Consider the Impact** – Ask: "Could this information put someone at risk?"

✓☐ **Stay Legally Informed** – Keep updated on international and regional data protection laws.

Ethical and legal considerations are essential in image and geolocation-based OSINT. While these techniques provide valuable insights, they must be used responsibly to avoid harming individuals, violating privacy laws, or enabling malicious surveillance. By understanding privacy risks, legal restrictions, and best ethical practices, OSINT practitioners can ensure their investigations serve the public interest while respecting human rights.

2. Reverse Image Searching: Techniques & Tools

In this chapter, we will explore the powerful techniques and tools available for reverse image searching, a crucial method in the OSINT analyst's toolkit. By leveraging image-based search engines and specialized platforms, analysts can trace the origin of images, uncover hidden details, and verify the authenticity of visual content. We will cover various approaches, from using metadata to utilizing AI-powered reverse search engines, as well as understanding the challenges and limitations of these techniques. Mastery of reverse image searching allows analysts to expose disinformation, track the spread of images, and gain deeper insights into the visual data they encounter.

2.1 How Reverse Image Searching Works

Reverse image searching is a fundamental technique in OSINT (Open-Source Intelligence) investigations, enabling analysts to trace the origins of an image, find similar images, and uncover hidden connections. Unlike traditional keyword searches, which rely on text input, reverse image searches use visual data to identify matches across the internet. This chapter explores how reverse image search works, the underlying technology, and its practical applications in OSINT.

1. The Basics of Reverse Image Searching

Reverse image search is a process where an image is used as a query instead of text. Search engines and specialized tools analyze the image's visual characteristics and compare it to indexed images across the web. The goal is to:

- Identify the original source of an image.
- Detect altered or edited versions of an image.
- Find higher-resolution copies of an image.
- Verify claims and debunk misinformation by tracing the image's history.

How It Differs from Regular Image Searches

Feature	Regular Image Search	Reverse Image Search
Input Type	Keywords/Text	Image file/URL
Results Based On	Metadata, keywords	Visual patterns, pixel analysis
Use Cases	Finding new images	Identifying sources, tracking usage

Reverse image search is particularly useful in OSINT investigations for fact-checking, geolocation, social media analysis, and uncovering image manipulation.

2. The Technology Behind Reverse Image Search

Reverse image search engines rely on advanced technologies to compare images and generate matches. The key components include:

2.1 Image Hashing & Fingerprinting

Image hashing converts an image into a unique mathematical signature or "fingerprint." Even if the image is slightly modified (cropped, resized, color adjusted), hashing algorithms can detect similarities. Common hashing techniques include:

- **pHash (Perceptual Hashing):** Detects similarities even in altered images.
- **dHash (Difference Hashing):** Fast, lightweight hashing method for image comparisons.
- **aHash (Average Hashing):** Uses pixel averaging for fast image matching.

2.2 Feature Extraction & Pattern Recognition

Search engines use computer vision and machine learning to analyze an image's distinct features, including:

- Shapes, colors, and textures
- Facial recognition (for some tools like PimEyes)
- Object detection (cars, landmarks, text on signs, etc.)

2.3 AI & Neural Networks

Modern reverse image search tools utilize deep learning algorithms trained on massive datasets. AI can detect:

- Contextual elements in an image (urban vs. rural, specific landmarks, etc.)
- Face matches across different photos (if supported by the tool)
- Text within images using Optical Character Recognition (OCR)

3. How to Perform a Reverse Image Search

Step 1: Choose a Reverse Image Search Tool

Different search engines and tools provide varying levels of accuracy and database coverage. Some of the most widely used options include:

Tool	Best For	Strengths	Weaknesses
Google Images	General searches	Largest database, fast	Struggles with altered images
Yandex	Finding people & locations	Strong AI, facial recognition	Indexes mostly Russian sites
TinEye	Image tracking & copyright checks	Tracks image history	Limited database
Bing Visual Search	Object & product recognition	Identifies objects well	Smaller index than Google
PimEyes	Face recognition	Identifies faces across web	Privacy concerns, paid tool

Step 2: Upload or Paste the Image URL

Most tools allow you to either:

✓ Upload an image from your device.

✓ Paste an image URL from the web.

Step 3: Analyze the Results

The search engine will return:

- Exact or similar image matches
- Websites where the image appears
- Higher-resolution versions of the image

- Possible modifications or cropped versions

Step 4: Cross-Check & Verify

- Use multiple search engines for broader coverage.
- Compare timestamps to track when an image first appeared online.
- Check for contextual clues (e.g., website credibility, captions, metadata).

4. OSINT Applications of Reverse Image Search

Reverse image searching plays a crucial role in various OSINT investigations:

4.1 Identifying Misinformation & Fake News

- Detect when an image is misrepresented (e.g., an old war photo used to depict a recent conflict).
- Find original sources to check if the image was altered or taken out of context.
- **Example**: A viral protest photo turns out to be from a different country and year.

4.2 Geolocating Photos & Verifying Locations

- Use reverse image search to identify landmarks, street signs, or unique buildings.
- Cross-check with mapping tools (Google Earth, Street View, Yandex Maps).
- **Example**: A social media post claims to be from Paris, but a reverse image search reveals the photo was taken in Montreal.

4.3 Tracking Down Stolen or Misused Images

- Journalists and photographers can check if their images are being used without permission.
- Businesses can find unauthorized commercial use of product images.
- **Example**: An artist discovers their painting being sold on an unlicensed website.

4.4 Unmasking Fake Identities & Sock Puppets

- Scammers often use stolen profile pictures from other social media accounts.
- Reverse image search helps identify stolen photos used in catfishing schemes.
- **Example**: A person on a dating app claims to be "John from New York," but a reverse image search shows the photo belongs to a model in Italy.

4.5 Analyzing War Crimes & Human Rights Violations

- Investigators can verify whether images of war or protests are genuine.
- NGOs and law enforcement can track perpetrators through leaked images.
- **Example**: A video frame from a conflict zone is matched to a known location using satellite imagery.

5. Challenges & Limitations of Reverse Image Search

5.1 Limited Database Coverage

- No search engine indexes all images on the internet.
- Private websites and encrypted platforms (e.g., WhatsApp, Telegram) are not included.

5.2 Difficulty with Altered or Cropped Images

- Reverse image search may fail if an image is heavily edited, flipped, or color-adjusted.
- Solution: Manually adjust brightness or crop sections before re-searching.

5.3 Privacy & Ethical Concerns

- Searching for someone's face without consent can raise legal and ethical issues.
- Some tools (e.g., PimEyes) allow people to request removal from databases.

5.4 Identifying Fake AI-Generated Images

- Deepfake images may not be recognized in searches.
- Solution: Use forensic tools like InVID, Forensically, or FotoForensics.

Reverse image searching is a powerful tool in OSINT investigations, helping analysts verify images, track sources, and expose misinformation. Understanding how it works—from image hashing and AI pattern recognition to searching across multiple platforms—is crucial for any investigator. However, limitations exist, and OSINT practitioners must combine reverse searching with other techniques like metadata analysis and forensic image examination for the most accurate results.

By mastering reverse image search techniques, OSINT analysts can uncover hidden connections, debunk false claims, and contribute to fact-based investigations in the digital age.

2.2 Using Google Lens, TinEye & Other Reverse Image Search Engines

Reverse image search is one of the most powerful tools in OSINT investigations, allowing analysts to trace images back to their sources, detect manipulations, and uncover hidden connections. Several search engines specialize in image analysis, with Google Lens, TinEye, and Yandex among the most widely used. This chapter explores how these tools work, their strengths and weaknesses, and how OSINT investigators can maximize their effectiveness.

1. Understanding Reverse Image Search Engines

Reverse image search engines operate by analyzing an image's visual features—such as shapes, colors, and textures—then comparing them against an extensive database of indexed images. Unlike traditional text-based searches, these engines rely on computer vision and pattern recognition to find matches.

Each search engine has unique capabilities, covering different image sources and providing varying levels of accuracy. Here's a brief comparison:

Search Engine	Strengths	Weaknesses
Google Lens	Large database, integrates with Google search, AI-powered object recognition	Removes metadata, struggles with altered images
TinEye	Tracks image history, finds exact matches, allows bulk searches	Limited database, doesn't recognize objects
Yandex	Strong facial recognition, works well for geolocation and landmarks	Mostly Russian websites, occasional false positives
Bing Visual Search	Good for product identification and object recognition	Smaller index than Google
PimEyes	Specialized in face recognition, strong accuracy	Privacy concerns, paid tool

Each tool serves different investigative purposes. Google Lens and Yandex are ideal for geolocation and object detection, while TinEye excels in tracking image history.

2. Using Google Lens for Reverse Image Search

2.1 What is Google Lens?

Google Lens is an AI-powered tool that can identify objects, landmarks, text, and products within an image. It integrates directly with Google Search, making it useful for quick OSINT investigations.

2.2 How to Use Google Lens for OSINT

Method 1: Using Google Lens on a Mobile Device

- Open the Google app or the Google Lens app (available on iOS and Android).
- Tap the camera icon and upload an image or take a new photo.
- Google Lens will analyze the image and suggest related searches, visually similar images, and website sources.

Method 2: Using Google Lens on Desktop (via Google Images)

- Go to Google Images.
- Click the camera icon in the search bar.
- Upload an image or paste an image URL.
- Google will return results with visually similar images and source pages.

2.3 OSINT Applications of Google Lens

- **Verifying misinformation** – Checking if an image has been misused in fake news.
- **Identifying landmarks** – Matching photos to known locations.
- **Extracting text from images** – Using Optical Character Recognition (OCR) for document analysis.
- **Recognizing objects and logos** – Identifying products or corporate branding.

2.4 Limitations of Google Lens

✗ **Struggles with edited images** – Cropped, filtered, or manipulated photos may not yield accurate results.
✗ **No metadata analysis** – Google Lens removes EXIF data, limiting forensic analysis.

✗ **Poor facial recognition** – Unlike Yandex or PimEyes, Google does not specialize in face matching.

3. Using TinEye for Image Tracking

3.1 What is TinEye?

TinEye is a specialized reverse image search engine focused on tracking the origins and history of images. Unlike Google Lens, TinEye does not analyze objects but instead looks for exact matches or slightly modified versions of an image.

3.2 How to Use TinEye

- Visit TinEye.
- Upload an image or enter an image URL.
- TinEye will return a list of matching images along with:
- First appearance of the image online.
- Any altered or cropped versions.
- Higher-resolution copies.

3.3 OSINT Applications of TinEye

- **Tracking image usage** – Finding where an image has been published.
- **Detecting manipulated images** – Identifying altered versions of an original photo.
- **Investigating copyright violations** – Checking if an image has been used without permission.

3.4 Limitations of TinEye

✗ **Smaller database** – TinEye's index is not as extensive as Google's.

✗ **No object or face recognition** – It only finds exact or near-exact matches.

✗ **No geolocation capabilities** – Cannot identify places within an image.

4. Using Yandex for Reverse Image Search

4.1 Why Yandex is a Powerful OSINT Tool

Yandex, the Russian search engine, has a superior facial and object recognition algorithm, making it useful for finding:

✓ People's photos across the web (e.g., tracking fake social media accounts).

✓ Geolocating images using street signs, buildings, and landmarks.

4.2 How to Use Yandex for OSINT

- Go to Yandex Images.
- Click the camera icon and upload an image or paste a URL.
- Yandex will return visually similar images, sometimes with precise facial matches.

4.3 OSINT Applications of Yandex

- **Facial recognition** – Matching a face to online social media profiles.
- **Locating unknown places** – Identifying landmarks, buildings, and street signs.
- **Unmasking fake accounts** – Finding stolen images used in fraudulent profiles.

4.4 Limitations of Yandex

✗ **Bias toward Russian content** – Mostly indexes Russian-language websites.

✗ **Privacy concerns** – Strong facial recognition may raise ethical concerns.

5. Other Useful Reverse Image Search Engines

5.1 Bing Visual Search

- Good for product identification and object recognition.
- Smaller database than Google and lacks advanced geolocation capabilities.

5.2 PimEyes (Face Recognition)

- Focuses on finding images of people across the internet.
- Highly accurate, but raises privacy concerns due to face-tracking capabilities.

5.3 Berify & Social Catfish

- Paid tools specializing in social media and dating site image searches.
- Useful for tracking scammers and catfish accounts.

6. Best Practices for Reverse Image Searching in OSINT

🔍 **Use multiple search engines** – No single tool has full coverage. Combine Google, Yandex, and TinEye for best results.

🔍 **Analyze variations** – Slightly crop or adjust brightness to detect altered versions.

🔍 **Cross-check metadata** – If available, extract EXIF data before searching.

🔍 **Verify context** – Just because an image appears on a site does not mean it originated there.

Google Lens, TinEye, and Yandex each provide unique strengths for reverse image searching. Google Lens is excellent for object and landmark recognition, TinEye is best for tracking image history, and Yandex excels in facial and geolocation analysis. By combining these tools, OSINT investigators can verify sources, track image alterations, and uncover hidden information more effectively. However, analysts must always consider privacy laws, ethical concerns, and the potential for false positives when using these technologies.

2.3 Advanced Search Operators for Finding Image Matches

Reverse image searching is a powerful OSINT (Open-Source Intelligence) technique, but sometimes, standard searches do not yield precise results. To refine and enhance investigations, OSINT analysts can use advanced search operators—specialized commands that help filter and narrow down image-related searches.

This chapter explores various search operators that work across Google, Bing, Yandex, and other search engines, explaining their functions, use cases, and practical examples for finding image matches, verifying sources, and uncovering hidden connections.

1. Understanding Advanced Search Operators in OSINT

Search operators are text-based commands that modify or refine search results. These operators help OSINT analysts:

✅ Find high-resolution versions of an image.

✅ Locate the first appearance of an image online.

✅ Identify image duplicates across different websites.

✅ Filter searches by file type, domain, or publication date.

✓ Combine text and reverse image search for deeper analysis.

By using these operators, investigators can bypass irrelevant results, pinpoint sources more quickly, and uncover hidden information.

2. Google Search Operators for Image OSINT

Google is one of the most powerful tools for OSINT investigations. However, default image searches often yield millions of results, making it difficult to find the right match. Using search operators refines the results significantly.

2.1 Filtering by File Type: filetype:

◆ **Purpose**: Finds images in specific formats (JPG, PNG, GIF, etc.).
◆ **Use Case**: Searching for high-quality versions of an image.

Example:

filetype:png "protest in Hong Kong"

◆ **What it does**: Returns only PNG images related to Hong Kong protests.

2.2 Searching by Domain: site:

◆ **Purpose**: Restricts results to a specific website.
◆ **Use Case**: Checking if an image has appeared on a particular site.

Example:

site:bbc.com "forest fire in California"

◆ **What it does**: Finds all BBC articles containing forest fire images in California.

2.3 Finding Cached & Deleted Images: cache:

◆ **Purpose**: Retrieves the last cached version of a webpage, even if it has been deleted.
◆ **Use Case**: Recovering an image that was removed from a website.

Example:

cache:example.com/missing-image.jpg

- ◆ **What it does**: Attempts to retrieve a deleted image from Google's cache.

2.4 Finding Similar Images: related:

- ◆ **Purpose**: Locates websites with visually similar images.
- ◆ **Use Case**: Discovering alternative sources for an image.

Example:

related:example.com/image1.jpg

- ◆ **What it does**: Shows other sites hosting similar versions of image1.jpg.

2.5 Searching by Date: before: & after:

- ◆ **Purpose**: Finds images published within a specific time frame.
- ◆ **Use Case**: Tracking when an image first appeared online.

Example:

"earthquake damage" before:2022-01-01

- ◆ **What it does**: Returns images of earthquake damage published before 2022.

3. Using Search Operators for Reverse Image Search

Most reverse image search tools do not have built-in operators, but analysts can combine text-based searches with reverse image lookups to refine results.

3.1 Combining Reverse Image Search with Google Operators

If an OSINT investigator reverse searches an image on Google but cannot find a reliable match, they can extract visual clues and use text operators for deeper searches.

Example: Investigating a Protest Image

- A reverse image search returns no clear matches for a photo of a protest.
- The investigator notices a banner with non-English text in the image.

Instead of relying solely on image search, they try:

"protest banner" site:twitter.com OR site:reddit.com

◆ **What it does**: Searches for text-based discussions about the protest banner on Twitter and Reddit.

3.2 Using Reverse Image Search Links with Operators

If Google Lens or Yandex provides a partial match, analysts can refine results using the inurl: operator.

Example:

inurl:/photo/ "suspicious image"

◆ **What it does**: Searches for URLs containing "/photo/" (common for image pages) related to suspicious images.

4. Yandex & Bing Search Operators for Image OSINT

Google isn't the only search engine with powerful operators. Yandex and Bing offer their own advanced filtering methods.

4.1 Yandex Search Operators

Yandex is known for its superior face recognition and geolocation capabilities. Investigators can combine operators to improve accuracy.

◆ **Searching for Faces on Russian Websites:**

site:vk.com "profile picture"

◆ **What it does**: Finds profile pictures on VK (a Russian social media platform).

◆ **Tracking Images by Date:**

"missing person" after:2021-06-01

◆ **What it does**: Finds missing person images published after June 2021.

4.2 Bing Search Operators

Bing's image search is less advanced but still useful for finding object-based matches.

◆ **Searching for Images by License:**

license:free "wildlife photography"

◆ **What it does**: Finds freely usable wildlife images.

◆ **Finding Local News Images:**

location:California "flood damage"

◆ **What it does**: Searches for California-based flood images.

5. Combining Multiple Search Operators for Maximum Accuracy

🔍 Scenario 1: Finding the First Appearance of an Image

A journalist wants to verify when a viral image of a fire first appeared online.

✅ **Step 1**: Perform a reverse image search using Google, Yandex, and TinEye.
✅ **Step 2**: If no clear date is found, use:

"forest fire" before:2019-01-01 filetype:jpg

✅ **Step 3**: Check archived pages with:

cache:example.com/fire-image.jpg

◆ **Outcome**: The investigator finds that the image was first published in 2018, not 2023 as claimed.

Advanced search operators are essential tools for OSINT analysts working with images. By refining searches using file types, domains, dates, and reverse image links, investigators can uncover hidden details, verify sources, and improve accuracy in their findings.

The most effective approach is to combine different search engines (Google, Yandex, TinEye) with precise search operators, ensuring comprehensive and accurate results in OSINT investigations.

2.4 Reverse Searching Images Across Social Media Platforms

Social media platforms are a goldmine of visual intelligence, often hosting original images before they spread across the internet. For OSINT analysts, reverse image searching on social media helps track image origins, verify accounts, expose fake profiles, and analyze geolocated content. However, unlike Google and TinEye, most social media platforms do not provide built-in reverse image search tools, requiring investigators to use alternative methods.

This chapter explores the best techniques for reverse searching images across Facebook, Twitter, Instagram, TikTok, LinkedIn, and other platforms, along with tools and strategies for effective investigations.

1. Why Reverse Image Search on Social Media?

Many OSINT investigations require tracing an image's social media footprint for various purposes:

✓ **Verifying social media profiles** – Identifying fake accounts using stolen profile pictures.

✓ **Locating the original source of an image** – Determining where an image was first uploaded.

✓ **Tracking image misuse or disinformation** – Finding how images are manipulated or taken out of context.

✓ **Identifying locations or events** – Geolocating images shared in real-time.

✓ **Finding more information about a person or entity** – Connecting profiles across different social platforms.

Since social media often acts as the first point of upload for many images, reverse searching in this space is crucial for OSINT work.

2. Challenges of Reverse Image Search on Social Media

Unlike standard websites indexed by Google, many social media platforms have closed ecosystems that make direct reverse image searches difficult. Common challenges include:

✗ **Limited searchability** – Platforms like Facebook and Instagram do not allow direct image searching within their networks.

✗ **Privacy restrictions** – Some profiles and images are hidden due to privacy settings.

✗ **Content removal** – Users can delete images, making it harder to trace the original source.

✗ **Modified images** – People often crop, filter, or edit images, making exact matches harder to find.

✗ **Watermarks and overlays** – Meme pages and fake news sites frequently add text or overlays to obscure original sources.

Despite these limitations, several workarounds and external tools exist for tracing images across social platforms.

3. Reverse Searching Images on Specific Social Media Platforms

3.1 Facebook Image Search Techniques

Facebook does not offer a built-in reverse image search feature, but analysts can use alternative methods:

Method 1: Using Google Reverse Image Search for Facebook Photos

- **Go to Google Images**: images.google.com
- Click the camera icon and upload a photo or paste an image URL.

Add the Facebook domain filter to focus the search:

site:facebook.com "profile picture"

- If the image is a profile picture, check the Facebook numeric ID (explained below).

Method 2: Extracting Facebook's Image Numeric ID

Every image uploaded to Facebook has a unique numeric identifier embedded in its file name:

https://scontent.fbxx1-1.fna.fbcdn.net/v/t1.0-9/102938475_10158399234512345_12345678890123456789_n.jpg

- The middle number (10158399234512345) represents the Facebook user ID.
- Searching for this number on Google may lead to the original Facebook profile.

3.2 Twitter (X) Image Search

Twitter is more open than Facebook for OSINT investigations, and images can often be traced back to their original tweets.

Method 1: Using Google Reverse Image Search for Twitter Photos

Use Google Images with the site:twitter.com filter:

site:twitter.com "earthquake aftermath photo"

This narrows results to Twitter-hosted images.

Method 2: Using Twitter's Advanced Search

- Go to Twitter Advanced Search.
- Use keywords related to the image (e.g., "fire in California").
- Filter by dates to locate the first tweet containing the image.

Method 3: Checking Twitter Metadata (for unedited images)

- Download the image from Twitter.
- Check the EXIF metadata (only works if the original uploader did not strip metadata).

3.3 Instagram Image Search

Instagram is one of the hardest platforms for reverse image searching due to:

✗ Strict privacy settings (profiles may be private).

✗ No built-in image search options.

✗ High use of filters and edits, making reverse searching less effective.

Method 1: Using Google Reverse Image Search for Instagram Photos

site:instagram.com "beach sunset"

◆ **What it does**: Searches for public Instagram images matching "beach sunset."

Method 2: Searching for Hashtags and Locations

If an image contains location clues or objects, try searching Instagram manually:

- Go to Instagram Explore (www.instagram.com/explore).
- Use hashtags related to the image (e.g., #parisview).
- Check posts in geotagged locations if the image suggests a specific place.

3.4 TikTok Reverse Image Search

TikTok does not support reverse image searching directly, but images from TikTok videos can sometimes be found elsewhere.

Method 1: Extracting Video Thumbnails for Reverse Search

- Open a TikTok video and take a screenshot of a key frame.
- Use Google Reverse Image Search or Yandex to check if the image appears elsewhere.

Method 2: Searching TikTok by Keywords

If a screenshot includes text overlays or a username, try:

site:tiktok.com "funny cat video"

◆ **What it does**: Searches for TikTok posts containing "funny cat video."

3.5 LinkedIn Reverse Image Search

LinkedIn is a valuable source for tracking professional headshots and exposing fake job profiles.

Method 1: Using Google Reverse Image Search for LinkedIn Photos

site:linkedin.com "John Doe"

⧫ **What it does**: Finds LinkedIn profiles matching "John Doe."

Method 2: Using Yandex for Face Recognition

Yandex reverse image search is exceptionally good at matching profile pictures, even if they are slightly edited.

Steps:

- Upload the image to Yandex Reverse Image Search.
- If a LinkedIn profile exists with the same picture, Yandex may return it.

4. OSINT Tools for Reverse Image Searching on Social Media

Besides Google and Yandex, various third-party tools specialize in social media image searches:

Tool	Best For
PimEyes	Face recognition across multiple platforms
Social Catfish	Finding social media accounts linked to an image
Berify	Reverse image search for copyrighted content
IntelTechniques Image Tools	Various social media image lookup methods
ExifTool	Extracting metadata from unedited images

Reverse image searching on social media is more complex than on traditional websites, but with the right techniques, OSINT analysts can track down original images, verify accounts, and uncover hidden connections.

⧫ Google and Yandex are essential for finding social media images across multiple platforms.

◆ Platform-specific techniques (e.g., Facebook numeric ID, LinkedIn headshot search) can reveal hidden data.

◆ Third-party OSINT tools can enhance investigations, especially for face recognition and profile tracking.

By combining these methods, OSINT investigators can effectively trace images back to their source—a crucial step in verifying authenticity, debunking misinformation, and conducting digital forensics.

2.5 Identifying Modified, Cropped & Edited Images

In OSINT investigations, a crucial challenge is determining whether an image has been altered, cropped, or manipulated to mislead viewers. Images can be edited to remove crucial details, misrepresent events, or spread misinformation, making it essential for analysts to verify their authenticity.

This chapter explores how to detect modifications, analyze cropped images, and identify edited content using various forensic techniques, metadata analysis, and reverse search strategies.

1. Why Image Manipulation Matters in OSINT

Images are frequently edited for different reasons:

✅ **Propaganda & Misinformation** – Altered photos are used to push false narratives.

✅ **Fake News & Hoaxes** – Edited images can support fabricated stories.

✅ **Fraud & Scams** – Scammers modify images to deceive victims.

✅ **Social Media Virality** – Cropped or edited images may misrepresent real events.

✅ **Digital Censorship** – Details in an image may be blurred or removed to hide the truth.

Understanding how images are manipulated helps analysts verify authenticity, uncover deception, and prevent the spread of false information.

2. Identifying Cropped & Resized Images

Cropping and resizing images are common ways to hide important details or make it harder to perform reverse image searches.

2.1 How Cropping Affects Reverse Image Search

- If an image is cropped, reverse image search tools like Google Lens, TinEye, and Yandex may fail to find matches.
- The more an image is cropped or resized, the harder it becomes to trace its original source.

Solution: Reverse Searching Variants of an Image

✓ **Try Yandex**: Yandex reverse search performs better with cropped images compared to Google.

✓ **Use Multiple Tools**: Compare results from Google Lens, TinEye, and Bing.

✓ **Look for Context Clues**: If a cropped image includes unique elements (e.g., a building, a logo), perform text-based searches related to those details.

2.2 Detecting Cropping Using Image Metadata

Some images contain metadata (EXIF data) that reveals if an image has been cropped.

✓ Use ExifTool or Jeffrey's Image Metadata Viewer to check:

- Original dimensions vs. current dimensions
- Cropping indicators in the metadata
- Software used to edit the image (e.g., Photoshop, Snapseed, Lightroom)

3. Detecting Edited & Manipulated Images

Edited images can be photoshopped, color-adjusted, blurred, or distorted to deceive viewers.

3.1 Using Forensic Tools to Detect Edits

Several OSINT tools specialize in detecting image manipulation:

Tool	Function
FotoForensics	Analyzes JPEG compression to reveal digital edits
Forensically (29a.ch)	Detects cloned areas, hidden objects, and inconsistencies
Image Edited?	Compares an image against known originals
Error Level Analysis (ELA)	Highlights altered sections in an image
Ghiro	Performs deep image forensics analysis

3.2 Error Level Analysis (ELA) for Detecting Edits

Error Level Analysis (ELA) is a technique that reveals inconsistencies in JPEG compression, exposing areas of an image that have been digitally altered.

How to Perform ELA Analysis:

- Upload an image to FotoForensics or Forensically.
- The tool generates an ELA heatmap where edited areas glow brighter than the rest of the image.
- If certain areas stand out, it suggests that those parts of the image were altered separately from the rest.

Example of ELA in Action:

🔍 **Scenario**: A viral image claims to show an explosion in a war zone.

✅ **ELA Analysis**: Reveals that the explosion was pasted onto the image, proving it is fake.

4. Identifying Faces or Objects That Have Been Manipulated

4.1 Cloning & Object Duplication

- Fake images often contain cloned objects to make scenes appear larger or more dramatic.
- Tools like Forensically's Clone Detection can highlight duplicated patterns in an image.

Example:

🔍 A protest image appears to show thousands of identical people.

✓ Clone Detection reveals repeated figures, proving that the crowd was artificially increased.

4.2 Deepfake & AI-Generated Image Detection

AI-generated and deepfake images are increasingly used for disinformation campaigns and identity fraud.

Tools to Detect AI-Generated Images:

- **PimEyes** (Face recognition for reverse searching images)
- **Deepware Scanner** (Detects deepfake manipulation)

Hugging Face Deepfake Detection

🔍 **Key Signs of AI-Generated Images:**

✓ **Irregular backgrounds** – Blurred or distorted details around faces.
✓ **Asymmetry** – Inconsistencies in earrings, glasses, or reflections.
✓ **Unrealistic skin textures** – Over-smooth, plastic-like appearances.

5. Identifying Filtered, Color-Adjusted, or Blurred Images

Some images are subtly altered using filters, brightness changes, or color corrections to mislead viewers.

5.1 Reverse Searching Color-Edited Images

- Some platforms allow searching by grayscale versions of images to bypass color alterations.
- Convert the image to black & white before running a reverse image search.

5.2 Checking for Blurring or Pixel Manipulation

- Some images have blurred backgrounds or pixelated sections to remove critical details (e.g., logos, timestamps).
- AI de-blurring tools like Remini or Let's Enhance can restore clarity.

6. Case Study: Uncovering a Cropped & Edited Image in Disinformation

🔍 **Scenario**: A news outlet publishes an image claiming to show a politician in an illegal meeting.

✅ OSINT Analysis:

- **Reverse Image Search** – Finds an uncropped version showing the politician in a public event, not a secret meeting.
- **ELA Analysis** – Detects digital editing around the politician's face.
- **Metadata Check** – Reveals the original photo was taken in a different year than claimed.

📌 **Conclusion**: The image was cropped and edited to mislead the public.

7. Conclusion: Best Practices for Identifying Image Manipulation

◆ **Use multiple reverse image search tools** – Google Lens, Yandex, and TinEye handle modifications differently.

◆ **Perform forensic analysis** – Tools like ELA and Clone Detection reveal hidden edits.

◆ **Check metadata when available** – It may expose cropping, editing software, or timestamps.

◆ **Compare multiple sources** – Find the uncropped or unedited version of an image for context.

◆ **Use AI detection tools** – Deepfake and face recognition tools help verify authenticity.

By applying these techniques, OSINT investigators can expose altered images, prevent misinformation, and ensure accurate digital investigations.

2.6 Case Study: Identifying a Fake Profile Using Reverse Image Search

The rise of fake profiles on social media has become a significant challenge in OSINT investigations. Fraudsters, scammers, catfishers, and even intelligence operatives create false identities using stolen or AI-generated images to deceive individuals or organizations. In this case study, we will walk through an OSINT investigation where a fake profile was uncovered using reverse image search and forensic analysis.

1. The Scenario: A Suspicious LinkedIn Profile

An investigative journalist received a LinkedIn connection request from an individual named "Mark Stevenson," who claimed to be a cybersecurity expert working for a well-known tech company.

🔍 Red Flags That Raised Suspicion:

✓ The profile was recently created (less than a month old).

✓ It had only one profile picture and minimal activity.

✓ The work history listed prestigious roles, but with vague job descriptions.

✓ No mutual connections or endorsements.

✓ The profile picture looked too polished—like a stock photo or AI-generated image.

To verify if the profile was legitimate, an OSINT image-based investigation was launched.

2. Step 1: Performing a Reverse Image Search

The first step was to run the profile picture through multiple reverse image search engines:

Method 1: Google Reverse Image Search

- Downloaded the LinkedIn profile picture.
- Uploaded it to Google Images (images.google.com).
- Google returned no exact matches, but a similar image appeared on a stock photo website.

Method 2: Yandex Reverse Image Search

- Uploaded the same image to Yandex Images (yandex.com/images).
- Yandex found a perfect match—the image belonged to a real estate agent in Germany whose photo had been stolen.

🔎 **Conclusion**: The profile picture was not of "Mark Stevenson" but belonged to someone else.

3. Step 2: Checking for AI-Generated Images (Deepfake Profile Detection)

Since some fake profiles use AI-generated faces, the next step was to determine if the image was created by AI rather than stolen from an existing person.

✅ **Tools Used:**

- **PimEyes** (Facial recognition search)
- **This Person Does Not Exist** (Comparing with AI-generated images)
- **Sensity.AI** (Deepfake detection)

🔍 **Findings:**

The image was not AI-generated but was a real person's photo misused for deception.

📖 **Conclusion**: The profile creator likely stole the image instead of generating a deepfake.

4. Step 3: Cross-Checking Social Media & Web Presence

If "Mark Stevenson" was a real person, there should be traces of him online. The next step was to investigate:

Method 1: Searching for the Name on Google

- A Google search of "Mark Stevenson cybersecurity" yielded no relevant LinkedIn or work-related results.
- No articles, interviews, or previous social media activity—unusual for a cybersecurity expert.

Method 2: Cross-Checking on Other Social Platforms

- Facebook & Twitter searches showed no matching personal accounts.
- Instagram had no photos resembling the LinkedIn profile picture.

📖 **Conclusion**: The person did not exist outside of LinkedIn.

5. Step 4: Verifying the Claimed Workplace

The profile stated that "Mark Stevenson" worked at a well-known cybersecurity firm. To verify:

✓ **Checked the company's official website** – No employee named Mark Stevenson.

✓ **Searched for the name in employee directories** – No LinkedIn mentions.

✓ **Looked for past conference talks or published work** – Nothing found.

🚨 **Final Conclusion:**

- The profile was completely fake.
- The image was stolen from a real person.
- No digital footprint or employment records existed for "Mark Stevenson."

6. Why Was This Fake Profile Created? (Possible Motives)

Fake profiles on LinkedIn and other platforms are often used for:

1️⃣ **Social Engineering Attacks** – Building trust to scam or gather intelligence.

2️⃣ **Phishing Attempts** – Sending malicious links disguised as job offers.

3️⃣ **Corporate Espionage** – Gaining access to employees and sensitive company data.

4️⃣ **Influence Operations** – Spreading misinformation or political propaganda.

5️⃣ **Romance Scams & Fraud** – Using fake identities for financial scams.

Based on the findings, "Mark Stevenson" was likely created for cyber espionage or scam purposes.

7. Key Takeaways: How to Spot & Investigate Fake Profiles Using Reverse Image Search

✓ **Reverse Image Search is Crucial** – Use Google, Yandex, and PimEyes to find stolen images.

✓ **Check for AI-Generated Faces** – Tools like Sensity.AI detect deepfake profile pictures.

✓ **Verify Online Presence** – Real professionals have a history of work, mentions, and social activity.

✓ **Analyze Profile Details** – Watch for generic descriptions, recent accounts, and lack of connections.

✓ **Confirm Employment Claims** – Use official websites and employee directories to verify work history.

By following these OSINT techniques, investigators can quickly detect and expose fake profiles, preventing fraud, misinformation, and cyber threats.

3. EXIF Metadata & Digital Forensics

In this chapter, we will dive into the world of EXIF metadata and its critical role in digital forensics. EXIF (Exchangeable Image File Format) data embedded in images holds a wealth of information, including details about the device used to capture the image, timestamp, GPS coordinates, and even the software used for editing. By extracting and analyzing this metadata, OSINT analysts can uncover crucial clues about the origin, authenticity, and history of digital images. We will explore the tools and techniques for accessing and interpreting EXIF data, as well as the importance of digital forensics in validating information and ensuring the integrity of the intelligence collected.

3.1 What is EXIF Data & How It Can Be Used in Investigations

In the world of OSINT (Open-Source Intelligence), digital images are more than just pixels—they often contain hidden metadata known as EXIF data (Exchangeable Image File Format). EXIF data can provide critical information about an image's origin, including the device used, time and date, GPS coordinates, camera settings, and even software edits. This makes EXIF data an essential tool in verifying authenticity, tracing locations, and uncovering digital manipulation.

1. Understanding EXIF Data

1.1 What is EXIF Data?

EXIF (Exchangeable Image File Format) data is embedded metadata stored within digital photos and videos. When an image is taken with a smartphone or camera, the device automatically saves technical and contextual details as part of the image file.

1.2 Common Information Stored in EXIF Metadata

Category	Metadata Details
Camera Details	Brand, model, lens type
Image Settings	Resolution, ISO, shutter speed, aperture
Date & Time	When the photo was taken
GPS Location	Latitude, longitude, altitude (if enabled)
Software Used	Editing tools like Photoshop, Lightroom
File Properties	File name, size, format

🔍 **Example**: A photo taken on an iPhone 14 may contain metadata like:

- **Device**: Apple iPhone 14 Pro
- **Time Stamp**: 2024-01-05 14:32:10
- **Location**: 40.7128° N, 74.0060° W (New York City)
- **Software Used**: Adobe Photoshop (indicating edits)

2. How EXIF Data is Used in OSINT Investigations

2.1 Geolocation Tracking: Finding Where an Image Was Taken

One of the most powerful aspects of EXIF data is GPS coordinates. If location services were enabled on the device, the metadata may reveal exact latitude, longitude, and altitude.

✅ **Use Case:**

- An OSINT investigator receives an anonymous threat image.
- By extracting EXIF data, they find GPS coordinates leading to a remote location.
- Cross-referencing with Google Maps reveals it was taken near a known extremist hideout.

🔍 **How to Extract GPS Data from Images:**

- Use ExifTool or Jeffrey's EXIF Viewer to extract metadata.
- Look for latitude and longitude entries.
- Enter coordinates into Google Maps for precise location tracking.

⚠ **Limitations:**

- Social media platforms strip EXIF data when images are uploaded.
- Users may disable location tagging on their devices.

2.2 Verifying Authenticity & Detecting Manipulation

EXIF data helps verify whether an image is authentic or altered. If an image has been modified using software, EXIF metadata may reveal the editing history.

✅ Use Case:

- A journalist receives an image claiming to be from a recent protest.
- Checking the EXIF data shows the image was taken three years ago and edited in Photoshop.
- The claim is false, and the image is being used for misinformation.

🔍 Key EXIF Clues for Fake Images:

- **Date inconsistencies** – Does the timestamp match the event's claimed date?
- **Editing software detected** – If Photoshop, Lightroom, or Snapseed is listed, the image has been altered.
- **Camera mismatch** – A photo allegedly from a smartphone but shows DSLR metadata is suspicious.

🚨 Limitations:

- Some users remove EXIF data before sharing images.
- Fake images can be created without EXIF data, making other OSINT methods necessary.

2.3 Unmasking Identities & Fake Accounts

EXIF data has been used to track down criminals, expose fake social media profiles, and uncover scams.

✅ Use Case:

- A fraudster sends a victim a selfie claiming to be in Paris.
- EXIF data reveals GPS coordinates from Russia, exposing the deception.

- The victim avoids a romance scam.

🔍 Common Clues in EXIF for Identifying Fake Profiles:

- **Camera metadata** – Is the photo from a high-end DSLR but claims to be a casual selfie?
- **Location mismatch** – Does the GPS data contradict what the person claims?
- **Editing software used** – Was the profile picture altered in FaceApp or Photoshop?

📷 Limitations:

Social media platforms like Facebook, Twitter, and Instagram strip EXIF data for privacy reasons.

3. How to Extract & Analyze EXIF Data

There are various tools available for extracting EXIF metadata from images:

3.1 Online Tools (No Installation Needed)

✓ Jeffrey's Image Metadata Viewer

✓ Exifmeta

3.2 Software Tools for Deeper Analysis

✓ **ExifTool** (Command-line tool for detailed analysis)
✓ **Photo Sherlock** (Mobile app for EXIF extraction)
✓ **Ghiro** (Forensic-level image analysis)

🔍 How to Use ExifTool (Command Line)

exiftool image.jpg

This command extracts metadata and displays all available EXIF data.

4. How Criminals Try to Remove or Alter EXIF Data

Since EXIF data can expose locations and identities, criminals and hackers often remove metadata before sharing images.

4.1 How Metadata is Removed or Altered

⊘ **EXIF Removers** – Tools like ExifPurge, ImageOptim, or Photoshop can delete metadata.
⊘ **Social Media Uploads** – Facebook, Twitter, and WhatsApp automatically strip EXIF data.
⊘ **Metadata Editors** – Advanced users may modify GPS data to mislead investigators.

✓ OSINT Countermeasure: Even if EXIF is missing, investigators can still:

- Reverse image search to find unedited versions.
- Analyze shadows and landmarks for geolocation clues.
- Use AI forensic tools like FotoForensics to detect tampering.

5. Case Study: Using EXIF Data to Solve a Crime

🔍 Real-World Example: Identifying a Kidnapper's Location

In a high-profile criminal case, a kidnapper sent a photo of the victim to authorities. Investigators extracted EXIF data, revealing GPS coordinates from an abandoned warehouse. Law enforcement used this data to rescue the victim and apprehend the suspect.

📖 **Takeaway**: Even when criminals try to cover their tracks, EXIF data can expose hidden details and aid investigations.

6. Ethical Considerations & Legal Aspects

While EXIF analysis is a powerful OSINT tool, investigators must follow ethical and legal guidelines:

⚖️ **Respect Privacy** – Extracting EXIF data from personal photos without consent may violate privacy laws.
⚖️ **Legality Varies by Country** – Some jurisdictions restrict metadata collection for OSINT purposes.

⚖️ **Responsible Use** – Always verify findings through multiple sources before making claims.

✅ **Best Practice**: EXIF should be used to verify authenticity, detect manipulation, and aid investigations, not for unauthorized tracking.

7. Conclusion: Why EXIF Data is a Game-Changer for OSINT

📌 EXIF data reveals hidden details in digital images, from camera settings to GPS coordinates.

📌 It is crucial for verifying authenticity, tracking locations, and uncovering fraud.

📌 Criminals may remove metadata, but other OSINT techniques can still expose deception.

📌 Legal and ethical guidelines must always be followed when using EXIF data in investigations.

By mastering EXIF analysis, OSINT investigators can uncover hidden truths, verify sources, and track digital footprints with precision.

3.2 Extracting Metadata from Images Using OSINT Tools

Metadata embedded within digital images holds valuable clues for OSINT (Open-Source Intelligence) investigations. These hidden details—such as camera information, timestamps, GPS coordinates, and editing history—can provide critical intelligence when analyzing images. Extracting metadata can help validate sources, trace locations, detect digital manipulation, and unmask fraudulent activities.

In this chapter, we explore the tools and techniques used to extract metadata from images effectively.

1. Understanding Image Metadata & Its Role in OSINT

Every digital image contains hidden metadata that provides context about how, when, and where it was created. The most common type of metadata is EXIF (Exchangeable Image File Format) data, but images may also include IPTC, XMP, and other metadata formats.

1.1 What Types of Metadata Are Embedded in Images?

Category	Metadata Details
Camera Data	Brand, model, serial number
Image Settings	ISO, shutter speed, aperture
Date & Time	When the photo was taken
GPS Location	Latitude, longitude, altitude (if enabled)
Software Used	Photoshop, Lightroom, Snapseed (if edited)
File Properties	File name, format, size, compression

🔍 **Example**: A photo taken with an iPhone may contain:

- **Device**: Apple iPhone 14 Pro
- **Timestamp**: 2024-02-18 12:45:30
- **GPS Data**: 51.5074° N, 0.1278° W (London, UK)
- **Software Used**: Adobe Photoshop (indicating possible edits)

Why does this matter?

- Investigators can geolocate where an image was taken.
- Metadata can expose fake images by revealing editing history.
- Law enforcement can track criminal activities using GPS data.

2. OSINT Tools for Extracting Image Metadata

There are multiple free and paid tools available for extracting metadata from images. These tools vary in complexity, from web-based EXIF viewers to advanced forensic analysis software.

2.1 Online EXIF Viewers (Quick & Easy Tools)

✅ **Jeffrey's Image Metadata Viewer**

- Upload an image or enter a URL.
- Displays EXIF, IPTC, and XMP metadata.

✅ **Exifmeta**

- Fast, web-based tool for viewing metadata.
- Works with JPG, PNG, and TIFF files.

✅ FotoForensics

- Provides deep analysis of metadata.
- Detects possible image manipulation.

🚀 **Best for**: Quick metadata extraction without installation.

2.2 Software-Based Tools for Detailed Analysis

✅ ExifTool (by Phil Harvey)

- Command-line tool for deep EXIF metadata analysis.
- Can extract, edit, or remove metadata.
- Works on Windows, Mac, and Linux.

📌 **Example: Running ExifTool in a terminal:**

exiftool image.jpg

This command extracts and displays all metadata from the image.

✅ Exif Pilot

- GUI-based EXIF tool for Windows.
- Allows metadata extraction and editing.

✅ Ghiro (Forensic-Level Image Analysis)

- Detects metadata manipulation.
- Includes image hashing and forensic tools.

🚀 **Best for**: Investigators needing in-depth metadata extraction.

2.3 Mobile Apps for EXIF Analysis

✓ Photo Sherlock (iOS & Android)

- Extracts EXIF data directly from a phone's gallery.
- Offers reverse image search integration.

✓ Metapho (iOS)

- View and remove metadata from images.

🖋 **Best for**: Field investigators who need mobile-friendly EXIF tools.

3. Extracting Metadata: Step-by-Step Guide

Let's walk through how to extract metadata from an image using different tools.

3.1 Extracting EXIF Data Using an Online Tool

- **Step 1**: Open Jeffrey's Image Metadata Viewer (link).
- **Step 2:** Upload an image or paste a URL.
- **Step 3**: Click "Submit" to view metadata.
- **Step 4**: Analyze the date, location, and software history for clues.

📌 **Example Findings:**

- The photo was taken on March 5, 2023 in Berlin, Germany.
- The software used was Adobe Lightroom (suggesting it was edited).

3.2 Extracting Metadata Using ExifTool (Advanced Users)

- **Step 1:** Install ExifTool on your system.
- **Step 2**: Open the command line (Terminal or Command Prompt).
- **Step 3**: Run the following command:

exiftool image.jpg

Step 4: Review the extracted metadata, including:

- Camera model
- GPS coordinates

- Editing software

📌 **Example Findings:**

- The image was taken with a Canon EOS 5D Mark IV.
- GPS data shows the image was captured in Los Angeles, USA.
- The image was edited using Photoshop CC 2022.

3.3 Extracting Metadata from Social Media Images

Most social media platforms strip metadata when an image is uploaded. However, some forensic techniques can still uncover useful information.

✅ **Step 1**: Perform a reverse image search using Google, Yandex, or TinEye.

✅ **Step 2**: Look for original versions of the image that still contain EXIF data.

✅ **Step 3:** Use FotoForensics to check for digital alterations.

✅ **Step 4:** Analyze shadows, objects, and context clues to estimate location manually.

⚠ **Warning**: Social media images may have altered metadata, so always cross-check findings.

4. Detecting Metadata Manipulation & Removal

Criminals and scammers often delete or alter EXIF data to cover their tracks. Here's how to detect tampering:

4.1 How Metadata is Removed or Modified

🚫 **EXIF Removal Tools** – Software like ExifPurge deletes metadata.

🚫 **Social Media Uploads** – Facebook, Instagram, and Twitter strip EXIF data automatically.

🚫 **Manual Editing** – Metadata fields can be modified using tools like ExifTool.

4.2 Detecting Manipulation

✅ **Compare timestamps** – Do the metadata dates align with the claim?

✅ **Check for missing metadata** – If an image has zero metadata, it was likely stripped.

✅ **Analyze file history** – Metadata may show which software edited the image.

🖋 **Countermeasure**: Use AI-based forensic tools like Ghiro or FotoForensics to detect inconsistencies.

5. Case Study: Using EXIF Data to Solve a Crime

📌 **Real-World Example: Identifying a Terrorist's Location**

- A journalist receives an anonymous threat photo.
- Investigators extract EXIF GPS data, showing a remote desert area in Syria.
- The GPS coordinates match a known terrorist training camp.
- Law enforcement uses this intelligence for a successful counterterrorism operation.

🖋 **Key Takeaway**: Even small metadata details can expose critical intelligence.

6. Ethical & Legal Considerations in Metadata Extraction

⚖ **Respect Privacy** – Extracting metadata from personal photos without consent may violate privacy laws.

⚖ **Legal Restrictions** – Some countries have strict regulations on metadata analysis.

⚖ **Responsible Use** – Metadata should only be used for verifying authenticity, digital forensics, and lawful investigations.

✓ **Best Practice**: Always verify findings with multiple OSINT techniques before drawing conclusions.

7. Conclusion: Why Metadata Analysis is Essential for OSINT

📌 EXIF metadata provides hidden clues that help verify images, track locations, and detect tampering.

📌 Multiple OSINT tools (ExifTool, Jeffrey's Viewer, FotoForensics) can extract metadata.

📌 Social media images strip metadata, but forensic techniques can still uncover details.

📌 Ethical considerations must be followed to ensure responsible metadata analysis.

By mastering metadata extraction, OSINT analysts can uncover hidden truths, detect deception, and strengthen digital investigations.

3.3 Identifying Camera Models, GPS Coordinates & Timestamps

Digital images contain hidden metadata that can reveal which camera was used, when the image was taken, and where it was captured. This information is embedded in the EXIF (Exchangeable Image File Format) data, a crucial element for OSINT (Open-Source Intelligence) investigations. Analysts can use this metadata to verify image authenticity, track locations, and uncover manipulation attempts.

In this chapter, we will explore how to identify camera models, extract GPS coordinates, and analyze timestamps to enhance OSINT investigations.

1. Understanding EXIF Metadata & Its Importance

When a digital camera or smartphone captures a photo, it automatically embeds technical details about the image in its metadata. This includes:

- Camera make and model
- Lens specifications
- Timestamp (date & time of capture)
- GPS coordinates (if enabled)

These details help investigators trace the origin of an image, verify claims, and detect inconsistencies.

2. Identifying Camera Models & Device Information

2.1 How Camera Metadata Helps OSINT Investigations

Every camera records unique information in an image's EXIF metadata. By analyzing this data, investigators can:

✅ **Determine the camera make & model** – Helps identify whether an image was taken with a smartphone, DSLR, or security camera.
✅ **Detect fake claims** – If someone says a photo was taken with an iPhone 15, but metadata shows a Samsung Galaxy S21, they may be misleading.
✅ **Identify image sources** – Some images have unique device serial numbers, which can help track specific cameras.

2.2 Extracting Camera Details from an Image

Method 1: Using Online EXIF Viewers

- Visit Jeffrey's EXIF Viewer or Exifmeta.
- Upload the image or enter its URL.
- Review the "Camera Model" and "Make" fields.

📌 Example:

- **Make**: Canon
- **Model**: EOS 5D Mark IV
- **Lens**: EF 24-70mm f/2.8L

Method 2: Using ExifTool (Advanced Users)

- Install ExifTool on your computer.
- Open a command-line interface (CMD, Terminal, or PowerShell).

Run the following command:

exiftool image.jpg

Locate Make and Model fields in the output.

📌 **Key Insight**: If an image is claimed to be from a high-end DSLR but metadata shows it was taken with an inexpensive smartphone, the image may have been staged or manipulated.

3. Extracting GPS Coordinates from an Image

3.1 How GPS Metadata Helps OSINT Investigations

Many modern cameras and smartphones record latitude and longitude coordinates in an image's metadata when GPS is enabled. Investigators can:

✅ **Determine where a photo was taken** – Useful for verifying locations.

✅ **Track suspect movements** – Law enforcement can trace where a suspect was based on location data.

✓ **Cross-check claims** – If an image is claimed to be from New York, but GPS metadata shows it was taken in Tokyo, it may be misleading.

3.2 Extracting GPS Coordinates from an Image

Method 1: Using an Online EXIF Viewer

- Open Jeffrey's Image Metadata Viewer.
- Upload the image or enter its URL.
- Scroll down to the GPS section to find latitude and longitude.
- Click the Google Maps link to see the exact location.

📌 **Example Output:**

- **Latitude**: 48.858844° N
- **Longitude**: 2.294351° E
- **Location**: Eiffel Tower, Paris, France

Method 2: Using ExifTool for GPS Data

Open a command-line interface.

Run:

exiftool -GPSLatitude -GPSLongitude -GPSAltitude image.jpg

Copy the coordinates and check them on Google Maps.

3.3 What If an Image Has No GPS Data?

📌 **Reasons GPS metadata might be missing:**

- The camera's GPS setting was turned off.
- The image was uploaded to social media, which strips metadata.
- The metadata was manually removed using EXIF-cleaning tools.

📌 **Alternative methods to determine location:**

- Reverse image search (Google Lens, TinEye) to find similar images.
- Visual clues analysis (landmarks, signs, shadows).

- Cross-referencing social media posts with geotagged content.

📌 **Pro Tip**: Even if GPS data is missing, other metadata (such as the camera model and timestamp) can still provide useful intelligence.

4. Extracting & Analyzing Timestamps

4.1 Why Timestamps Matter in OSINT

Timestamps in image metadata can:

✅ **Confirm when an image was taken** – Useful in investigations and fact-checking.
✅ **Expose timeline inconsistencies** – If a suspect claims they were in one place, but metadata shows they took a photo elsewhere at the same time, it raises red flags.
✅ **Detect manipulation** – If an image's timestamp doesn't match the context, it may have been altered.

4.2 How to Extract Image Timestamps

Method 1: Using an Online Tool

- Upload the image to Exifmeta or Jeffrey's EXIF Viewer.
- Find the Date/Time Original field.

📌 **Example Output:**

- **Date Taken**: 2024-02-18 14:30:15
- **Time Zone**: UTC+2

Method 2: Using ExifTool (Command Line)

Run:

exiftool -DateTimeOriginal image.jpg

📌 **Example Output:**

Date/Time Original : 2024:02:18 14:30:15

4.3 Detecting Timestamp Manipulation

Criminals may alter timestamps to mislead investigators. Here's how to detect inconsistencies:

✅ **Compare EXIF timestamps with other sources** – Social media metadata, CCTV footage, or witness accounts.
✅ **Look for inconsistencies in shadow lengths** – If an image's shadows don't match the claimed time of day, it may be fake.
✅ **Analyze metadata history** – Tools like Ghiro can detect if a timestamp was modified.

🚀 **Real-World Example:**

In a cybercrime investigation, a fraudster claimed an image was taken on March 1, 2024, but metadata analysis showed the actual capture date was December 12, 2023. This discrepancy exposed the fraud.

5. Key Takeaways

✦ Camera model metadata can help identify the device used to capture an image.
✦ GPS coordinates can geolocate an image, but metadata may be removed or altered.
✦ Timestamps help verify when an image was taken and detect inconsistencies.
✦ EXIF tools like ExifTool, Jeffrey's Viewer, and FotoForensics help extract metadata.
✦ Even without metadata, visual clues and reverse image search can provide intelligence.

By mastering camera model identification, GPS tracking, and timestamp analysis, OSINT analysts can validate sources, track digital footprints, and detect manipulation attempts in image-based investigations.

3.4 How Metadata Can Be Removed, Altered or Faked

Metadata plays a crucial role in OSINT investigations, as it provides essential details about an image's origin, timestamp, and location. However, this metadata can be removed, altered, or even faked—either to protect privacy or to mislead investigators. Understanding these manipulations is vital for verifying images and detecting potential deception.

In this section, we will explore how metadata can be erased, modified, or falsified, the tools used for these purposes, and the methods OSINT analysts can employ to detect tampering.

1. Why People Remove or Alter Metadata

There are several reasons why individuals or organizations might manipulate metadata:

✅ **Privacy Protection** – Journalists, whistleblowers, and activists may remove metadata to prevent tracking.

✅ **Anonymity in Social Media** – Users may strip metadata before posting to avoid revealing sensitive details.

✅ **Criminal Intent** – Fraudsters, cybercriminals, and propagandists may alter metadata to spread misinformation.

✅ **False Alibis** – Someone may change timestamps to fabricate a false narrative in legal cases.

✅ **Hiding the Origin of an Image** – Fake accounts and disinformation campaigns often remove metadata to obscure the source of their images.

Regardless of intent, removing or modifying metadata affects image verification and can complicate OSINT investigations.

2. How Metadata is Removed from Images

2.1 Social Media Platforms Strip Metadata Automatically

Most major social media sites automatically remove metadata from uploaded images to protect user privacy. For example:

Platform	Removes EXIF Metadata?
Facebook	✅ Yes
Twitter/X	✅ Yes
Instagram	✅ Yes
WhatsApp	✅ Yes (on sent images)
Telegram	❌ No (if sent as a file)

📌 **Key Takeaway**: If an image is downloaded from a social media post, it likely has no metadata. Analysts must rely on reverse image search, visual clues, and context analysis instead.

2.2 Using EXIF Removal Tools

There are many tools available that allow users to completely wipe metadata from an image. Some of the most common ones include:

- **EXIF Purge** (Online tool)
- **ExifCleaner** (Open-source desktop tool)
- **GIMP/Photoshop** (Metadata can be stripped when saving images)
- **Preview (Mac) & Windows Properties** (Allows manual metadata removal)

Example: Removing Metadata Using ExifTool

To strip all metadata from an image, a user can run:

exiftool -all= image.jpg

This command removes all embedded metadata, making it impossible to retrieve location, timestamps, or camera details.

3. How Metadata is Altered or Faked

While removing metadata erases important details, modifying metadata can be even more deceptive. A skilled user can alter timestamps, change GPS coordinates, or even make an image appear as though it was taken with a different device.

3.1 Tools for Modifying Metadata

There are various tools that allow metadata modification:

- **ExifTool** – Command-line tool that enables editing EXIF data.
- **Exif Pilot** – GUI-based tool for modifying metadata.
- **JPEG & PNG Stripper** – Can both remove and edit metadata.
- **Photoshop/Lightroom** – Allows users to edit metadata before exporting images.

Example: Changing Metadata Using ExifTool

A user can alter the timestamp of an image with the following command:

exiftool -DateTimeOriginal="2024:01:01 12:00:00" image.jpg

Similarly, they can modify GPS coordinates to mislead investigators:

exiftool -GPSLatitude=37.7749 -GPSLongitude=-122.4194 image.jpg

📌 **Real-World Impact**: A criminal could alter GPS data to make an image appear as if it were taken in San Francisco, when it was actually taken elsewhere.

4. Detecting Metadata Manipulation

4.1 Comparing Multiple Metadata Fields

If an image's metadata has been tampered with, inconsistencies may appear between fields. Investigators should compare:

✓ **Date/Time Original vs. File Modification Date** – If the original capture time is different from the file modification date, the image may have been altered.
✓ **Camera Make & Model vs. Expected Device** – If someone claims a photo was taken on an iPhone 14, but metadata shows a Samsung Galaxy S22, there may be deception.
✓ **File Size Changes** – If an image is unusually small or heavily compressed, it may have been edited or resaved multiple times.

4.2 Reverse Image Search to Find the Original

Even if metadata is altered, a reverse image search using Google Lens, TinEye, or Yandex may reveal older versions of the image with original metadata intact.

- How to Conduct a Reverse Image Search
- Upload the image to Google Lens or TinEye.
- Check if older versions of the image exist.

If older images have different metadata, the newer image may have been manipulated.

4.3 Cross-Checking Metadata with External Sources

OSINT analysts can verify metadata accuracy by cross-referencing it with other sources:

- **Google Earth & Street View** – If GPS coordinates suggest an image was taken in Paris, but no matching landmarks are visible, the data might be faked.
- **Weather & Sun Positioning** – If an image's timestamp claims it was taken at 5 PM but shadows suggest midday, the timestamp may have been altered.
- **Social Media Posts** – If a person claims to have taken an image at a certain time, but their social media activity shows them elsewhere, their metadata may have been modified.

★ **Example**: If an OSINT analyst is investigating a suspect who claims an image was taken in June, but metadata suggests it was taken in December, it raises red flags.

5. Key Takeaways

✓ Social media platforms strip metadata, making it harder to trace images.

✓ Metadata removal tools like ExifCleaner and Photoshop can erase identifying details.

✓ Metadata modification tools like ExifTool can alter timestamps, GPS data, and device information.

✓ Reverse image search and cross-referencing can help verify an image's authenticity.

✓ Analyzing inconsistencies in metadata fields can reveal if an image has been tampered with.

By understanding how metadata can be removed, altered, or faked, OSINT investigators can develop strategies to detect deception, verify sources, and ensure the accuracy of image-based intelligence.

3.5 Cross-Verifying EXIF Data with Other OSINT Techniques

Extracting EXIF metadata from an image is only the first step in an OSINT investigation. While metadata can provide valuable details like camera model, timestamps, and GPS coordinates, it is not always reliable—metadata can be removed, altered, or faked. To ensure accuracy, investigators must cross-verify EXIF data with other OSINT techniques such as reverse image search, geolocation analysis, weather verification, and social media tracking.

This section explores methods for verifying EXIF data against external sources to confirm authenticity and detect manipulation.

1. Why Cross-Verification is Essential in OSINT

EXIF metadata can be misleading or incomplete for several reasons:

✖ **Metadata can be removed** – Social media platforms strip metadata from uploaded images.
✖ **Metadata can be altered** – Fraudsters may change timestamps or GPS coordinates to deceive investigators.
✖ **Metadata may not exist** – Some images (e.g., screenshots, scans) lack EXIF data entirely.

To counter these issues, analysts must use multiple OSINT methods to verify details.

2. Reverse Image Search to Validate Metadata

2.1 Confirming an Image's Origin with Reverse Search

Even if an image's metadata has been altered, a reverse image search can reveal its original version. If an older copy of the image exists online with different metadata, the newer version may have been manipulated.

2.2 How to Conduct a Reverse Image Search

1☐ Upload the image to Google Lens, TinEye, or Yandex.

2☐ Check if older versions of the image exist.

3☐ Compare metadata from older versions with the metadata of the image being analyzed.

📌 **Example**: If an image claims to be from 2023, but an identical version is found online from 2019, it's likely an old image being misrepresented.

3. Geolocation Verification: Matching GPS Data with Map Tools

3.1 Cross-Checking EXIF GPS Coordinates with Online Maps

If an image contains GPS metadata, analysts can verify it using Google Maps, Google Earth, or OpenStreetMap.

✅ Steps to Verify GPS Coordinates

- Extract GPS data using ExifTool or an online EXIF viewer.
- Enter the latitude and longitude into Google Maps.
- Compare the mapped location with the image's visual content (buildings, landmarks, terrain).

📌 **Example**: If an image's GPS metadata claims it was taken in Paris, but no Eiffel Tower or Parisian architecture is visible, the metadata may have been altered.

3.2 Using Street View for Verification

Google Street View can help confirm whether the scenery in an image matches the claimed location.

✅ How to Use Street View for Verification

- Navigate to the GPS coordinates in Google Street View.
- Compare visible elements (roads, signs, buildings) with those in the image.
- If discrepancies exist, the image's metadata may be falsified.

📌 **Example**: If an image's metadata claims it was taken at Times Square, New York, but a Street View search shows a different layout, the metadata could be fake.

4. Sunlight & Shadows: Verifying Timestamps with Solar Data

4.1 Using Sun Position to Check Date & Time

The angle of sunlight and shadows in an image can be compared with solar data to confirm or refute a timestamp.

✅ Tools for Sun Position Analysis

- **Suncalc.org** – Shows the sun's position based on date, time, and location.
- **Timeanddate.com** – Provides historical sunrise/sunset data.

✅ **How to Analyze Shadows for Verification**

- Extract the timestamp from EXIF data.
- Identify shadows and sun position in the image.
- Compare with Suncalc.org for that date, time, and location.

📌 **Example**: If an image claims to be taken at 3 PM but the shadows indicate early morning, the timestamp may have been manipulated.

5. Weather Data: Comparing Conditions with EXIF Timestamps

5.1 Using Historical Weather Data to Verify an Image's Date

Weather patterns can be cross-checked against the EXIF timestamp to confirm an image's authenticity.

✅ **Sources for Historical Weather Data**

- **Wunderground.com** – Past weather reports.
- **Timeanddate.com** – Historical temperature and conditions.

✅ **How to Cross-Check Weather with EXIF Data**

- Check the weather conditions recorded in EXIF metadata.
- Look up historical weather for that location and date.
- Compare cloud cover, rain, or temperature with what's visible in the image.

📌 **Example**: If an image claims to be from July 2023 in London, but the image shows heavy snowfall, the timestamp is likely fake.

6. Cross-Checking Social Media Activity & Metadata

6.1 Verifying an Image's Source with Social Media Analysis

If an image appears on social media, analysts can:

✅ Use social media metadata tools (e.g., Exif.tools, FotoForensics) to extract any remaining EXIF data.

☑️ **Analyze post timestamps** – Compare when the image was uploaded versus when it was supposedly taken.

☑️ **Check user interactions** – Comments, likes, and reposts may indicate the actual date of the image.

📌 **Example**: If a suspect claims an image was taken in 2024, but reverse search shows it was posted on Twitter in 2021, their claim is false.

7. Case Study: Detecting Fake Metadata in a Crime Investigation

Scenario

A suspect claims they were in Los Angeles on March 1, 2024, and provides an image as proof. The image's EXIF metadata shows:

- **Date Taken**: 2024-03-01
- **GPS Coordinates**: 34.0522° N, 118.2437° W (Los Angeles)
- **Camera Model**: iPhone 14

Cross-Verification Steps

1️⃣ **Reverse Image Search** – Finds the same image posted in 2021, proving it's not new.

2️⃣ **GPS Check** – Google Maps shows that the street layout does not match recent changes in Los Angeles.

3️⃣ **Sunlight Analysis** – Shadows suggest the photo was taken in winter, not early March.

4️⃣ **Weather Comparison** – March 1, 2024, was cloudy in Los Angeles, but the image shows clear skies.

5️⃣ **Social Media Tracking** – The suspect's Instagram posts from that day show them in New York, not LA.

📌 **Conclusion**: The suspect falsified the image's metadata to create a false alibi.

8. Key Takeaways

☑️ EXIF metadata alone is not always reliable—cross-verification is essential.

☑️ Reverse image search can reveal older versions of an image with original metadata.

✓ GPS coordinates should be matched with online maps and Street View.

✓ Sunlight, shadows, and weather data help verify timestamps.

✓ Social media activity and historical posts provide additional verification.

By combining EXIF data with OSINT techniques, investigators can detect manipulated images, fake timestamps, and falsified locations, ensuring the integrity of their findings.

3.6 Case Study: Finding a Location from an Image's EXIF Data

In OSINT investigations, EXIF metadata can provide critical location details embedded in an image, particularly GPS coordinates. However, analysts must verify this data to confirm authenticity, as metadata can be altered or removed. This case study demonstrates how an investigator used EXIF data to determine an image's location and validate it using additional OSINT techniques.

1. Case Scenario: Identifying a Suspicious Image's Location

Background

A journalist receives a tip that a high-profile fugitive is hiding in an unknown location. The source provides a photo allegedly taken recently, claiming it shows the fugitive near a secluded safe house. However, the journalist needs to verify:

1️⃣ Is the image genuine, or has it been altered?
2️⃣ Does the EXIF data provide accurate location information?
3️⃣ Can the location be confirmed using OSINT tools?

2. Extracting EXIF Data from the Image

Step 1: Checking for Embedded Metadata

The investigator uses ExifTool to analyze the image's metadata:

exiftool suspect_image.jpg

📌 **Key EXIF Data Extracted:**

- **Camera Model**: iPhone 13 Pro
- **Date & Time**: 2024:02:10 14:30:45
- **GPS Coordinates**: 48.858844, 2.294351
- **Altitude**: 85.2 meters

Step 2: Decoding GPS Coordinates

The extracted GPS coordinates (48.858844, 2.294351) are entered into Google Maps:

☞ The location matches the Eiffel Tower in Paris, France.

Possible Red Flag: If the fugitive was last reported in South America, why does the image's metadata show Paris?

3. Verifying Location with Additional OSINT Techniques

Step 3: Cross-Checking Image with Google Street View

To confirm if the image was actually taken at the Eiffel Tower:

✅ Google Street View is used to compare landmarks, buildings, and surrounding elements.

✅ The background buildings and lampposts in the image match Google Street View of the Eiffel Tower area.

📌 **Conclusion**: The physical environment matches the extracted location.

Step 4: Reverse Image Search to Find Older Copies

The investigator uploads the image to Google Lens, TinEye, and Yandex to check if it has been previously published.

✅ **Google Lens & TinEye Results**: The image appears in a 2019 travel blog, proving it is not a recent photo.

✅ **Yandex Image Search**: Shows the same photo used in an unrelated Instagram post from 2020.

📌 **Key Finding**: The image is not recent—it was likely downloaded and repurposed to mislead investigators.

Step 5: Checking Weather & Shadows for Timestamp Accuracy

Since the EXIF timestamp states February 10, 2024, at 14:30 (2:30 PM), the investigator checks historical weather data.

✅ Using Timeanddate.com & Wunderground.com:

- The actual weather in Paris on February 10, 2024, at 2:30 PM was cloudy with rain.
- The image shows clear skies and bright sunlight, contradicting historical weather records.

✅ Sunlight & Shadow Analysis with Suncalc.org:

- The sun's angle and shadows in the image suggest a mid-summer afternoon, not a winter day.

📌 **Conclusion**: The timestamp in EXIF data was altered to make an old image seem recent.

Step 6: Investigating the Source & Identifying Deception

At this point, the investigator suspects that the image was staged or manipulated. To confirm this:

✅ The journalist contacts the original photographer from the 2019 blog post.

✅ The photographer confirms the image was taken in July 2019, proving it was stolen and misrepresented.

📌 **Final Conclusion:**

- The image was not taken in February 2024.
- The fugitive is not in Paris—the image was used to spread false information.

4. Key Takeaways from the Investigation

✓ EXIF data can provide GPS coordinates, but it must be verified.

✓ Reverse image searches can reveal older versions of an image.

✓ Google Maps & Street View help confirm physical locations.

✓ Historical weather data and sunlight analysis can detect timestamp forgery.

✓ Contacting the original source can confirm image authenticity.

This case highlights the importance of cross-verifying EXIF metadata before drawing conclusions in OSINT investigations.

4. Analyzing Photos for Clues: Shadows, Objects & Context

In this chapter, we will focus on the art of analyzing photos for hidden clues by examining elements like shadows, objects, and context. Beyond just the visual content, photographs often contain subtle yet telling details that can reveal crucial information about a location, time, and even the intentions behind an image. By studying the direction of light, the positioning of objects, and the environmental context, OSINT analysts can piece together valuable intelligence that might not be immediately apparent. We will cover methods for scrutinizing images for these hidden clues, providing practical examples to enhance your skills in uncovering critical insights from even the most seemingly mundane photographs.

4.1 How to Analyze Lighting & Shadows for Time & Direction

In OSINT investigations, analyzing lighting and shadows in an image can provide valuable clues about the time of day, direction, and even the location where the photo was taken. By understanding how sunlight interacts with objects, investigators can estimate a photo's timestamp, detect manipulated images, and verify claims about when and where an image was captured.

1. Why Shadow & Light Analysis Matters in OSINT

☑ **Verifying timestamps** – If an image claims to be taken at 3 PM, but the shadows indicate early morning, the timestamp might be fake.
☑ **Determining cardinal direction** – Shadows reveal the sun's position, helping pinpoint the camera's orientation.
☑ **Detecting manipulated images** – If shadows in an image don't align correctly, it may be digitally altered.
☑ **Cross-checking locations** – Sunlight angles can help verify whether an image was taken in the northern or southern hemisphere.

2. Understanding How Shadows Work

Shadows are created when an object blocks light, and their length and direction depend on:

◆ **Time of Day** – Shadows are longer in the morning and evening, and shorter around noon.

◆ **Season** – The sun is higher in the sky during summer, casting shorter shadows, while winter shadows are longer.

◆ **Latitude** – Near the equator, shadows are shorter throughout the year, while closer to the poles, they are longer.

◆ **Sun's Position** – The sun rises in the east, moves across the sky, and sets in the west (varies by hemisphere).

📌 **Example**: If an image shows a long shadow pointing toward the west, it was likely taken in the morning (sun in the east).

3. Tools for Analyzing Shadows & Sunlight

🔍 **Suncalc.org** – Provides the sun's position and shadow direction based on time and location.

🔍 **Timeanddate.com** – Gives sunrise/sunset times and historical weather data for verification.

🔍 **Google Earth Pro** – Allows users to see sunlight angles and shadows for a specific location.

🔍 **Shadow Calculator Apps** – Mobile apps that help analyze and predict shadow lengths.

📌 **Example**: If an image claims to be taken in London at noon, but Suncalc shows the sun should be low on the horizon, the timestamp might be fake.

4. Step-by-Step Shadow Analysis for OSINT

Step 1: Identify the Shadows in the Image

- Look at buildings, trees, people, or objects casting shadows.
- Note the direction and length of the shadows.

Step 2: Determine the Sun's Position

- The sun is opposite the direction of the shadows.
- A shadow pointing north means the sun is south.
- A short shadow suggests midday, while a long shadow suggests morning or late afternoon.

Step 3: Use Suncalc.org to Cross-Check

- Enter the GPS coordinates (if available) or approximate location.
- Adjust the date and time to see how the sun and shadows align.

Step 4: Compare Shadows with Other Clues

- Look at streetlights, signs, or landmarks to confirm orientation.
- Check EXIF metadata to compare timestamps.
- If the shadows don't match the expected sun position, the image may be altered.

5. Case Study: Detecting a Fake Timestamp Using Shadows

Scenario:

A viral image claims to show a political leader at a public event at 2 PM. Investigators suspect the image is old or manipulated.

Shadow Analysis Process:

✅ **Step 1**: The image shows long shadows pointing west, suggesting early morning.

✅ **Step 2**: Using Suncalc.org, investigators find that at 2 PM, shadows should be short, not long.

✅ **Step 3**: Historical weather data shows it was cloudy on that date, but the image has clear skies.

✅ **Step 4**: Reverse image search reveals an identical image from 2018, proving it's not recent.

📌 **Conclusion**: The timestamp was falsified, and the image was reused to spread misinformation.

6. Key Takeaways

✅ Shadows provide clues about time, direction, and season.

✅ The sun is always opposite the shadow's direction.

✅ Tools like Suncalc and Google Earth can verify timestamps.

✅ Comparing shadows with metadata helps detect image manipulation.

✓ Shadow analysis is a powerful OSINT technique for verifying authenticity.

By combining shadow analysis with OSINT tools, investigators can validate images, debunk misinformation, and verify locations with high accuracy.

4.2 Identifying Objects & Recognizing Patterns in Photos

Object identification and pattern recognition are essential skills in OSINT image analysis. By examining the elements within a photo, investigators can extract crucial details that reveal locations, events, timelines, or even the authenticity of an image. This subchapter explores methods and tools used to identify objects, recognize patterns, and draw meaningful conclusions in OSINT investigations.

1. Why Object & Pattern Recognition Matters in OSINT

🔎 **Determining Image Location**: Recognizing landmarks, street signs, architecture, or unique environmental features helps pinpoint where an image was taken.
🔎 **Validating Authenticity**: Identifying inconsistencies, such as mismatched objects, can reveal edited or misleading images.
🔎 **Tracking Individuals & Groups**: Objects like clothing, accessories, or vehicles can help connect people to events or locations.
🔎 **Verifying Timelines**: Certain objects, such as seasonal decorations or weather conditions, can help confirm or dispute an image's claimed date.

📌 **Example**: A photo claims to be from New York in July, but visible Christmas decorations suggest otherwise.

2. Key Elements to Analyze in a Photo

To effectively analyze a photo, investigators should focus on the following key elements:

A. Landmarks & Background Elements

- Buildings, monuments, bridges, or unique geographical features can help identify locations.
- Compare these elements with Google Images, Google Earth, or Street View to verify locations.

✓ **Example**: A photo features the Eiffel Tower, suggesting it was taken in Paris.

B. Signs, Text, & Language

- Street signs, billboards, shop names, and vehicle license plates provide geographic clues.
- Use OCR (Optical Character Recognition) tools like Tesseract or Google Lens to extract and translate text.

✓ **Example**: A blurry sign in a photo is analyzed with OCR, revealing it contains Cyrillic text, indicating a possible Russian-speaking country.

C. Vehicles & License Plates

- Vehicle models, colors, and license plate formats can indicate specific countries or regions.
- Check license plate formats using CarPlates.app or WorldLicensePlates.com.

✓ **Example**: A car in an image has a yellow rear license plate, common in the UK and Netherlands.

D. Clothing & Accessories

- Uniforms, cultural clothing, or fashion trends can indicate geographic or temporal clues.
- Logos or insignias on clothing can be linked to organizations, companies, or affiliations.

✓ **Example**: A person wearing a specific military uniform can be identified using military database images.

E. Weather & Environmental Clues

- Snow, rain, shadows, or dry landscapes can suggest seasonal or geographic context.
- Compare weather conditions with historical weather data from Timeanddate.com.

✓ **Example**: A photo claims to be from Dubai in August, but the presence of snow suggests it was taken elsewhere.

F. Digital Artifacts & Inconsistencies

- Pixelation, mismatched lighting, or distortion may indicate photo manipulation.
- Use tools like Forensically, FotoForensics, or InVID to detect digital tampering.

✅ **Example**: An image has blurred edges around a person, suggesting Photoshop editing.

3. Tools for Object Identification & Pattern Recognition

📌 **Google Lens & TinEye** – Identifies objects, buildings, and people through reverse image search.

📌 **Yandex Image Search** – Excellent for finding similar images, faces, and landmarks.

📌 **EXIF Tools (ExifTool, Jeffrey's Image Metadata Viewer)** – Extracts metadata like camera details and timestamps.

📌 **Street View & Google Earth** – Helps match locations and verify landmarks.

📌 **OCR Software (Tesseract, Google Cloud Vision API)** – Extracts text from images for analysis.

📌 **Forensically & FotoForensics** – Detects image alterations and inconsistencies.

4. Case Study: Identifying a Secret Meeting Location

Scenario:

A whistleblower shares a leaked photo of a private political meeting, but the location is unknown. Investigators use object recognition and pattern analysis to determine where it was taken.

Step 1: Examining Background Elements

✅ The image shows a large window overlooking a waterfront with skyscrapers.

✅ Investigators search Google Images for similar city skylines and match it to Shanghai, China.

Step 2: Identifying Text & Signs

✅ A restaurant menu in the background contains Chinese characters.

✅ Using OCR tools, investigators extract the text and translate it, confirming the location is in Shanghai.

Step 3: Analyzing Objects & Environmental Clues

✅ A calendar on the wall shows the month April.

✅ Checking historical weather data, investigators find Shanghai was rainy on that day, but the image shows sunshine.

✅ This suggests the photo was taken on a different date than claimed.

📌 **Conclusion**: The image was indeed taken in Shanghai, but at an earlier date than suggested, proving it was being misrepresented.

5. Key Takeaways for OSINT Analysts

✅ Analyze background elements (landmarks, signs, vehicles) to determine location.

✅ Use OCR to extract and translate text from images.

✅ Check weather conditions to verify the claimed date.

✅ Compare objects and patterns with known databases (military insignias, license plates, etc.).

✅ Detect inconsistencies using forensic analysis tools.

By combining object identification, pattern recognition, and OSINT tools, analysts can effectively verify image authenticity, track events, and uncover deception in digital investigations.

4.3 Understanding Depth, Perspective & Photo Manipulation

In OSINT investigations, analyzing depth, perspective, and signs of manipulation in photos is crucial for detecting deception, verifying authenticity, and extracting key intelligence. Understanding how images are composed, how perspective affects perception, and how digital forgeries can be identified allows analysts to distinguish between genuine and altered photos.

1. Why Depth & Perspective Matter in OSINT

✅ **Verifying Image Authenticity** – Perspective analysis helps detect distorted, stretched, or manipulated photos.

✅ **Identifying Digital Alterations** – Changes in lighting, inconsistent depth, or unusual angles may indicate photoshopped elements.

✅ **Locating Camera Position** – Depth clues reveal whether a photo was taken close or far, affecting its reliability.

✅ **Reconstructing Scene Context** – Understanding spatial relationships between objects helps confirm or challenge image claims.

📌 **Example**: A viral image claims to show a collapsed building, but incorrect depth cues suggest it is a miniature model.

2. Understanding Depth & Perspective in Photos

Depth and perspective refer to how objects appear smaller as they move further away and how lines converge toward a vanishing point.

A. Perspective & Vanishing Points

- Parallel lines (e.g., railway tracks, roads, buildings) appear to converge at a vanishing point.
- If objects don't align properly with expected perspective, the image may be manipulated.

✅ **Example**: A building appears tilted in an image, but checking other photos of the same location confirms it was digitally altered.

B. Foreground vs. Background Analysis

- Objects in the foreground should appear larger and sharper, while background elements appear smaller and blurrier.
- If a background object is too sharp or doesn't match the expected size, it may have been added digitally.

✓ **Example**: A person in a protest photo looks too large compared to surrounding people, suggesting they were inserted artificially.

C. Focal Length & Lens Distortion

- Different lenses (e.g., wide-angle vs. telephoto) affect depth perception.
- Wide-angle lenses exaggerate depth, while telephoto lenses compress distances between objects.
- If depth doesn't match the expected focal length, the image may have been manipulated.

✓ **Example**: A fake UFO sighting photo appears distorted due to incorrect depth cues.

3. Detecting Signs of Photo Manipulation

To detect digital alterations, analysts must look for inconsistencies in depth, lighting, and perspective.

A. Shadow & Lighting Discrepancies

- Shadows should align correctly based on the light source.
- If different objects in an image cast shadows in different directions, the image may have been manipulated.

✓ **Example**: A political photo shows a crowd of supporters, but shadow analysis suggests some people were added digitally.

B. Edges & Blending Errors

- Objects added to an image may have unnatural edges that don't blend well.
- Look for blurred outlines, inconsistent textures, or color mismatches.

✓ **Example**: A celebrity deepfake had mismatched edges where the face met the neck, proving it was AI-generated.

C. Cloning & Repeated Patterns

- Some manipulated images use copy-paste techniques, leading to identical objects appearing multiple times.
- Use error-level analysis (ELA) tools to detect repeated patterns.

✓ **Example**: A war photo showed identical people in different parts of the image, revealing Photoshop cloning.

D. Metadata & Digital Fingerprints

- Use EXIF tools to check if an image's metadata suggests editing software was used.
- Many forgeries remove metadata, which itself is a red flag.

✓ **Example**: A controversial news image had no EXIF data, suggesting possible tampering.

4. OSINT Tools for Detecting Image Manipulation

📌 **FotoForensics** – Provides error-level analysis (ELA) to detect edited areas.
📌 **Forensically** – Detects cloning, noise patterns, and inconsistent lighting.
📌 **InVID** – Analyzes videos and images for deepfake detection.
📌 **Google Reverse Image Search** – Helps find original versions of edited photos.
📌 **EXIF Tools (ExifTool, Jeffrey's Image Viewer)** – Extracts metadata to check for editing software usage.

5. Case Study: Exposing a Fake Viral Image

Scenario:

A viral image claims to show a military attack on a civilian area, but analysts suspect it has been digitally altered.

Step 1: Reverse Image Search

✓ Google Reverse Image Search finds an older version of the image without explosions.

Step 2: Checking Perspective & Depth

✓ The explosion appears flat and lacks realistic depth.

✅ Using FotoForensics, analysts detect a different noise pattern in the explosion area, suggesting it was added later.

Step 3: Shadow & Lighting Analysis

✅ The explosion's light source doesn't match the sun's position in the rest of the image.

📌 **Conclusion**: The image was manipulated to spread misinformation.

6. Key Takeaways for OSINT Analysts

✅ Depth & perspective help verify authenticity.

✅ Vanishing points and shadow direction reveal manipulations.

✅ Edges, blending, and repeated patterns indicate Photoshop edits.

✅ Use forensic tools to analyze metadata, lighting, and digital fingerprints.

✅ Always compare suspect images with original sources using reverse image search.

By mastering depth, perspective, and manipulation detection, OSINT investigators can debunk fake images, verify sources, and uncover digital deception with precision.

4.4 Using Contextual Clues for Location & Time Estimation

One of the most powerful techniques in OSINT image analysis is extracting contextual clues from photos to determine where and when they were taken. Even when metadata is stripped, images still contain valuable details such as landmarks, weather, signs, clothing, and lighting, which can help estimate time and location. This subchapter explores methods and tools used to analyze contextual clues for geolocation and time verification.

1. Why Context Matters in OSINT Investigations

Understanding the context of an image can:

✅ Verify or disprove claims about an image's origin or timeline.

✅ Determine the location of an event or person.

✅ Expose misinformation by identifying inconsistencies.

✅ Corroborate other OSINT findings with visual evidence.

📌 **Example**: A viral image claims to be from a recent protest in London, but analysis of weather conditions and billboards suggests it was actually taken years earlier in Hong Kong.

2. Identifying Location Clues in Images

Geolocation techniques rely on recognizing physical, cultural, and environmental clues to determine where an image was taken.

A. Landmarks & Architecture

- Skylines, bridges, towers, and unique buildings help pinpoint locations.
- Compare these features with Google Earth, Street View, or image search engines.

✅ **Example**: A photo includes a distinct pagoda-style roof, suggesting it was taken in Japan or China.

B. Street Signs, Billboards & Language

- Text in the image can reveal the local language and writing system.
- Road signs and shop names can be translated to identify cities or regions.
- Use Google Translate or OCR tools (Tesseract, Google Lens) to extract and analyze text.

✅ **Example**: A blurry sign in a photo contains Arabic text, indicating it was taken in a Middle Eastern country.

C. Vehicle Types & License Plates

- Some countries have specific car models, colors, or license plate formats.
- Use resources like WorldLicensePlates.com to match plate designs.

✅ **Example**: A car in the image has a blue and white license plate with Chinese characters, confirming it was taken in China.

D. Environmental & Vegetation Clues

- Trees, plants, and terrain types provide regional clues.
- Dry deserts suggest Middle East, Africa, or U.S. Southwest.
- Dense jungles suggest Southeast Asia or South America.

✓ **Example**: A photo with palm trees and Spanish signage suggests it was taken in Florida, Spain, or Latin America.

3. Estimating the Time & Date of an Image

Time estimation is possible by analyzing shadows, weather, clothing, and event clues.

A. Shadow Length & Sun Position

- Shadows change based on time of day and geographic location.
- Use tools like Suncalc.org to estimate when an image was taken.

✓ **Example**: A photo shows long shadows from a westward sun, indicating it was taken in late afternoon.

B. Weather & Seasonal Indicators

- Snow, rain, and fog can help verify or challenge an image's timestamp.
- Compare image conditions with historical weather data from Timeanddate.com.

✓ **Example**: An image claims to be from Paris in July, but shows snow-covered streets, proving it was taken in winter.

C. Clothing & Fashion Trends

- Clothing styles, uniforms, and accessories reflect local climate and time period.
- Event-specific outfits (e.g., Halloween costumes) help estimate the date.

✓ **Example**: A group photo features football jerseys for a team's new season, helping confirm the year.

D. Public Events & Advertisements

- Posters, billboards, and signs with dates or event names can verify time.
- News coverage or social media posts can confirm if an event was recent.

✓ **Example**: A street photo includes a billboard advertising a concert on March 15, 2023, suggesting the image was taken around that time.

4. OSINT Tools for Contextual Analysis

🔍 **Google Earth & Street View** – Match landmarks, roads, and terrain.

🔍 **Google Lens & TinEye** – Reverse search for matching images and locations.

🔍 **Suncalc.org** – Estimate time of day based on shadows.

🔍 **Timeanddate.com** – Check historical weather reports.

🔍 **WorldLicensePlates.com** – Identify license plate origins.

🔍 **Google Translate & Tesseract OCR** – Extract and analyze text in images.

5. Case Study: Geolocating a War Zone Image

Scenario:

An anonymous image claims to show a recent bombing in Kyiv, Ukraine, but investigators suspect it's from an older conflict.

Step 1: Checking Landmarks & Buildings

✓ The skyline features a distinctive Soviet-era tower.

✓ Using Google Earth, analysts match the tower to Grozny, Chechnya, not Kyiv.

Step 2: Analyzing Signs & Language

✓ A damaged billboard in the image has text in Cyrillic script, confirming it's from a Russian-speaking region.

Step 3: Checking Weather Conditions

✓ The image shows heavy snow, but Kyiv was experiencing mild temperatures that week.

✓ Timeanddate.com confirms the weather does not match recent conditions.

📌 **Conclusion**: The image was from the Chechen War in the 1990s, not a recent attack in Ukraine.

6. Key Takeaways for OSINT Analysts

✓ Landmarks, signs, and language reveal geographic clues.

✓ Weather, shadows, and seasonal details help estimate time.

✓ Reverse image search helps verify original sources.

✓ Using multiple OSINT tools improves accuracy in location tracking.

✓ Contextual clues are crucial in debunking misinformation.

By combining contextual analysis, OSINT tools, and investigative techniques, analysts can accurately determine when and where an image was taken, exposing misinformation and uncovering hidden truths.

4.5 How to Spot AI-Generated & Deepfake Images

The rise of AI-generated images and deepfakes has created new challenges in OSINT investigations. Malicious actors use AI to create fake profile pictures, propaganda, and deceptive media, making it harder to distinguish real from fake. OSINT analysts must develop skills to detect AI-generated and deepfake images using visual analysis, metadata checks, and forensic tools.

1. Understanding AI-Generated Images & Deepfakes

A. What Are AI-Generated Images?

AI-generated images are created using machine learning models like:

- **Generative Adversarial Networks (GANs)** – Used to create fake human faces (e.g., ThisPersonDoesNotExist.com).
- **Stable Diffusion, MidJourney & DALL·E** – Generate artificial landscapes, objects, or fake event images.

- **Face Morphing AI** – Merges real and synthetic images to create fake profiles and fake identities.

✅ **Common Use Cases**: Fake social media profiles, misinformation campaigns, digital impersonation.

B. What Are Deepfakes?

Deepfakes use AI to replace faces, alter video footage, or generate lifelike fake images.

- Can be used for political propaganda, scams, fake evidence, or revenge attacks.
- Typically created using DeepFaceLab, FaceSwap, or AI video synthesis tools.

✅ **Common Use Cases**: Fake celebrity scandals, disinformation videos, impersonation fraud.

2. Visual Clues to Detect AI-Generated Faces

AI-generated faces often have subtle mistakes that reveal their synthetic nature.

A. Asymmetry in Facial Features

- AI struggles with symmetry – look for mismatched eyes, ears, or face alignment.
- One eye may be slightly larger than the other.
- Teeth are often uneven or blurred together.

✅ **Example**: A fake social media profile has one earlobe larger than the other, indicating AI generation.

B. Strange Background Artifacts

- AI-generated images often blur or distort backgrounds.
- Jewelry, glasses, or hair may blend awkwardly with the background.

✅ **Example**: A profile picture has a hand in the background that appears deformed, signaling AI manipulation.

C. Inconsistent Lighting & Shadows

- AI often miscalculates light sources, causing shadows to appear unnatural.

- One side of the face may be lit differently than the rest of the image.

✓ **Example**: A "news photo" of an explosion has multiple inconsistent shadow directions, proving it was AI-generated.

D. Irregular Text & Logos

- AI struggles with text generation – letters appear distorted or unreadable.
- Fake news images may contain gibberish writing on signs or banners.

✓ **Example**: An AI-generated protest photo has misspelled words on banners, exposing it as fake.

3. Deepfake Detection: How to Spot Manipulated Faces & Videos

A. Unnatural Facial Movements

- AI struggles with lip-syncing and blinking in deepfake videos.
- Blinking may be too fast, too slow, or missing entirely.

✓ **Example**: A political deepfake video shows a speaker not blinking for minutes, proving it's fake.

B. Skin Texture & Facial Flickering

- Deepfakes often have unnatural skin textures or pixelation around the face.
- Skin may appear too smooth or lack normal wrinkles and pores.

✓ **Example**: A deepfake video of a CEO announcing a fake company deal shows blurry facial edges, exposing manipulation.

C. Speech & Audio Sync Issues

- Lip movements may not match speech timing.
- AI voices may lack emotion or sound robotic.

✓ **Example**: A leaked "celebrity confession video" has lagging lip-sync, confirming it's a deepfake.

4. Technical & Metadata Analysis for AI Image Detection

OSINT analysts can use forensic tools to analyze image metadata and structure.

A. Checking EXIF Metadata

- AI-generated images often lack normal EXIF metadata (camera model, GPS, timestamp).
- Use ExifTool or Jeffrey's Image Metadata Viewer to inspect metadata.

✅ **Example**: A news agency claims a warzone photo was taken in 2024, but EXIF analysis shows it was created with an AI tool in 2023.

B. Error Level Analysis (ELA)

- ELA detects manipulated parts of an image by highlighting compression differences.
- Use FotoForensics to reveal edited areas in AI or deepfake images.

✅ **Example**: A viral image claims to show a politician in a scandal, but ELA analysis reveals the face was edited onto a different body.

C. Reverse Image Search

- AI-generated images often don't appear in past databases because they're newly created.
- Use Google Reverse Image Search, TinEye, or Yandex to verify source images.

✅ **Example**: A deepfake image of a historical event is reverse-searched and has no prior record, indicating AI creation.

5. OSINT Tools for AI & Deepfake Detection

🔍 **Deepware Scanner** – Detects deepfake videos.
🔍 **Hugging Face Deepfake Detector** – AI tool to analyze facial forgeries.
🔍 **ThisPersonDoesNotExist Detector** – Identifies AI-generated profile images.
🔍 **Sensity.ai** – Scans images/videos for deepfake indicators.
🔍 **Microsoft Video Authenticator** – Flags manipulated videos.
🔍 **Google Reverse Image Search & TinEye** – Checks if images have prior records.
🔍 **FotoForensics** – Analyzes error levels in images.

6. Case Study: Exposing an AI-Generated Fake Journalist

Scenario:

An investigative team finds an online journalist, "Emma Carter," who writes political reports. Suspicious elements lead analysts to check her profile image.

Step 1: Reverse Image Search

✅ Google Reverse Image Search finds no past versions of Emma's photo, raising red flags.

Step 2: Facial Symmetry & Background Check

✅ Emma's earrings don't match on both sides, suggesting an AI-generated face.
✅ Her hair blends unnaturally into the background.

Step 3: EXIF & Metadata Inspection

✅ ExifTool reveals the image was created with AI software, confirming it's fake.

📌 **Conclusion**: "Emma Carter" was a fake persona created using AI to spread disinformation.

7. Key Takeaways for OSINT Analysts

✅ AI-generated faces often have symmetry flaws, distorted backgrounds, and unnatural lighting.
✅ Deepfakes show unnatural blinking, lip-sync issues, and facial inconsistencies.
✅ EXIF metadata, error-level analysis, and reverse image search help verify authenticity.
✅ Specialized AI detection tools can identify manipulated images and videos.
✅ Always cross-check with other OSINT techniques to confirm results.

As AI-generated content becomes more advanced, OSINT investigators must stay ahead by mastering deepfake detection techniques. By combining forensic analysis, metadata verification, and AI tools, analysts can expose fake images and protect the integrity of digital investigations.

4.6 Case Study: Verifying an Image's Authenticity Through Context Analysis

In early 2023, an image surfaced online claiming to show a military airstrike on a civilian building in Eastern Europe. The image was widely shared on social media, fueling political tensions and misinformation. However, OSINT analysts suspected the image might be old or manipulated. This case study demonstrates how analysts used context analysis, metadata checks, and OSINT tools to verify the image's authenticity.

Step 1: Reverse Image Search – Identifying Previous Uses

The first step in verifying an image is to check if it has appeared online before.

Actions Taken:

- The image was run through Google Reverse Image Search, TinEye, and Yandex.
- Results showed similar images had been published in 2017, raising suspicion.

✅ **Finding**: The image closely matched a photo from a 2017 explosion in Syria, suggesting it was being reused with a false claim.

Step 2: Checking Metadata for Creation Date & Source

If the image was taken in 2023, its metadata should confirm this.

Actions Taken:

The image was analyzed using ExifTool and Jeffrey's Image Metadata Viewer.

The EXIF data revealed:

- **Creation date**: 2017 (not 2023).
- **Camera model**: Canon EOS 5D (matching known war photographers from Syria).

- **GPS data**: No location data present, but time zone information matched the Middle East, not Eastern Europe.

✅ **Finding**: The metadata confirmed that the image was taken in 2017, not 2023, and was not from Eastern Europe.

Step 3: Contextual Clues – Analyzing Visual Elements

Since metadata can be altered, analysts examined the image itself for contextual inconsistencies.

Actions Taken:

Weather conditions:

- The image showed a clear sky, but historical weather data (from TimeandDate.com) revealed that the alleged location had heavy snowfall on the reported date.
- Mismatch suggests image was not taken on that day.

Language & signage analysis:

- A partially visible billboard in the background contained Arabic text, not the expected local language.
- Google Lens OCR translation revealed the billboard advertised a Damascus-based business, linking it to Syria.

Clothing analysis:

- Some civilians in the image wore light summer clothing, which was inconsistent with the alleged region's cold winter at that time.

✅ **Finding**: The environmental details (clear sky, Arabic signage, and clothing inconsistencies) contradicted the claimed location and time.

Step 4: Cross-Referencing with News Reports & Satellite Imagery

To further verify, analysts cross-checked with official news sources and satellite imagery.

Actions Taken:

News Verification:

- No reputable news agencies reported an airstrike on the given date.
- A similar attack was reported in Syria in 2017, matching the image's context.

Satellite Imagery (Google Earth & Sentinel-2):

- The supposed bombed building did not exist in Eastern Europe.
- Satellite imagery from 2017 showed a matching destroyed structure in Damascus, Syria.

✅ **Finding**: The satellite images and news reports confirmed the original attack was in Syria, not Eastern Europe.

Final Conclusion: The Image Was Misleading

Through OSINT techniques, analysts determined:

- The image was originally from a 2017 explosion in Syria.
- The metadata confirmed it was not taken in 2023.
- Weather, language, clothing, and signage inconsistencies exposed the deception.
- Satellite imagery and news reports verified the real event.

📛 **Verdict**: The image was misleadingly repurposed to spread false information about an unrelated event in 2023.

Key Takeaways for OSINT Analysts

✅ Reverse image search helps identify previously used images.

✅ Metadata analysis can confirm or challenge image claims.

✅ Environmental clues (weather, signage, clothing) are crucial in verification.

✅ Cross-referencing with satellite imagery and news sources strengthens findings.

✅ A single deceptive image can spread misinformation—OSINT is essential to debunk false claims.

By combining technical analysis, visual examination, and contextual clues, OSINT analysts can detect manipulated images, debunk misinformation, and verify authenticity in digital investigations.

5. Social Media Image Tracking

In this chapter, we will explore the techniques and strategies used for social media image tracking, a vital skill in the OSINT analyst's toolkit. Social media platforms are a treasure trove of visual content, often containing geotagged images, timestamps, and contextual data that can lead to valuable intelligence. By leveraging reverse image search engines, AI tools, and data scraping techniques, analysts can trace the origin of images, track their spread across platforms, and uncover connections between individuals, locations, and events. We will discuss methods for identifying patterns, verifying image authenticity, and using social media images to support investigations in real-time.

5.1 How Social Media Platforms Store & Process Images

Social media platforms play a crucial role in image-based OSINT investigations, but understanding how these platforms store, compress, and process images is essential for analysts. When a user uploads an image to platforms like Facebook, Instagram, Twitter (X), LinkedIn, or TikTok, the image undergoes various transformations. These include compression, metadata stripping, and unique fingerprinting, all of which impact the way images are stored and retrieved.

1. Image Storage & Hosting on Social Media

Each platform stores images in distributed cloud servers. When an image is uploaded, it is often stored in multiple resolutions for optimized loading across devices.

♦ **Facebook & Instagram**: Images are hosted in Meta's cloud infrastructure and delivered through a Content Delivery Network (CDN).
♦ **Twitter (X):** Stores images in Amazon Web Services (AWS) and generates unique media URLs.
♦ **TikTok & Snapchat:** Images and videos are stored temporarily and undergo AI-based content moderation.

✅ **OSINT Tip**: Analysts can often retrieve the direct image URL from a post's source code or inspect the file naming conventions to infer where the image is hosted.

2. Image Processing: Compression & Resizing

To save storage space and ensure fast loading times, social media platforms automatically compress and resize images.

◆ **Compression Algorithms Used:**

- JPEG compression (lossy) for photos
- WebP compression for optimized loading
- PNG/GIF formats preserved for logos & transparent images

◆ **Resizing Standards:**

- Facebook resizes images to 720px, 960px, or 2048px width.
- Twitter converts images to 1024px width for previews.
- Instagram uses 1080px as the max width.

✅ **OSINT Tip**: Higher resolution images often retain more details. If possible, analysts should try to retrieve original-sized uploads instead of preview versions.

3. Metadata Stripping & Its Impact on OSINT

Most social media platforms strip EXIF metadata upon upload, removing information like GPS coordinates, timestamps, and camera details.

Platform	EXIF Metadata Preserved?	Notes
Facebook	✖ No	Removes EXIF data but retains internal tracking tags.
Instagram	✖ No	Strips metadata but may keep internal records.
Twitter (X)	✅ Yes (Until 2019) / ✖ No (After 2019)	EXIF was removed in 2019 update.
TikTok	✖ No	Stores metadata internally but removes it from public images.
LinkedIn	✖ No	Strips all metadata from uploaded images.

✅ **OSINT Tip**: Since metadata is stripped, analysts must rely on contextual clues, visual analysis, and platform-specific data to verify an image's origin.

4. Image Hashing & Unique Identifiers

Many platforms assign unique identifiers or hash values to images. These hashes help detect duplicate content, prevent reposts, and enable automated moderation.

◆ Perceptual Hashing:

- Platforms like Facebook, Instagram, and Twitter (X) use hashing techniques to detect similar images, even if they've been modified (cropped, resized, or slightly altered).
- **Example**: Facebook uses PhotoDNA hashing to detect child exploitation material and misinformation images.

◆ File Naming Conventions:

- Some platforms rename images upon upload, embedding a unique identifier.
- **Example**: Facebook's image URLs contain fbcdn.net, showing they are stored in Meta's servers.

✔ **OSINT Tip**: If an image's hash or unique filename can be retrieved, analysts may be able to track similar uploads across different accounts.

5. How Social Media Processes Image-Based Content Moderation

Most social media platforms use AI-based moderation tools to detect:

- Inappropriate content (nudity, violence, misinformation)
- Fake news & manipulated images
- Copyrighted material (using Content ID systems)

These AI tools flag or remove certain images, which may affect their availability in OSINT investigations.

✔ **OSINT Tip**: If an image disappears after being flagged, analysts can check cached versions using tools like Google Cache, the Wayback Machine, or Archive.today.

6. Retrieving Images for OSINT Analysis

To gather useful intelligence, OSINT analysts use several techniques to extract images from social media.

◆ Inspecting Page Source:

Right-click on an image → "Inspect" → Locate direct image URLs.

◆ Using Reverse Image Search:

Search an image across platforms using Google Reverse Image Search, TinEye, and Yandex.

◆ Accessing Archived Versions:

Use archive services to retrieve deleted images.

✓ **OSINT Tip**: Investigators can use Twitter's Advanced Search, Facebook Graph Search (deprecated but archived), and Google Dorks to locate images posted by specific users.

Key Takeaways for OSINT Analysts

✓ Social media platforms heavily compress, resize, and store images using CDNs.

✓ EXIF metadata is removed upon upload, requiring alternative verification methods.

✓ Hashing techniques are used to track image duplicates and prevent reposts.

✓ AI-based moderation can remove or censor sensitive images, affecting OSINT access.

✓ Archived image retrieval and reverse search are crucial for historical investigations.

Understanding how images are processed, stored, and manipulated on social media enhances an OSINT investigator's ability to track and analyze visual intelligence effectively.

5.2 Extracting Hidden Clues from Social Media Photos

Social media photos often contain hidden details that OSINT analysts can use to gather intelligence, verify claims, and track individuals or events. Even though platforms strip metadata, visual and contextual clues remain embedded in the images themselves. This section explores techniques for extracting hidden clues from social media images, including background details, reflections, geolocation hints, and digital fingerprints.

1. Background Details & Environmental Context

A social media photo often contains more than just its main subject. Background elements—such as street signs, billboards, store logos, or architectural features—can provide location clues.

Key Techniques:

◆ **Street Signs & Billboards**: Language, phone numbers, or website URLs may indicate a specific city or country.
◆ **License Plates & Vehicles**: Certain vehicle models, license plate formats, and road markings vary by region.
◆ **Weather & Season Clues**: Snow, greenery, or shadows can help determine the time of year or climate.
◆ **Advertisements & Storefronts**: Local business names can be cross-referenced with Google Maps or business directories.

✓ **OSINT Tip**: Use Google Street View or Mapillary to compare the background against real-world locations.

2. Reflections & Shadows: Uncovering Hidden Details

Sometimes, the most revealing clues in an image are not in the main frame but in reflections or shadows.

How to Analyze Reflections:

◆ **Mirrors & Glass Surfaces**: Sunglasses, car mirrors, or store windows may reflect nearby objects or the person taking the photo.
◆ **Shiny Surfaces**: Look at metal objects, polished floors, or water puddles for subtle reflections.
◆ **Car Windows**: Often reveal additional details, such as landmarks or bystanders.

How to Analyze Shadows:

◆ **Shadow Length & Direction**: The position of shadows can help estimate time of day using tools like SunCalc.
◆ **Object Shadows**: A shadow might reveal something outside the frame, such as a hidden individual or camera setup.

✅ **OSINT Tip**: Use SunCalc.net to calculate time and location based on the angle of shadows.

3. Clothing, Accessories & Fashion Trends

Clothing styles, uniforms, and accessories can hint at a person's location, affiliation, or time period.

What to Look For:

◆ **Uniforms & Insignias**: Military, police, or company uniforms can be linked to organizations.
◆ **Fashion Trends**: Styles of dress, popular brands, or traditional clothing can indicate culture or regional trends.
◆ **Wristwatches & Time Displays**: If a watch or digital clock is visible, it can help determine the exact time the photo was taken.

✅ **OSINT Tip**: Reverse search logos or uniforms using Google Lens or Yandex Image Search.

4. Social Media Filters, Watermarks & Hidden Digital Markers

Many social media platforms apply filters, watermarks, or unique compression artifacts that can help track an image's origin.

Identifying Watermarks & Filters:

◆ **Instagram & Snapchat Filters**: Certain filters are unique to specific years, locations, or events.
◆ **TikTok & Snapchat Watermarks**: Reveal the original uploader's username even if reposted elsewhere.
◆ **Compression Artifacts**: Different platforms compress images differently, helping to determine which site hosted it first.

✅ **OSINT Tip**: Use PhotoForensics to analyze compression patterns and detect signs of image tampering.

5. Geolocation Clues: Extracting Location Data Without Metadata

Even without EXIF data, visual landmarks, terrain features, and local details can help geolocate an image.

How to Geolocate an Image:

♦ **City Skylines & Landmarks**: Compare with known cityscapes using Google Earth.
♦ **Mountain Ranges & Coastlines**: Terrain features can be matched with satellite imagery.
♦ **Power Lines & Street Lamps**: Utility pole designs and streetlights vary by region.

✓ **OSINT Tip**: Use PeakFinder to identify mountain silhouettes and Google Earth Pro for terrain matching.

6. Cross-Referencing with Other Social Media Content

Images often appear on multiple platforms, allowing OSINT analysts to track reposts and find additional context.

How to Cross-Reference an Image:

♦ **Reverse Image Search**: Use TinEye, Google Lens, or Yandex to find where else an image appears.
♦ **Check Video Screenshots**: If an image is from a video, extract key frames and search for matching clips.
♦ **Search for Similar Hashtags**: Hashtags and geotags can lead to more images from the same event.

✓ **OSINT Tip**: If an image is part of a larger album or event, look for similar posts by other users.

7. Case Example: Tracking Down a Protest Location

A social media user posted an anonymous protest photo claiming it was taken in Berlin, Germany. However, OSINT analysts suspected otherwise.

Steps Taken:

Background Analysis:

A billboard in the background contained Spanish text, raising doubts about the claimed location.

Clothing & Weather Check:

Protesters wore light clothing, but Berlin's temperature that day was near freezing.

Reverse Image Search & Hashtags:

Reverse searches found a similar protest in Buenos Aires, Argentina.

Google Street View Comparison:

A distinctive building in the photo matched a location in Buenos Aires.

✅ **Conclusion**: The image was falsely attributed to Berlin—it was actually from a protest in Argentina.

Key Takeaways for OSINT Analysts

✅ Background details like billboards, signs, and architecture provide location hints.

✅ Reflections in sunglasses, windows, and puddles can reveal hidden information.

✅ Shadows help estimate the time of day using SunCalc.

✅ Clothing, uniforms, and watches provide cultural and temporal clues.

✅ Geolocation can be achieved without metadata by analyzing terrain and buildings.

✅ Cross-referencing images on multiple platforms reveals additional context.

By combining these techniques, OSINT analysts can extract valuable intelligence from social media photos—even when metadata is stripped.

5.3 Cross-Referencing Images Across Multiple Platforms

Social media images rarely exist in isolation. They are often shared, reposted, and altered across different platforms, making it crucial for OSINT analysts to cross-reference images to uncover source origins, duplicates, and additional context. This chapter explores strategies, tools, and techniques to track images across multiple platforms and verify their authenticity.

1. Why Cross-Referencing Matters in OSINT Investigations

Cross-referencing images is essential for:

♦ Verifying authenticity: Ensuring an image hasn't been manipulated or misrepresented.
♦ Tracking reposts: Identifying where and how an image has been used online.
♦ Finding additional context: Discovering related posts, comments, or discussions.
♦ Attributing sources: Determining the original uploader and possible motivations behind sharing.

✅ **Example**: A viral image claiming to show a current conflict zone may have actually originated from a different event years earlier.

2. Reverse Image Searching Across Multiple Platforms

The first step in cross-referencing an image is to conduct reverse image searches on multiple search engines.

Key Reverse Image Search Tools:

Tool	Strengths	Best Use Cases
Google Lens	Largest index, AI-enhanced search	Finding well-known or widely shared images
TinEye	Tracks image modifications, detects older versions	Checking for altered, cropped, or edited images
Yandex	Advanced facial & object recognition	Finding similar images or cross-checking social media
Bing Visual Search	AI-powered image analysis	Complementary to Google & Yandex searches
PimEyes	Specialized in facial recognition	Finding people's images across platforms

✅ **OSINT Tip**: Each search engine has different algorithms, so running an image through multiple tools increases the chances of finding useful matches.

3. Identifying Platform-Specific Image Variations

Different social media platforms process, resize, and store images differently, which can impact the search results.

How Platforms Modify Images:

◆ **Compression & Resizing** – Facebook, Instagram, and Twitter reduce image quality for faster loading.
◆ **EXIF Metadata Stripping** – Most platforms remove metadata, but some, like Telegram and Discord, may preserve it.
◆ **Unique File Naming Conventions** – Some sites rename images upon upload, embedding timestamps or user IDs.

How to Use This in OSINT:

✓ If an image appears slightly different across platforms (cropped, resized, or altered), use Yandex or TinEye, which detect similar images even with modifications.

✓ If an image retains its original filename, it may be possible to track the exact source by looking at how different platforms rename files.

4. Tracking an Image Across Social Media Platforms

Platform-Specific Cross-Referencing Strategies:

Facebook & Instagram (Meta)

◆ **Use site-specific searches:**

site:facebook.com "image caption text"
site:instagram.com "hashtags or keywords"

◆ Check image URLs – Facebook CDN links often contain a user's unique ID.
◆ Reverse search profile pictures to detect fake accounts.

Twitter (X)

◆ **Use Twitter Advanced Search:**

Search by date, keywords, or hashtags to locate posts containing an image.

◆ Use Google Reverse Image Search for image previews stored in Twitter CDNs.
◆ Look for reply chains—original posters may provide additional details.
Reddit & Other Forums

◆ **Search using Google Dorks:**

site:reddit.com inurl:comments "keyword"
site:4chan.org "filename or keyword"

◆ Reverse search meme images—many viral images originate from Reddit.

Telegram & Dark Web Forums

◆ Some EXIF data may still be present in Telegram images.
◆ Use Telegram search bots to locate public groups sharing similar content.
◆ Dark web marketplaces often reuse the same scam images—cross-checking these can expose fraudulent listings.

✅ **OSINT Tip**: If a deleted post contained an image, try retrieving it via Google Cache, the Wayback Machine, or Archive.today.

5. Cross-Referencing Video Screenshots & Frames

Images extracted from videos often circulate as stills. OSINT analysts must cross-check frames from videos to determine their origin.

How to Reverse Search Video Frames:

◆ **Use YouTube DataViewer (Amnesty International)** – Extracts timestamps & metadata.
◆ Take screenshots of key frames and reverse search using Google Lens or Yandex.
◆ If a video was posted on TikTok, Instagram, or YouTube Shorts, check hashtags or related videos for context.

✓ **OSINT Tip**: Altered video frames (cropped, color-adjusted) may require contrast-enhancing techniques before reverse searching.

6. Case Study: Unmasking a Fake News Image Through Cross-Referencing

A widely shared image claimed to depict a recent natural disaster in Japan. However, OSINT analysts suspected it might be old or misattributed.

Investigation Steps:

1️⃣ Reverse Image Search

Google Lens & Yandex found matches from five years earlier in Indonesia.

2️⃣ Checking File Names & URLs

The original image file had a date stamp of 2018, contradicting claims that it was from 2024.

3️⃣ Cross-Referencing on Twitter & Reddit

Older discussions on Reddit matched descriptions of the 2018 tsunami in Sulawesi.

4️⃣ Using Google Earth for Location Matching

The damaged buildings in the image were found using Google Earth's historical imagery.

✓ **Conclusion**: The image was misleadingly labeled as a new disaster, but it actually originated from 2018 in Indonesia.

7. Key Takeaways for OSINT Analysts

✓ Use multiple reverse image search tools (Google, Yandex, TinEye) for better accuracy.

✓ Cross-reference platform-specific modifications—different sites alter images differently.

✓ Leverage search operators (site:facebook.com, site:reddit.com) for deeper searches.

✅ Extract video frames for reverse searching—some images originate from viral videos.

✅ Check filenames, EXIF data, and unique platform identifiers to track images accurately.

✅ Use archival tools like the Wayback Machine to retrieve deleted images.

Cross-referencing images across multiple platforms is a critical skill in OSINT investigations, helping analysts verify authenticity, track sources, and uncover deeper intelligence.

5.4 Finding Original Image Sources & Tracing Reuploads

Images often spread across the internet in altered, cropped, or manipulated forms, making it difficult to determine their true origin. Whether investigating misinformation, verifying authenticity, or tracking reuploads, OSINT analysts must employ multiple techniques to trace an image back to its original source. This chapter explores strategies, tools, and methodologies for tracking down the first known upload of an image and identifying modified versions.

1. Why Finding the Original Source Matters in OSINT

Tracing an image's first appearance helps analysts:

◆ **Verify authenticity** – Determine if an image is being misrepresented or falsely attributed.
◆ **Track misinformation** – Identify how an image has been altered or taken out of context.
◆ **Find high-quality versions** – Locate uncompressed or uncropped images that may contain more details.
◆ **Uncover additional sources** – Identify the uploader, related images, or original context.

✅ **Example**: A viral image claiming to show a military conflict in 2024 might actually be from an unrelated event in 2015.

2. Reverse Image Searching to Identify the First Upload

Using Reverse Image Search Tools Effectively

Tool	Strengths	Best Use Cases
Google Lens	Largest index, best for popular images	Searching for well-known images & news content
TinEye	Tracks image modifications & finds earliest versions	Finding old uploads & detecting altered versions
Yandex	Strong object & facial recognition	Locating similar images & cross-checking social media
Bing Visual Search	AI-powered analysis	Complementary tool for alternative results
Photo Sherlock	Mobile-friendly image search	Quick searches from smartphones

✅ **Best Practice**: Always use multiple search engines to maximize results, as each has a different index and algorithm.

3. Identifying the Earliest Known Upload Date

Steps to Determine the First Appearance of an Image

1⃞ Use TinEye to Track Earliest Uploads

TinEye allows users to sort results by oldest first, which helps in finding the first known appearance of an image.

✅ **Steps:**

◆ Upload the image to TinEye.
◆ Click "Sort by Oldest" to see the earliest known instances.
◆ Compare timestamps to determine the first recorded upload.

2⃞ Check Image Timestamps in Search Results

Some platforms display timestamps next to search results. Compare results from:

◆ **Google Lens & Yandex** – Look for news articles or forum discussions referencing the image.

◆ **Wayback Machine & Archive.today** – Check if an image appeared on an archived page before it went viral.

3⃞ Use EXIF Metadata (If Available)

If an uncropped, original-quality image is found, extract its metadata using tools like:

◆ ExifTool
◆ Jeffrey's Image Metadata Viewer
◆ Forensicly

✓ **OSINT Tip**: Even if social media strips EXIF data, older versions from web archives or blogs may still retain it.

4. Tracking Reuploads & Modifications

Images often spread online in different versions (cropped, edited, watermarked). To track reuploads:

1⃞ Compare Image Variations Using TinEye & Yandex

◆ TinEye detects cropped & altered versions.
◆ Yandex can find color-adjusted, filtered, or slightly modified images.

2⃞ Use Google Search Operators for Reupload Detection

◆ Find reuploads on a specific site:

site:twitter.com "image filename" OR "caption text"
site:instagram.com inurl:p "image keywords"

◆ Find similar images without exact matches:

intitle:"image description" filetype:jpg

✓ **OSINT Tip**: If an image appears with different timestamps on different websites, the earliest timestamp likely indicates the original upload.

5. Checking Social Media & Forum Archives

Many images first appear on social media, image boards, or forums before spreading widely. Checking these sources can reveal early uploads.

Where to Look:

◆ **Twitter (X) & Facebook** – Use Advanced Search or Google Dorks to find early versions.
◆ **Reddit & 4chan Archives** – Search past threads with keywords related to the image.
◆ **Telegram Channels** – Use OSINT tools like TGStat to track image-based discussions.

✅ **OSINT Tip**: If an image first appears on an obscure forum, its poster may be the original source.

6. Case Study: Debunking a Fake News Image

Scenario:

A widely shared image claimed to show a flood disaster in 2023. OSINT analysts suspected it might be an old image being misused.

Investigation Steps:

1️ Reverse Image Search

Google Lens & Yandex returned results from 2017.

2️ TinEye Search for Earliest Upload

The first known instance appeared on a news site from India in 2017.

3️ Comparing Image Versions

The 2023 viral version had a different caption & increased contrast, making it seem newer.

4️ Checking Web Archives

The original 2017 news article was found on the Wayback Machine.

✅ **Conclusion**: The image was misrepresented as a recent event, but it actually depicted a flood in India from 2017.

7. Key Takeaways for OSINT Analysts

✅ Use multiple reverse image search engines to track down the first known upload.

✅ Sort TinEye results by "Oldest First" to identify early appearances.

✅ Check timestamps in Google & Yandex results to estimate the original upload date.

✅ Use web archives (Wayback Machine, Archive.today) to locate older versions of pages with the image.

✅ Cross-reference social media, forums, and dark web sources for early appearances.

✅ Analyze modified versions using image comparison tools to detect alterations.

By applying these techniques, OSINT analysts can trace the true origin of an image, detect misinformation, and uncover hidden details in investigations.

5.5 Tracking Social Media Trends Through Image Analysis

Images play a significant role in shaping and spreading trends across social media platforms. OSINT analysts can leverage image analysis techniques to monitor viral content, emerging trends, and disinformation campaigns. This chapter explores how to track social media trends using reverse image searches, metadata analysis, and AI-driven tools, helping investigators gain deeper insights into how images influence digital narratives.

1. Why Image Analysis is Key for Tracking Social Media Trends

Social media trends are often driven by visual content—memes, viral photos, and manipulated images that spread rapidly. Tracking these trends helps analysts:

◆ **Monitor disinformation** – Identify fake images, deepfakes, and manipulated visuals.
◆ **Detect emerging trends** – Understand which topics are gaining traction based on image shares.

◆ **Track influencers & sources** – Discover who is creating or amplifying viral images.
◆ **Analyze sentiment & reactions** – Determine how an image is being perceived or interpreted online.

✅ **Example**: A political meme might originate from a small forum, spread to Twitter, and later be amplified by mainstream news outlets.

2. Using Reverse Image Search to Track Viral Images

Step 1: Identify & Collect Trending Images

To begin tracking a trend, analysts need to identify key images associated with the trend.

◆ Use Twitter Trending Topics, Reddit Popular Posts, and TikTok Hashtags to find images gaining traction.
◆ Check Google Trends & CrowdTangle (for Facebook & Instagram) to track which images are being shared most.
◆ Use automated tools like VisualPing to monitor image changes on key websites.

Step 2: Conduct Reverse Image Searches

Run collected images through multiple reverse image search engines to:

◆ Identify where they first appeared online.
◆ Track modifications & reposts across different platforms.
◆ Uncover who is amplifying the content.

✅ **Best Tools for Trend Analysis:**

Tool	Use Case
Google Lens	Finding reposts & modified versions
TinEye	Identifying oldest known version of an image
Yandex	Tracking social media image propagation
Bing Visual Search	AI-driven image recognition for trends

3. Detecting Manipulated Images in Trends

Viral images are often edited, cropped, or deepfaked to fit a certain narrative. Detecting image manipulation is crucial for understanding how trends are being altered or weaponized.

How to Spot Altered Trend Images:

◆ Compare different versions using TinEye's image tracking.

◆ Use photo forensics tools like FotoForensics & Forensically to detect pixel inconsistencies.

◆ Check for EXIF metadata (if available) to verify when & where an image was taken.

◆ Cross-reference video stills to see if an image originated from a longer, contextual clip.

✅ **Case Example:**

A photo of a protest was edited to remove police presence, making it seem more chaotic. OSINT analysts compared the original image (archived on Wayback Machine) to the viral one and exposed the manipulation.

4. Tracking Hashtags & Image Mentions Across Platforms

How to Monitor Image-Based Trends on Social Media

1️⃣ Twitter & Instagram

◆ **Use Twitter Advanced Search:**

#TrendImage since:2024-01-01 → Finds posts using a specific image hashtag.

filter:images → Narrows down tweets containing images.

◆ Check Instagram Hashtags (via third-party tools like Hashtagify) to see how an image spreads.

2️⃣ Reddit & 4chan

◆ Use Reddit's Advanced Search with keywords related to the trend.

◆ Search 4chan archives (via yuki.la or DesuArchive) for early versions of viral images.

3⃞ TikTok & YouTube

◆ Use TikTok's search bar to look for videos containing a viral image.
◆ Screenshot key video frames and reverse search them to find earlier uploads.

✅ **OSINT Tip**: Some images go viral in different forms (GIFs, screenshots from videos). Run multiple types of reverse searches to track them properly.

5. AI & Automation for Image Trend Analysis

Using AI to Identify Social Media Trends

◆ **Google Vision AI & Amazon Rekognition** – Can scan large datasets of images to detect recurring trends.
◆ **Trend Aggregators (BuzzSumo, CrowdTangle)** – Analyze which images are shared most frequently.
◆ **Fake News Detectors (InVID)** – Identify misleading images in news articles.

✅ **Example**: A misleading political meme was flagged by an AI tool, which detected it had been posted across multiple disinformation networks.

6. Case Study: Tracking a Viral Misinformation Image

Scenario:

An image claiming to show a protest in Paris in 2024 started trending on Twitter. OSINT analysts suspected it might be old or misleading.

Investigation Steps:

1⃞ Reverse Image Search (Google Lens & TinEye)

Found the same image from a protest in 2019, proving it wasn't recent.

2⃞ Hashtag Analysis on Twitter & Instagram

The hashtag #ParisProtests2024 was trending, but older posts linked the image to a 2019 protest.

3️⃣ Web Archives & Context Matching

Checking Wayback Machine revealed that the original news source had different captions.

✅ **Conclusion**: The image was misused to fuel a false narrative, and OSINT analysts debunked it using reverse searches & trend tracking.

7. Key Takeaways for OSINT Analysts

✅ Use reverse image searches to track how viral images spread over time.

✅ Monitor trending hashtags & keywords to identify emerging social media trends.

✅ Detect manipulated images using forensic analysis tools.

✅ Cross-check social media platforms (Twitter, Reddit, TikTok) to find image origins.

✅ Leverage AI-powered tools to automate trend detection.

Tracking social media trends through image analysis helps analysts understand digital narratives, detect misinformation, and uncover hidden patterns in online content.

5.6 Case Study: Identifying a Viral Image's Source

Images can spread rapidly across the internet, often detached from their original context. Misattributed or manipulated photos play a significant role in misinformation campaigns, political propaganda, and viral hoaxes. In this case study, we'll walk through an OSINT investigation to trace a viral image's true origin, demonstrating the techniques and tools that analysts use in real-world scenarios.

1. The Viral Image & Initial Claims

In January 2024, an image began circulating on Twitter (X), Telegram, and Facebook, depicting a burning building with people running in panic. The image was widely shared with captions claiming it showed a recent airstrike in Ukraine, fueling discussions on geopolitical tensions.

◆ **Key claims made by viral posts:**

- "Massive airstrike hits Ukraine today! 💔"
- "Another war crime—civilians targeted in Ukraine."
- "Breaking: Explosion in Kyiv, January 2024."

OSINT analysts suspected the image might be older or from a different event. The goal was to determine its true origin.

2. Initial Reverse Image Search

Step 1: Running Reverse Image Searches

The first step was to conduct reverse image searches using multiple tools:

- ◆ **Google Lens** – Found multiple similar images but no definitive source.
- ◆ **TinEye** – Identified older versions of the image dating back to 2020.
- ◆ **Yandex Reverse Image Search** – Matched the image to a 2017 news article.

Key Finding: The image predated 2024, contradicting the viral claims.

3. Verifying the Image's Context & Location

Since the image was not new, the next step was to identify where and when it was actually taken.

Step 2: Checking EXIF Metadata (If Available)

Unfortunately, social media platforms strip EXIF metadata, so no direct GPS or timestamp data was available.

Step 3: Analyzing Visual Elements

- ◆ The architecture and street signs suggested a European city.
- ◆ A billboard in the background had Cyrillic text, suggesting a Russian or Ukrainian location.
- ◆ The fire truck design matched those used in Russia, raising suspicion that the image was not from Ukraine.

✓ **Conclusion**: The image likely originated from Russia, not Ukraine.

4. Locating the Image's Original Publication

Step 4: Using Advanced Google Search Operators

To track down the original news report, analysts used:

◆ **Reverse keyword search:**

"burning building" site:rt.com OR site:ria.ru (Russian news sites)
"fire in Russia" before:2020-12-31

◆ **Translation & Cross-referencing:**

The Cyrillic text in the image was translated and searched in Russian-language sources.

✓ **Breakthrough**: A 2017 Russian news article reported a gas explosion in Magnitogorsk, Russia, featuring the exact same image.

5. Confirming the Findings with Open-Source Mapping

To further verify the location, the team:

◆ Used Google Earth & Yandex Maps to find buildings matching the image.
◆ Cross-checked local Russian news reports from 2017.
◆ Found a YouTube video from 2017 with the same scene.

✓ Final Conclusion:

The image was not from Ukraine in 2024, but from a gas explosion in Magnitogorsk, Russia, in 2017.

6. Outcome & Disinformation Impact

After the OSINT team published their findings:

◆ Fact-checkers debunked the claim, and major news outlets corrected their reports.
◆ Social media platforms flagged posts sharing the false claim.

◆ The viral narrative lost traction, reducing misinformation impact.

Key Lessons for OSINT Analysts

✓ Always conduct reverse image searches before trusting viral photos.

✓ Use multiple tools (Google Lens, TinEye, Yandex) to track image origins.

✓ Check visual clues (architecture, signs, vehicles) to identify locations.

✓ Verify with mapping tools & archived reports to confirm authenticity.

By following these steps, OSINT analysts can accurately trace viral images and combat misinformation.

6. Identifying Landmarks & Locations in Photos

In this chapter, we will focus on the techniques used to identify landmarks and locations within photographs, an essential skill for any OSINT analyst working with visual data. Whether it's a famous landmark, a unique architectural feature, or a subtle geographic marker, photos often contain valuable clues that can reveal the exact location or context of an image. We will explore various tools and approaches for recognizing landmarks, analyzing geographical features, and cross-referencing visual data with online resources. By developing the ability to pinpoint locations from photos, analysts can enhance their investigative capabilities and add depth to their geospatial intelligence work.

6.1 How to Recognize Key Landmarks & Environmental Features

Identifying key landmarks and environmental features in an image is a critical OSINT skill for geolocation analysis. By analyzing buildings, landscapes, and other visual cues, investigators can determine where a photo or video was taken. This chapter explores the techniques and tools used to recognize and verify locations based on architectural styles, natural geography, road signs, and urban infrastructure.

1. Understanding the Importance of Landmarks in OSINT

Landmarks provide crucial reference points in geolocation investigations. They help analysts:

* **Confirm the authenticity of an image or video** – Does the location match the claim?
* **Track the movement of individuals or events** – Where was an image taken, and what does it reveal?
* **Verify locations in crisis mapping** – Humanitarian organizations use geolocation to confirm reports.
* **Uncover disinformation** – Fake or misattributed locations can be debunked through landmark verification.

✅ **Example**: A viral video claimed to show a protest in London, but by identifying street signs and buildings, OSINT analysts confirmed it was actually filmed in Toronto.

2. Recognizing Key Landmark Categories

Landmarks can be broadly classified into man-made structures and natural geographic features:

A. Man-Made Structures

1 Skyscrapers & Unique Buildings

- **Example**: Eiffel Tower (Paris), Burj Khalifa (Dubai)
- **Tools**: Google Earth, Wikimapia, OpenStreetMap

2 Bridges & Monuments

- **Example**: Golden Gate Bridge (San Francisco), Colosseum (Rome)
- **Tools**: Reverse image search, historical archives

3 Stadiums & Arenas

- **Example**: Camp Nou (Barcelona), Madison Square Garden (NYC)
- **Tools**: Sports databases, Street View

4 Religious Buildings

- **Example**: St. Basil's Cathedral (Moscow), Notre Dame (Paris)
- **Tools**: Google Images, local tourism sites

B. Environmental & Natural Features

1 Mountains & Hills

- **Example**: Mount Fuji (Japan), Table Mountain (South Africa)
- **Tools**: PeakFinder, NASA Earth Observatory

2 Rivers, Lakes & Coastlines

- **Example**: River Thames (London), Great Lakes (USA/Canada)
- **Tools**: Google Earth, Mapillary

3️⃣ Forests & Deserts

- **Example**: Amazon Rainforest, Sahara Desert
- **Tools**: Satellite imagery, GIS tools

✅ **Case Example**: A photo of a mysterious desert structure was verified as a military base in Nevada using Google Earth and desert topology analysis.

3. Identifying Locations with Visual & Textual Clues

Step 1: Looking for Text-Based Clues

◆ **Street Signs** – Language, numbering systems, font styles can hint at the region.
◆ **Billboards & Advertisements** – Local brands, phone numbers, and web domains (.fr for France, .jp for Japan).
◆ **License Plates & Traffic Signs** – Plate colors, formats, and driving side rules vary by country.

✅ **Example**: A viral image claimed to be from Mexico, but a billboard with a Russian domain (.ru) proved it was from Moscow.

Step 2: Analyzing Architectural Styles

◆ **European cities** – Historic cathedrals, cobblestone streets.
◆ **Middle Eastern regions** – Sandstone buildings, Islamic architecture.
◆ **Asian cities** – Neon signs, high-rise density, pagodas.

✅ **Example**: An apartment building's window style and air conditioning placement helped analysts confirm a photo was from Seoul, South Korea.

Step 3: Cross-Referencing Public Databases

- **Google Earth & Google Street View** – Compare landmarks with real-world imagery.
- **Wikimapia & OpenStreetMap** – Community-driven location databases.
- **Flightradar24 & MarineTraffic** – If aircraft or ships are visible, track their routes.

✅ **Example**: A drone image of a secluded mansion was geolocated by cross-referencing its driveway pattern with Google Earth historical imagery.

4. Using Satellite & Aerial Views for Landmark Recognition

Step 4: Analyzing Shadows & Terrain

- ◆ **Sun Position** – Shadows reveal approximate time & cardinal direction.
- ◆ **Elevation & Slopes** – Mountainous vs. flat areas help confirm the region.
- ◆ **Road Layouts & Grids** – Cities have unique patterns (e.g., New York's grid vs. London's winding streets).

✅ **Example**: A satellite image of a military base was identified using the shadow angles of structures, revealing it was in the Southern Hemisphere.

5. Tools for Identifying Landmarks & Locations

Best Open-Source Tools for Geolocation

Tool	Use Case
Google Earth	High-resolution satellite imagery for landmark comparison
Google Street View	Ground-level images to verify buildings & streets
Wikimapia	User-tagged landmarks with descriptions
PeakFinder	Identifies mountain peaks in images
Mapillary	Crowd-sourced street-level imagery
Flightradar24	Tracks aircraft visible in images
MarineTraffic	Tracks ships & ports seen in coastal photos

✅ **Example**: An OSINT analyst identified a mystery military airfield in Africa by cross-referencing Google Earth and Flightradar24 data.

6. Case Study: Identifying a Location from a Viral Image

Scenario:

A photo of a collapsed bridge started circulating on social media, claiming to show a recent disaster in India. OSINT analysts were tasked with verifying the image's location.

Investigation Steps:

◆ **Reverse Image Search** – No immediate matches, meaning it wasn't widely documented before.

◆ **Textual Clues** – A highway sign in the background had Spanish text, contradicting the India claim.

◆ **Architectural Analysis** – The bridge design matched those found in South America.

◆ **Google Earth & Street View** – Analysts searched Spanish-speaking countries with similar bridges.

◆ **Final Match** – The bridge was actually in Colombia, not India, and the image was from a 2018 earthquake.

By analyzing landmarks, text clues, and satellite imagery, analysts debunked the misinformation and corrected the record.

7. Key Takeaways for OSINT Analysts

✅ Use architectural styles & urban layouts to match images with real-world locations.

✅ Pay attention to environmental features (mountains, rivers, coastlines) to narrow down regions.

✅ Leverage text clues (street signs, billboards, license plates) to identify local languages and domains.

✅ Cross-reference images with Google Earth, Street View, and public databases for accuracy.

✅ Reverse search and compare multiple elements to debunk misinformation or confirm authenticity.

By mastering landmark recognition, OSINT analysts can accurately verify images, track locations, and expose false claims, strengthening the integrity of digital investigations.

6.2 Using AI & Machine Learning for Landmark Identification

As open-source intelligence (OSINT) techniques evolve, AI and machine learning (ML) have become powerful tools for geolocation analysis. These technologies assist in recognizing landmarks, detecting objects, and verifying locations more efficiently than manual methods. This chapter explores how AI-powered tools help analysts identify landmarks, analyze images, and cross-reference locations in OSINT investigations.

1. The Role of AI & Machine Learning in Landmark Identification

Traditionally, analysts used manual comparisons with Google Earth, Street View, and public databases to identify locations. However, this process can be:

◆ **Time-consuming** – Reviewing thousands of images manually takes hours.
◆ **Error-prone** – Human bias can lead to misidentifications.
◆ **Limited in scale** – A single analyst cannot analyze global data efficiently.

✓ AI-powered systems enhance this process by:

- Automatically detecting and classifying landmarks in images.
- Matching photos with global databases in seconds.
- Recognizing patterns in architecture, terrain, and signage.

Real-World Example:

In 2022, AI-powered OSINT tools helped analysts identify the location of a Russian military camp by recognizing unique building layouts and forest patterns in satellite images.

2. AI-Powered Tools for Landmark Recognition

Several AI tools are available for image-based geolocation:

A. Google Vision AI & Google Lens

◆ **Google Lens** – Instantly matches landmarks with Google's vast image database.
◆ **Google Vision AI** – Uses deep learning to analyze objects, landscapes, and text in images.

✓ **Example**: A photo showing a mosque with a unique dome shape was identified as Hagia Sophia in Turkey using Google Lens.

B. Microsoft Azure Cognitive Services

◆ Can recognize landmarks, buildings, and natural landscapes.
◆ Uses OCR (Optical Character Recognition) to extract text from signs and billboards.

✓ **Example**: Analysts used Azure AI to read a street sign in an unknown location, revealing a city name that led to successful geolocation.

C. Facebook's & Instagram's Image Recognition

◆ Meta's AI systems detect geographic locations in social media images.
◆ Social media platforms automatically tag locations based on landmarks.

✓ **Example**: A protest photo posted without a location tag was identified as being in Bogotá, Colombia, using AI-assisted landmark detection.

D. Reverse Image Search with AI Enhancement

◆ **Yandex Reverse Image Search** – More advanced than Google in finding similar architecture styles.
◆ **TinEye AI Search** – Finds earlier versions of an image, helping verify if a location claim is false.

✓ **Example**: An image falsely claimed to show a recent disaster in India, but AI-assisted reverse search proved it was actually from Mexico in 2017.

3. How AI Analyzes Landmarks in Images

Step 1: Object Detection & Feature Extraction

AI models break down an image into key elements, such as:

◆ **Building facades** – Recognizing unique architecture styles.
◆ **Natural features** – Identifying mountains, rivers, forests.

◆ **Street signs & text** – Extracting readable information for location clues.

✅ **Example**: AI can distinguish between Gothic-style European cathedrals and modern skyscrapers in Asia.

Step 2: Pattern Matching & Database Cross-Referencing

AI compares extracted features with large-scale image databases, such as:

◆ Google Earth & Street View images
◆ Open-source GIS (Geographic Information Systems)
◆ Historical satellite imagery

✅ **Example**: AI successfully matched a mountain backdrop in a viral video with a real location in Afghanistan using Google Earth's elevation data.

Step 3: Contextual Analysis with Metadata & Deep Learning

AI cross-references images with metadata (if available), including:

◆ **Time of day & lighting** – Matching shadows to known locations.
◆ **Weather conditions** – Checking against historical weather data.
◆ **Social media geotags** – Using existing location data to verify authenticity.

✅ **Example**: A video claiming to be filmed in winter in Ukraine was debunked when AI analysis showed green trees and dry roads, proving it was filmed in a different season.

4. AI for Satellite & Aerial Image Landmark Detection

A. Google Earth AI & Deep Learning Models

◆ AI-enhanced satellite imagery analysis detects changes in urban landscapes.
◆ Identifies roads, buildings, and environmental changes over time.

✅ **Example**: AI pinpointed a secret military airstrip by detecting newly built runways not visible in older satellite images.

B. ESA & NASA's AI-Based Geospatial Analysis

- Machine learning identifies coastline changes, deforestation, and urban expansion.
- Helps track disaster-struck areas for rapid response.

✓ **Example**: AI used thermal imaging data to confirm the real location of wildfires based on smoke and heat signatures.

5. AI's Role in Verifying Fake or Misattributed Landmarks

AI is also used to detect manipulated images or misattributed locations in misinformation campaigns.

- **Fake landmarks in deepfakes** – AI detects inconsistencies in architectural details.
- **AI-generated images (MidJourney, Stable Diffusion)** – Identifies distorted building features that don't exist in real life.
- **Manipulated geolocation claims** – AI compares historical images to detect fake edits.

✓ **Example**: AI detected a fake protest image that was actually a doctored version of an old event in Egypt, proving the claim false.

6. Case Study: Identifying a Hidden Military Base Using AI

Scenario:

OSINT analysts received an aerial photo of an alleged Russian military base but needed to confirm its exact location.

AI Investigation Steps:

1. **Google Earth AI Analysis** – Compared the terrain and building layouts with existing maps.
2. **Reverse Image AI Matching** – Cross-referenced structures with historical satellite imagery.
3. **Elevation & Shadow Analysis** – AI detected building heights and sun direction to estimate the latitude.
4. **Social Media Image Comparison** – AI searched for related images posted by locals.

✓ AI successfully matched the image with a remote military facility near Voronezh, Russia, debunking false claims that it was in Ukraine.

7. The Future of AI in OSINT & Landmark Identification

As AI and ML technologies continue to evolve, OSINT analysts will benefit from:

◆ More precise object recognition models for identifying lesser-known landmarks.
◆ Real-time AI-powered video analysis to geolocate events instantly.
◆ Enhanced deepfake detection tools to prevent misinformation.
◆ AI-driven 3D reconstruction models for verifying building structures from limited-angle photos.

✓ **Key Takeaways:**

- AI enhances landmark identification speed and accuracy.
- Machine learning improves pattern recognition in architecture and geography.
- AI-driven reverse search tools help debunk misinformation and locate original sources.
- Future developments will further automate geolocation verification and image authentication.

By integrating AI and machine learning, OSINT analysts can quickly and accurately identify locations, track global events, and counter misinformation in the digital age.

6.3 Analyzing Architecture & Street Signs for Location Clues

In OSINT investigations, analyzing architecture and street signs can provide valuable location clues. While landmark recognition tools can quickly match well-known sites, identifying lesser-known locations often requires a deeper understanding of regional architectural styles, street layouts, and signage systems. This chapter explores methods and tools to extract location data from buildings, road signs, and other urban elements.

1. The Importance of Architecture & Signage in Geolocation OSINT

◆ Architecture styles vary by region, culture, and historical influences. Recognizing common styles can help narrow down a location.

◆ Street signs and road markings follow specific national or municipal guidelines. This includes font types, colors, and symbols.

◆ Language, numbering systems, and traffic signs provide key hints about a country or city.

✅ **Example:**

A photo showing colonial-style buildings with Spanish signage is more likely to be from Latin America than from Spain, where modern architecture is more common.

2. Analyzing Architectural Styles for Location Identification

Different regions have distinct architectural elements, including:

A. European vs. American vs. Asian Architecture

- **Europe**: Gothic cathedrals, Baroque palaces, narrow cobblestone streets.
- **North America**: Skyscrapers, grid-style streets, suburban homes with porches.
- **Asia**: Pagodas, curved roofs, compact urban layouts.

✅ **Example:**

A building with intricate wooden carvings and a curved roof suggests Japan, while a white stucco villa with red-tiled roofs is typical of Mediterranean countries.

B. Identifying Unique Regional & Historical Styles

◆ **Soviet-era architecture** – Boxy, concrete apartment blocks (common in Russia, Ukraine, and former USSR states).

◆ **Islamic architecture** – Domes, minarets, and geometric patterns (Middle East, North Africa, parts of Asia).

◆ **Brutalist architecture** – Harsh concrete structures, common in Eastern Europe and some parts of South America.

✅ **Example:**

An apartment block with concrete paneling and repetitive designs is likely from Eastern Europe, while a colorful colonial-style building with wooden balconies could be from Cuba or the Philippines.

3. Analyzing Street Signs for Clues

Street signs provide direct hints about location through language, colors, numbering systems, and design conventions.

A. Language & Script Recognition

- **English & Latin alphabet** – Common in the US, UK, Australia, and Western Europe.
- **Cyrillic script** – Found in Russia, Ukraine, Bulgaria, and some parts of Central Asia.
- **Arabic script** – Used in the Middle East, North Africa, and parts of South Asia.
- **Chinese, Japanese, and Korean characters** – Found in East Asia.

✅ Example:

A road sign with Hangul characters (Korean script) immediately suggests South Korea, while a sign with Thai script eliminates all other possibilities.

B. Road Sign Colors & Shapes by Country

Different countries use distinct color codes for traffic and road signs:

- **Green highway signs** – Common in the US, Canada, and parts of Europe.
- **Blue street signs** – Found in Japan, France, and Italy.
- **Yellow road signs** – Common in Scandinavian countries.
- **Red-bordered speed limit signs** – Used across most of Europe, while the US uses black-and-white signs.

✅ Example:

A speed limit sign with red borders and "km/h" notation suggests Europe or Latin America, whereas a yellow diamond-shaped road sign points to the United States or Canada.

C. Unique National Sign Features

- **UK** – "Give Way" instead of "Yield," black-on-white speed signs.
- **Germany** – Yellow road signs indicate town entry, blue signs show highways.
- **France** – Green highway signs for major roads, blue for secondary roads.
- **Brazil** – Portuguese-language signs with black-and-white numbering.

✅ Example:

A road sign with Portuguese text and a blue background suggests Brazil, not Portugal, as Portugal mostly uses white signs with black text.

4. Additional Urban Clues for Geolocation

Besides architecture and street signs, other elements help narrow down a location:

A. License Plates & Vehicle Clues

- **European license plates** – White background, blue EU strip on the left.
- **US license plates** – Vary by state, often colorful and unique.
- **Latin American plates** – Typically white with black text, some with country flags.

✅ Example:

A car with a white license plate and an "EU" blue strip is likely from Europe, while a brightly colored, state-specific plate suggests the US.

B. Public Transportation Systems

- **London's red double-decker buses** – Instantly recognizable.
- **New York's yellow taxis** – Strongly associated with the city.
- **Japanese Shinkansen bullet trains** – Found only in Japan.

✅ Example:

A subway station with French-language signage and white-tiled walls suggests Paris, not Montreal, which has different metro architecture.

C. Billboards & Advertisements

- Language, currency symbols, and branding provide location clues.
- Phone numbers with unique country codes (e.g., +44 for the UK, +1 for the US).

✅ **Example:**

An advertisement for "Vodafone UK" with a +44 phone number confirms a location in the United Kingdom.

5. Case Study: Locating an Unknown City from a Single Photo

Scenario:

An investigator received an unlabeled urban photo and needed to determine where it was taken.

Investigation Steps:

1☐ **Architecture Check** – The buildings had colonial-style facades with wooden balconies, suggesting a Latin American or Southeast Asian city.
2☐ **Street Signs & Language** – Signs showed Spanish text with yellow-bordered road markings, pointing to South America.
3☐ **Additional Clues** – A visible license plate had a blue stripe, matching Peruvian vehicle registration.
4☐ **Final Verification** – Using Google Street View, the investigator matched the buildings to a street in Lima, Peru.

✅ **Conclusion:**

The photo was correctly geolocated to downtown Lima, Peru using a combination of architecture, street signs, and vehicle clues.

6. Tools for Analyzing Architecture & Street Signs in OSINT

- **Google Street View & Earth** – Compare urban structures with real-world imagery.
- **Yandex & Baidu Maps** – Useful for analyzing locations in Russia and China.
- **Google Lens & Reverse Image Search** – Identify unique buildings.

◆ **Mapillary & OpenStreetMap** – Community-driven maps with street-level imagery.

◆ **AI-Powered Image Recognition (Google Vision, Microsoft Azure)** – Detects text and objects in images.

✅ **Example:**

An investigator used Google Lens to identify a distinctive street sign, confirming a location in Johannesburg, South Africa.

7. Summary & Key Takeaways

◆ Architecture and street signs provide crucial location clues in OSINT investigations.

◆ Regional architectural styles help narrow down possible countries or cities.

◆ Language, fonts, and road sign colors reveal national or municipal origins.

◆ Additional urban clues like license plates, billboards, and public transport signs aid geolocation.

◆ Combining multiple techniques and OSINT tools increases accuracy in image analysis.

By using these methods, analysts can extract critical location data from even the smallest architectural and signage details, making them powerful tools in geolocation-based OSINT investigations.

6.4 Understanding Cultural & Regional Markers in Photos

In OSINT investigations, identifying cultural and regional markers in images can be crucial for geolocation. While landmarks, street signs, and architecture provide direct clues, cultural and regional markers—such as clothing, festivals, food, religious symbols, and local customs—can help further pinpoint a location. This chapter explores how cultural elements in images can assist in geolocation analysis, common regional indicators, and tools for verification.

1. The Role of Cultural Markers in OSINT Geolocation

Cultural markers are unique, recognizable elements that are often specific to a particular country, region, or ethnic group. These can include:

◆ **Traditional clothing and fashion** – Unique attire or accessories that hint at a region.

◆ **Religious and spiritual symbols** – Mosques, churches, temples, and shrines can indicate location.

◆ **Language and text on signs** – Writing systems and language dialects can confirm regional identities.

◆ **Local food and dining styles** – Dishes, street food, and restaurant styles can help identify a country.

◆ **Vehicles, transportation, and license plates** – Common car brands, bus colors, and public transport styles vary by region.

◆ **Festivals and celebrations** – Local traditions and holidays provide seasonal and geographic context.

✅ **Example:**

A photo of a person wearing a sari suggests a location in India, Bangladesh, or Sri Lanka, whereas someone in a dirndl or lederhosen likely indicates Germany or Austria.

2. Traditional Clothing & Accessories as Regional Indicators

Clothing can offer strong location hints, particularly in rural areas or during cultural events.

A. Region-Specific Traditional Clothing

- **South Asia:** Sarees (India, Sri Lanka), Salwar Kameez (Pakistan, Bangladesh), Dhoti (Nepal, India).
- **Middle East & North Africa**: Thobe (Saudi Arabia, UAE), Abaya (Gulf countries), Djellaba (Morocco).
- **East Asia:** Kimono (Japan), Hanbok (Korea), Cheongsam/Qipao (China).
- **Africa**: Kente cloth (Ghana), Dashiki (West Africa), Boubou (Senegal).
- **Europe**: Kilts (Scotland), Bavarian Lederhosen (Germany, Austria), Flamenco dresses (Spain).

✅ **Example:**

A photo of people wearing colorful Kente cloth indicates a West African country like Ghana, while a man in a white thobe and red-checkered keffiyeh likely points to Saudi Arabia or Jordan.

3. Religious Symbols & Places of Worship as Location Clues

Religious buildings, symbols, and attire often provide strong geolocation hints.

A. Religious Structures & Their Regions

- **Mosques with minarets** – Found in Islamic countries (Middle East, North Africa, South Asia).
- **Churches with onion domes** – Common in Russia and Eastern Orthodox countries.
- **Buddhist temples with pagodas** – Seen in China, Thailand, Japan, Myanmar.
- **Hindu temples with ornate carvings** – Found in India, Nepal, and Bali (Indonesia).
- **Synagogues with Star of David symbols** – Jewish religious sites worldwide but concentrated in Israel, Europe, and the U.S.

✅ Example:

A golden stupa with intricate carvings suggests Myanmar or Thailand, while a white mosque with blue-tiled domes points to Turkey or Iran.

B. Religious Clothing & Accessories

◆ **Sikh Turbans** – Worn primarily in Punjab, India.

◆ **Hijabs, Niqabs, and Burqas** – Common in Muslim-majority countries, but styles vary (e.g., black abayas in Saudi Arabia, colorful hijabs in Indonesia).

◆ **Christian crosses on clothing** – Found in Catholic and Orthodox regions.

✅ Example:

A photo of a group of men in orange robes with shaved heads likely points to Buddhist monks in Thailand, Myanmar, or Sri Lanka.

4. Language, Text & Script as Regional Indicators

Text in an image—whether on street signs, billboards, or product labels—can be a strong location clue.

A. Writing Systems & Their Regions

- **Latin alphabet** – Used in North America, most of Europe, Latin America, parts of Africa.
- **Cyrillic script** – Russia, Ukraine, Bulgaria, Serbia.
- **Arabic script** – Middle East, North Africa, parts of South Asia (Pakistan).
- **Chinese, Japanese, Korean characters** – East Asia.
- **Devanagari script** – India (Hindi, Marathi), Nepal (Nepali).

✅ Example:

A billboard with Hangul characters (Korean script) confirms the location is South Korea, while a street sign with Cyrillic letters suggests Russia, Ukraine, or Bulgaria.

5. Local Food & Eating Customs as Clues

Food and dining habits vary significantly across regions and can help in geolocation.

A. Common Regional Food Markers

- ◆ **Chopsticks & rice bowls** – Common in China, Japan, Korea, Vietnam.
- ◆ **Street tacos & tortillas** – Indicate Mexico or Central America.
- ◆ **Spicy curries & naan bread** – Found in India, Pakistan, Bangladesh.
- ◆ **Bread, cheese, and olives** – Common in Mediterranean countries.

✅ Example:

A street vendor selling banh mi sandwiches and pho is likely from Vietnam, while a cart with arepas suggests Colombia or Venezuela.

6. Vehicles, Transportation & License Plates as Cultural Markers

Vehicles and transportation systems differ by country and can be useful location identifiers.

A. Recognizable Regional Vehicles

- **Tuk-tuks** – Common in Thailand, India, Sri Lanka, and Southeast Asia.
- **Jeepneys** – Unique to the Philippines.
- **Red double-decker buses** – London, UK.
- **Rickshaws** – Common in Bangladesh, India, Pakistan.

B. License Plate Clues

- **Blue strip with "EU" stars** – Found in European Union countries.
- **White plates with Arabic numerals** – Common in Middle East countries.
- **Yellow number plates** – Used in the UK and some African nations.

✅ **Example:**

A brightly colored Jeepney with passengers riding on top is exclusive to the Philippines, while a red taxi with Chinese characters suggests Hong Kong.

7. Festivals & Celebrations as Geolocation Indicators

Many cultures have unique public celebrations, which can reveal the time of year and location.

- ◆ **Chinese New Year (red decorations, dragon dances)** – China, Taiwan, Hong Kong, Singapore.
- ◆ **Oktoberfest (people in Bavarian attire, beer tents)** – Germany.
- ◆ **Holi (color powder celebrations)** – India, Nepal.
- ◆ **Carnival (elaborate costumes, parades)** – Brazil, Caribbean.

✅ **Example:**

A photo showing people throwing colored powder points to Holi celebrations in India or Nepal, while a costumed samba parade suggests Brazil.

8. Tools for Cultural & Regional Image Analysis

- ◆ **Google Reverse Image Search & Google Lens** – Identifies cultural artifacts, text, and landmarks.
- ◆ **Yandex Reverse Image Search** – Works well for identifying images from Russia and Eastern Europe.
- ◆ **Google Translate (Camera Mode)** – Helps decipher foreign text in images.
- ◆ **Wikimapia & OpenStreetMap** – Useful for matching cultural sites and local infrastructure.

✅ **Example:**

An investigator used Google Lens to identify a specific type of festival mask, confirming the photo was from a Day of the Dead celebration in Mexico.

9. Summary & Key Takeaways

- ◆ Clothing, religious symbols, food, and transportation can all reveal a photo's origin.
- ◆ Writing systems and text on signs help confirm national and regional identities.
- ◆ Local festivals, customs, and unique celebrations provide time and place context.
- ◆ Using multiple OSINT tools together increases accuracy in cultural-based geolocation.

By recognizing subtle cultural markers, analysts can extract critical location data from even the most ordinary images, making them a powerful asset in OSINT investigations.

6.5 Cross-Referencing Images with Publicly Available Datasets

In OSINT investigations, cross-referencing images with publicly available datasets is a powerful technique for verifying locations, identifying people or objects, and establishing timelines. By utilizing open databases, government records, crowdsourced imagery, and geospatial data, analysts can validate findings and uncover additional information that might not be evident from the image alone. This chapter explores key sources, methodologies, and best practices for cross-referencing images effectively.

1. The Importance of Cross-Referencing in OSINT

Images alone may not always provide enough context to confirm a location or identity. By comparing them with external datasets, investigators can:

✅ Verify the authenticity of an image by matching it with a known database.

✅ Determine the date and time of an event using timestamps from satellite imagery or social media archives.

✅ Identify people, vehicles, or objects by matching against databases like missing persons registries, vehicle identification services, or product catalogs.

✓ Corroborate location clues by comparing images to maps, real estate listings, or open archives.

For example, an image showing a unique street layout can be compared with OpenStreetMap (OSM) or Google Earth to pinpoint its exact location.

2. Key Publicly Available Datasets for Image Cross-Referencing

There are multiple free and open datasets that can aid OSINT analysts in geolocation and verification.

A. Satellite & Aerial Imagery Databases

◆ **Google Earth & Google Maps** – Provides satellite, terrain, and street-level imagery.
◆ **Bing Maps & Yandex Maps** – Alternative sources for geospatial verification.
◆ **Sentinel Hub (ESA Sentinel-2 data)** – Free, frequently updated satellite imagery from the European Space Agency.
◆ **NASA Worldview & USGS Earth Explorer** – High-resolution satellite images for long-term tracking.

✓ **Example:**

An analyst cross-references an image of a coastal area with Sentinel-2 imagery to determine whether the coastline matches the suspected region.

B. OpenStreetMap & Crowdsourced Geolocation Data

◆ **OpenStreetMap (OSM)** – Community-updated map data that includes roads, buildings, and points of interest.
◆ **Wikimapia** – A crowdsourced alternative to OSM with detailed user-contributed location information.
◆ **Mapillary & OpenAerialMap** – User-contributed street and aerial imagery.

✓ **Example:**

A photo containing a distinctively shaped intersection is compared with OSM road layouts to confirm a specific city.

C. Government & Institutional Databases

♦ **Property & land registries** – Useful for cross-referencing real estate and address information.

♦ **Census and municipal data** – Provides neighborhood-level insights.

♦ **FAO GeoNetwork** – Contains geographic and environmental datasets.

✅ Example:

An image of a building with a visible address number is matched against local property records to verify its authenticity.

D. Social Media & Image Repositories

♦ **Flickr & Wikimedia Commons** – Contains freely accessible geo-tagged images.

♦ **Geograph.org.uk** – A UK-based platform with thousands of location-specific images.

♦ **Panoramio (Archived on Google Earth)** – Historical user-contributed geographic photos.

♦ **Twitter, Instagram, Facebook** – Useful for tracking user-posted, geotagged images.

✅ Example:

An investigator finds an image of a protest with a visible banner and checks Twitter's geotagged posts to locate similar images from the same event.

E. Transportation & Vehicle Identification Databases

♦ **OpenVehicleData & Carfax** – Can help identify car models and regions based on license plate structures.

♦ **Plane Finder & MarineTraffic** – Useful for tracking aircraft and ships based on visible identifiers in images.

♦ **Bike-sharing and transit databases** – Helps place locations based on local transport branding.

✅ Example:

A photo of a bus stop with a unique bus number is cross-referenced with a city's transit database to identify its location.

3. Methodologies for Cross-Referencing Images with Datasets

A. Extracting and Analyzing Metadata

- Use EXIF readers (e.g., ExifTool, FotoForensics) to retrieve geotags, timestamps, and camera details.
- Compare timestamps with publicly available time-lapse satellite imagery.
- Validate GPS coordinates using Google Maps and OpenStreetMap.

✅ **Example:**

A journalist verifies a leaked image's metadata against NASA Worldview satellite data to confirm the date of capture.

B. Reverse Searching for Visual Matches

- Use reverse image search engines (Google Lens, TinEye, Yandex) to find similar or identical images.
- Check geotagged photo repositories (Flickr, Wikimedia) for matching landmarks or scenes.
- Compare background details (architecture, street signs) with historical images.

✅ **Example:**

An OSINT analyst confirms that a viral image of a burning building is an old 2018 news photo by cross-referencing it with archived news articles.

C. Correlating Geolocation Clues with GIS Tools

- Overlay images on satellite maps using Google Earth Pro's historical imagery feature.
- Use GIS tools like QGIS to analyze geographic patterns.
- Compare urban planning records for changes in infrastructure.

✅ **Example:**

An investigator overlays a photo of a construction site with historical satellite imagery to estimate when it was built.

D. Verifying Events & Timelines with Open Data

- Check weather archives (NOAA, Weather Underground) to match conditions with image metadata.
- Use news archives (Wayback Machine, FactCheck.org) to confirm event occurrences.
- Search law enforcement bulletins to verify claims of criminal activity.

✅ Example:

An OSINT analyst disproves a fake storm photo by checking historical NOAA weather data, which confirms that no such storm occurred that day.

4. Challenges & Limitations of Cross-Referencing

🖋 **Manipulated or faked metadata** – Some images may have altered EXIF data to mislead analysts.

🖋 **Lack of public datasets in certain regions** – Some countries have restricted mapping data.

🖋 **Time-sensitive information** – Certain databases, like social media archives, may become unavailable over time.

🖋 **Image degradation or compression** – Lower-quality images may reduce effectiveness in matching visual elements.

✅ **Solution**: Analysts should cross-check multiple sources to verify data consistency and use alternative investigative techniques when data is limited.

5. Case Example: Verifying a Viral War Image

📌 **Scenario**: A viral image claims to show a missile strike in Eastern Europe.

🔍 **OSINT Workflow:**

- Reverse image search reveals similar images dating back to 2016, not 2024.
- Satellite imagery (Sentinel-2) shows no evidence of damage at the claimed location.

- Weather databases confirm that clear skies were reported on the claimed date, contradicting the image's dark stormy background.
- Cross-referencing news archives finds the same image in a 2016 conflict report from a different country.

✅ **Conclusion**: The image was misrepresented and falsely attributed to recent events.

6. Summary & Key Takeaways

✓ Cross-referencing images with public datasets improves OSINT accuracy and verification.

✓ GIS tools, social media archives, and satellite imagery are valuable resources for geolocation.

✓ EXIF data, weather records, and vehicle registries can validate an image's authenticity.

✓ OSINT analysts must be aware of manipulated metadata and disinformation tactics.

By leveraging multiple open datasets, investigators can ensure greater accuracy, debunk misinformation, and enhance the reliability of image-based intelligence.

6.6 Case Study: Locating a Target Based on Background Details

In OSINT investigations, seemingly minor background details in images—such as architecture, signs, vegetation, and even weather conditions—can provide crucial clues for geolocation. This case study demonstrates how an analyst successfully pinpointed a target's location by analyzing these subtle elements in a photograph.

1. Scenario: Identifying the Location of an Anonymous Image

A journalist receives an image from an anonymous whistleblower claiming that a high-profile fugitive is hiding in a safe house. The image is cropped, showing only part of a balcony railing, a distant mountain range, and a few street signs in an unfamiliar language. The journalist needs to verify the location before publishing the story.

Key Details from the Image:

✓ A metal balcony railing with a unique design.

✓ A distant mountain range with snow-capped peaks.

✓ Two street signs with partial text in a non-Latin alphabet.

✓ A yellow taxi with a visible license plate format.

✓ A weather condition showing clear skies and bright sunlight.

Using OSINT techniques, analysts work to narrow down the possible location.

2. Step-by-Step OSINT Investigation

Step 1: Identifying the Language and Alphabet

The street signs contain partial text in a non-Latin script. Using Google Lens, OCR tools, and language detection software, analysts determine that the script is Cyrillic, commonly used in countries like Russia, Ukraine, Bulgaria, Serbia, and Kazakhstan.

✓ Eliminates countries without Cyrillic script (e.g., Western Europe, the Middle East).

✓ Narrows the search to specific regions where Cyrillic is used.

Step 2: Analyzing the Mountain Range

The image shows a snow-capped mountain range in the distance. Analysts use Google Earth, PeakFinder, and public databases of notable mountain ranges to compare the visible peaks.

By cross-referencing the mountain formations, they identify a match with the Tian Shan mountains, which stretch across Kazakhstan, Kyrgyzstan, and western China.

✓ Narrows the location to a Central Asian country.

Step 3: Examining the Taxi and License Plate Format

The image includes a yellow taxi with a partially visible license plate. Analysts use:

◆ Global license plate databases (e.g., Carplates.ai).

- Local taxi regulations from government websites.
- Social media images of taxis in various cities.

The format of the plate and color scheme match taxis commonly used in Almaty, Kazakhstan.

✓ Almaty, Kazakhstan is now the primary suspected location.

Step 4: Reverse Searching the Balcony Railing Design

The balcony railing has a distinctive pattern, which can be a helpful clue. Analysts conduct a reverse image search using:

- Google Lens & Yandex Images to find similar railings.
- Architectural forums & real estate listings in Almaty.
- Local Airbnb and hotel photos for visual matches.

A match is found in a real estate listing for an apartment in Almaty, confirming that the safe house is likely within this residential complex.

✓ Location narrowed to a specific neighborhood.

Step 5: Cross-Verifying with Street Signs

The partial street sign text provides an additional verification step. Analysts use:

- Google Translate to reconstruct the missing letters.
- OpenStreetMap (OSM) & Google Maps to check street names in Almaty.
- Local business directories to see if nearby landmarks match the image.

They find a street in central Almaty with a nearly identical name, confirming that the image was taken from an apartment overlooking this road.

✓ **Final location confirmed**: A specific residential complex in Almaty, Kazakhstan.

3. Outcome & Lessons Learned

With this evidence, the journalist verifies that the image is genuine and taken recently. The fugitive's whereabouts are confirmed, allowing authorities and media outlets to report accurately.

Key Takeaways from this Case Study:

✔ Background details (mountains, signs, objects) provide strong geolocation clues.

✔ Cross-referencing multiple OSINT techniques increases accuracy.

✔ Reverse image searches, GIS tools, and metadata extraction are essential.

✔ Even small elements, like railings or street signs, can pinpoint exact locations.

This case study highlights how OSINT analysts can use publicly available tools and datasets to uncover hidden details and track down key targets using only a single image.

7. Satellite & Street View OSINT

In this chapter, we will explore the use of satellite imagery and street view data for OSINT analysis, unlocking new layers of intelligence from overhead and ground-level perspectives. Satellite images provide a bird's-eye view of locations, offering insights into infrastructure, terrain, and even changes over time, while street view data allows analysts to virtually "walk" through neighborhoods and pinpoint specific locations with high accuracy. We will cover the tools and platforms available for accessing and interpreting satellite and street view imagery, as well as methods for combining these resources to corroborate findings, track developments, and uncover hidden details in a variety of investigative scenarios.

7.1 How Satellite Imagery Helps in OSINT Investigations

Satellite imagery is one of the most powerful tools in OSINT investigations, providing analysts with a bird's-eye view of locations, activities, and environmental changes across the globe. Whether tracking military movements, verifying humanitarian crises, or identifying illegal activities, satellite data allows OSINT practitioners to gather intelligence from a distance. This chapter explores how satellite imagery is used in investigations, the key sources available, and the techniques for analyzing imagery effectively.

1. The Role of Satellite Imagery in OSINT

Satellite imagery is valuable for validating claims, uncovering hidden details, and monitoring large-scale events. Some of its key uses include:

✓ **Geolocation Verification**: Confirming whether an image or video matches a real-world location.

✓ **Event Monitoring**: Tracking protests, conflicts, natural disasters, or infrastructure development.

✓ **Border & Military Surveillance**: Observing troop movements, border crossings, and military installations.

✓ **Illegal Activity Detection**: Identifying deforestation, smuggling routes, or hidden airstrips.

✓ **Disaster Response & Humanitarian Aid**: Assessing damage and planning relief efforts.

For example, analysts used satellite imagery to confirm the destruction of Mariupol's theater during the Russia-Ukraine war, proving that a civilian target was hit.

2. Key Sources of Satellite Imagery for OSINT

There are free and commercial satellite imagery providers available for OSINT analysis:

A. Free & Open-Source Satellite Imagery

◆ **Google Earth & Google Maps**: Provides high-resolution satellite views and historical imagery.
◆ **Sentinel-2 (European Space Agency):** Offers free, frequently updated imagery useful for environmental and crisis monitoring.
◆ **NASA Worldview**: Displays real-time global satellite imagery.
◆ **USGS Earth Explorer (Landsat):** Provides detailed imagery for historical comparisons.
◆ **NOAA Satellite Data**: Useful for weather tracking and environmental analysis.

✅ **Example Use:**

After an oil spill in the Gulf of Mexico, OSINT analysts used Sentinel-2 imagery to map the spread of the pollution.

B. Commercial Satellite Providers (Paid Access)

◆ **Maxar Technologies (formerly DigitalGlobe):** High-resolution imagery used by journalists and intelligence agencies.
◆ **Planet Labs**: Offers daily satellite updates for tracking changes over time.
◆ **Airbus Pleiades & SPOT**: High-detail imagery useful for military and security analysis.

✅ **Example Use:**

Maxar's high-resolution images were used to confirm mass graves in Bucha, Ukraine, refuting false claims that they were staged.

3. Techniques for Analyzing Satellite Imagery

A. Geolocation & Verification

Analysts use satellite images to verify if an image or video corresponds to a real-world location. This involves:

◆ Matching building layouts, road patterns, and terrain to known locations.
◆ Comparing satellite timestamps with other data sources.
◆ Using street view tools like Google Earth for ground-level verification.

✓ **Example:**

An image claiming to show a secret military base in Africa was debunked when analysts found that it was actually a mining facility using Google Earth.

B. Change Detection Over Time

Satellite imagery allows analysts to compare a location before and after an event to track changes.

◆ Tools like Sentinel Hub's EO Browser allow side-by-side comparisons.
◆ Analysts can detect new buildings, deforestation, or destroyed infrastructure.

✓ **Example:**

Satellite images from before and after wildfires in California helped confirm the extent of the damage.

C. Object Recognition & Pattern Analysis

AI and machine learning tools help detect:

◆ Military vehicles, aircraft, and ships from high-resolution images.
◆ Illegal deforestation, oil spills, or crop failures in environmental OSINT.
◆ Roadblocks, protest gatherings, or troop movements in conflict zones.

✓ **Example:**

Analysts used AI-powered tools to track Russian tank formations near Ukraine's border before the 2022 invasion.

D. Weather & Environmental Analysis

Satellite data can be used to:

- Cross-check weather conditions to confirm if a claimed event took place.
- Track climate change effects such as melting glaciers or rising sea levels.
- Detect flooding, hurricanes, and wildfires in real time.

✅ **Example:**

After a viral video claimed to show a flood in China, satellite weather data proved the footage was actually from Bangladesh in 2017.

4. Limitations & Challenges of Satellite OSINT

Despite its power, satellite imagery has some limitations:

❌ **Resolution Constraints**: Free imagery often lacks high detail, making object recognition difficult.
❌ **Cloud Coverage & Weather Conditions**: Obscured views can hinder analysis.
❌ **Time Lag**: Free images may be outdated, while real-time access is expensive.
❌ **Geopolitical Restrictions**: Some regions restrict access to high-quality satellite images.

✅ **Workaround**: Analysts combine multiple sources, including social media posts, to fill in missing details.

5. Case Study: Tracking Military Activity Using Satellite OSINT

📌 **Scenario:**

A military base expansion is rumored in North Korea, but official sources deny it.

🔍 **OSINT Investigation:**

- Google Earth historical imagery shows that an area near Pyongyang had new construction activity in the past six months.

- Planet Labs' daily imagery confirms that runway extensions and new barracks have appeared.
- Social media monitoring reveals recent satellite photos leaked by analysts on Twitter.
- Cross-referencing weather reports ensures the satellite images match real conditions.

✅ **Outcome:**

Journalists publish a report proving that North Korea is expanding its airbases, contradicting official statements.

6. Summary & Key Takeaways

✓ Satellite imagery is a powerful OSINT tool for tracking events, verifying locations, and uncovering hidden details.

✓ Free sources like Google Earth & Sentinel-2 provide valuable intelligence.

✓ Techniques like geolocation, change detection, and object recognition enhance investigations.

✓ Challenges include resolution limits, cloud cover, and restricted access to high-quality imagery.

✓ Combining satellite data with other OSINT techniques improves accuracy.

Satellite imagery remains an essential tool for investigative journalists, intelligence analysts, and researchers, offering a global, real-time perspective on unfolding events.

7.2 Using Google Earth, Bing Maps & OpenStreetMap for Geolocation

In OSINT investigations, geolocation plays a crucial role in verifying claims, identifying locations, and tracking individuals or events. While satellite imagery provides an overhead view, platforms like Google Earth, Bing Maps, and OpenStreetMap (OSM) offer powerful tools for analysts to cross-reference locations, examine terrain, and analyze geographic features. This chapter explores how each of these platforms can be used effectively in geolocation investigations.

1. The Importance of Mapping Platforms in OSINT

Mapping tools provide:

✅ High-resolution satellite imagery for verifying locations.

✅ Street-level views for identifying specific buildings, businesses, and signage.

✅ Historical imagery to track changes in a location over time.

✅ Crowdsourced data that can reveal local points of interest.

Common Use Cases:

◆ Verifying the authenticity of images/videos by matching background details.
◆ Tracking suspects by cross-referencing locations in photos.
◆ Monitoring events such as protests or conflicts.
◆ Investigating fraud by checking if a claimed business location exists.

For example, OSINT analysts used Google Earth to confirm the location of missile strikes in Syria by matching satellite imagery with social media footage.

2. Google Earth: A High-Resolution Mapping Tool for OSINT

Google Earth is one of the most comprehensive geolocation tools, offering:

✔ High-resolution satellite imagery

✔ Street View for ground-level verification

✔ Historical imagery for tracking changes

✔ 3D terrain mapping for elevation analysis

A. Key OSINT Features in Google Earth

1. Satellite & Aerial Imagery for Location Matching

Google Earth allows analysts to match landmarks, terrain, and road layouts with images or videos being investigated.

✅ **Example**: An analyst verifying the location of a terrorist training camp uses Google Earth to match building layouts and road intersections with intelligence reports.

2. Historical Imagery for Tracking Changes

Google Earth Pro allows users to view past satellite images, helping track:

- Deforestation & illegal land use.
- Military base expansions.
- Urban growth & infrastructure development.

✅ **Example**: Investigators used Google Earth's historical imagery to track China's construction of artificial islands in the South China Sea.

3. Street View for On-the-Ground Verification

Street View is invaluable for verifying details like:

- Road signs & business locations.
- Landmarks & building entrances.
- Traffic patterns & urban layouts.

✅ **Example**: A journalist used Street View to verify the location of a Russian spy by matching a bench in the UK where he was last seen with Google Street View imagery.

4. 3D Terrain Analysis for Environmental Context

Google Earth's 3D mode helps in:

- Analyzing elevation changes.
- Understanding visibility from a location.
- Verifying terrain features in images.

✅ **Example**: Analysts verified a sniper's possible vantage point by analyzing elevation differences in Google Earth's 3D mode.

3. Bing Maps: An Alternative with Unique Features

Bing Maps is a lesser-known but powerful alternative to Google Earth. While it lacks Google's historical imagery, it has unique features:

✓ **Bird's Eye View**: Provides 45-degree angled satellite imagery, offering a more detailed perspective of buildings and streets.

✓ **Different Satellite Providers**: Bing Maps sometimes has higher-quality imagery in areas where Google Earth is outdated.

✓ **Integration with Microsoft APIs**: Useful for cross-referencing locations with other Microsoft services.

A. Key OSINT Features in Bing Maps

1. Bird's Eye View for Angled Perspectives

Unlike traditional satellite imagery, Bird's Eye View offers a tilted, oblique angle, making it easier to:

◆ Identify building entrances, parking lots, and small structures.
◆ Spot vehicles, street furniture, and smaller urban details.
◆ Analyze shadow angles for estimating time of day.

✅ **Example**: Investigators used Bird's Eye View to map out cartel safe houses in Mexico, as the angled view revealed hidden entry points.

2. Superior Satellite Imagery in Some Regions

Bing's imagery is sometimes sharper in areas where Google Earth is outdated or lower resolution.

✅ **Example**: An analyst investigating North Korean infrastructure projects found Bing's satellite images to be newer than Google's, revealing new military installations.

3. Street Side (Street-Level Views in Some Cities)

While not as extensive as Google Street View, Bing's Street Side feature offers:

- Alternative street-level perspectives for verifying locations.
- Different image timestamps that may capture changes in an area.

✅ **Example**: Analysts confirmed the location of a suspected extremist in Europe by cross-referencing Bing's Street Side with Google's Street View, revealing slight differences in timestamps.

4. OpenStreetMap (OSM): A Crowdsourced Geospatial Database

OSM is an open-source, community-driven mapping platform. While it lacks satellite imagery, it is highly detailed in certain regions where commercial services fall short.

✓ Crowdsourced location data

✓ Detailed points of interest (POIs) not found on Google/Bing

✓ Offline access via tools like QGIS and OsmAnd

✓ Editable map data with community updates

A. Key OSINT Features in OSM

1. Identifying Points of Interest (POIs)

OSM is extremely detailed in regions where government data is restricted. Analysts can:

- Find businesses, safe houses, and meeting points.
- Locate infrastructure such as rail lines, tunnels, and pipelines.
- Identify protest locations and movement patterns.

✅ **Example**: Investigators tracked illegal mining operations in South America using OSM's detailed trails and industrial sites.

2. Offline Mapping for Field Investigations

OSM data can be used offline through apps like OsmAnd and MAPS.ME, making it useful for:

- On-the-ground investigations in restricted areas.

◆ Mapping rural or conflict zones where Google/Bing lack updates.

✅ **Example**: Humanitarian workers in war zones used OSM to navigate roads that were missing from commercial maps.

3. Custom Mapping & Data Export for Analysis

OSM allows users to:

◆ Download map data and analyze it with GIS tools.
◆ Overlay custom information, such as heatmaps of activity.

✅ **Example**: Journalists tracking Russian military movements used OSM's downloadable data to create custom geospatial intelligence layers.

5. Summary & Key Takeaways

✓ Google Earth is the most powerful tool for geolocation due to its high-resolution satellite imagery, Street View, and historical data.

✓ Bing Maps provides unique Bird's Eye views, sometimes offering better satellite updates than Google.

✓ OpenStreetMap is essential for finding hidden POIs, mapping offline, and analyzing community-driven data.

✓ Combining multiple tools improves accuracy, ensuring verified and cross-checked geolocation intelligence.

By mastering Google Earth, Bing Maps, and OSM, OSINT analysts can pinpoint locations, track movements, and verify digital content, making them essential tools for modern intelligence investigations.

7.3 Cross-Referencing Satellite & Street View Data for Accuracy

In OSINT investigations, geolocation accuracy is crucial. While satellite imagery provides a top-down, large-scale perspective, street-level imagery offers ground-level details. By cross-referencing these data sources, analysts can validate locations, detect inconsistencies, and confirm event timelines. This chapter explores how to effectively combine Google Earth, Bing Maps, OpenStreetMap, and other tools to ensure geolocation accuracy in OSINT investigations.

1. Why Cross-Referencing is Essential in OSINT

A. Verifying the Authenticity of an Image or Video

◆ **Example**: A viral video claims to show a riot in a specific city. Satellite imagery helps verify the existence of surrounding buildings, while Street View allows analysts to confirm storefront signs, road layouts, and local markers.

B. Detecting Misinformation & Edited Content

◆ **Example**: A social media post shows a destroyed building, claiming it is recent war damage. Analysts compare satellite imagery over time and discover the building was already abandoned years ago.

C. Tracking Changes Over Time

◆ **Example**: Investigators analyze deforestation in the Amazon by comparing older and newer satellite images while using Street View to check road developments and industrial activity in nearby towns.

2. Cross-Referencing Satellite Imagery with Street View

A. Identifying Key Landmarks

- Find a landmark or reference point in an image/video (e.g., a tower, river, bridge, or unique building).
- Use Google Earth or Bing Maps to locate the same landmark from a satellite perspective.

Switch to Google Street View or Bing Street Side to match finer details such as:

- Store signs
- Road layouts

- Vehicle models
- Language on billboards

✦ **Example**: Journalists investigating a military convoy video in Ukraine matched a gas station sign and road curvature in Street View with satellite imagery to confirm the exact location.

B. Verifying Road Networks & Urban Layouts

- Use satellite imagery to analyze road intersections, overpasses, and building positions.
- Use Street View to confirm pedestrian paths, road signs, or traffic signals that may be blurred in satellite views.

✦ **Example**: Investigators identified an illegal migrant route by cross-referencing dirt roads visible in satellite images with Street View evidence of makeshift camps near highways.

C. Confirming Water Bodies, Forests, & Terrain Features

- Use Google Earth to check elevation, hills, and vegetation coverage.
- Use Street View to analyze ground textures, tree types, and terrain differences.

✦ **Example**: An OSINT analyst investigating a reported cartel hideout in South America confirmed the exact location by matching satellite imagery of a river bend with Street View showing a bridge in the background of a suspect's video.

3. Cross-Checking with Multiple Mapping Platforms

A. Google Earth vs. Bing Maps

✓ **Google Earth**: Higher-resolution images, 3D terrain, and historical imagery.

✓ **Bing Maps**: Bird's Eye View (45-degree angles) offers a different perspective.

✦ **Example**: Analyzing a disputed military base, analysts found Google Earth had an outdated image, but Bing's Bird's Eye View revealed newly constructed buildings.

B. OpenStreetMap (OSM) for Additional Context

✓ OSM's crowdsourced data can confirm points of interest that may not be labeled in commercial maps.

✓ Some locations remove Street View access, but OSM still provides building outlines and road names.

✦ **Example**: A journalist tracking a war zone in Syria found that official maps lacked road details, but OSM contributors had mapped out key refugee camps.

4. Tools & Techniques for Cross-Referencing

A. Using Google Earth Pro for Historical Verification

- Compare past and present satellite images to check for building demolitions, new constructions, or environmental changes.
- Overlay old and new imagery to detect infrastructure shifts.

✦ **Example**: Analysts tracking Russian military activity used historical Google Earth images to confirm troop build-ups near Ukraine.

B. Using Sun Position & Shadows for Time Verification

- Satellite images are taken at different times of the day—shadow angles help verify time stamps.
- Use Suncalc.org to check if shadows in a video or photo match satellite images from the claimed date.

✦ **Example**: A Twitter post claimed an explosion happened at sunset, but shadow analysis in satellite images proved it was taken at noon.

C. Comparing Satellite Images with Video Geolocation

- Extract key frames from videos and match them with Google Earth terrain and street-level imagery.
- Identify key visual markers (mountains, unique buildings, road signs, or billboards).

✦ **Example**: An OSINT analyst geolocated a terrorist training camp in the Middle East by matching mountain ridges seen in a propaganda video with Google Earth's satellite view.

5. Case Study: Verifying a Conflict Zone Video

Step 1: Extract Key Details from the Video

- The footage showed a mosque, a destroyed bridge, and a hill in the background.
- A street sign was partially visible.

Step 2: Match Features in Google Earth

- Analysts searched for mosques near rivers in the claimed region.
- A satellite image showed a similar bridge with a collapsed section.

Step 3: Confirm Using Street View

- Google Street View verified the same mosque entrance and damaged road signs.
- A billboard in the background matched a social media post from the same region.

Step 4: Cross-Check with Other Mapping Sources

- Bing's Bird's Eye View showed the exact position of the collapsed bridge.
- OpenStreetMap confirmed the mosque's coordinates, which aligned with social media posts from locals.

✅ **Result**: The video was verified as authentic, confirming the reported location.

6. Key Takeaways

✓ Cross-referencing satellite and street-level data is essential for accuracy in OSINT investigations.

✓ Google Earth is best for satellite imagery, but Bing's Bird's Eye View offers unique perspectives.

✓ OpenStreetMap can provide missing details not found in commercial maps.

✓ Use shadow analysis and historical imagery to verify time-based claims.

✓ Combining multiple tools improves confidence in location verification.

By effectively cross-referencing satellite, street-level, and crowdsourced data, OSINT analysts can enhance investigative accuracy, expose misinformation, and uncover critical intelligence in real-world scenarios.

7.4 Identifying Changes in Location Over Time Using Historical Imagery

In OSINT investigations, tracking changes in locations over time is crucial for verifying claims, monitoring developments, and uncovering hidden details. Historical imagery—available through tools like Google Earth Pro, Sentinel Hub, Bing Maps, and Planet Labs—allows analysts to compare past and present visuals, identifying new constructions, environmental changes, conflict damage, and infrastructure development.

This chapter explores techniques for using historical imagery in OSINT, practical tools, and real-world case studies demonstrating how location changes reveal critical intelligence.

1. Why Historical Imagery Matters in OSINT Investigations

Historical satellite and street-view images help investigators:

A. Verify the Timeline of an Event

◆ **Example**: A news report claims that a hospital was bombed last week, but satellite imagery from a month ago already shows the building in ruins. The claim is false.

B. Detect Construction, Demolitions & Infrastructure Changes

◆ **Example**: A suspected underground bunker is identified by analyzing a forested area in past images that was later replaced with a cleared, paved section.

C. Monitor Environmental & Geopolitical Changes

◆ **Example**: Comparing satellite images of Arctic glaciers from 2010 to 2024 shows dramatic shrinkage, confirming climate change effects.

D. Track Military Build-Ups & Conflict Zones

♦ **Example**: OSINT analysts identified Russian troop movements near Ukraine by comparing Google Earth Pro images before and after the invasion.

2. Tools for Accessing Historical Imagery

A. Google Earth Pro

✓ Time Slider Feature allows users to access historical satellite images of locations worldwide.

✓ Best for monitoring urban development, deforestation, or military movements.

♦ **Use Case**: Tracking Syrian conflict zones by checking bombed-out buildings over several years.

B. Sentinel Hub (European Space Agency)

✓ Provides high-resolution satellite imagery with frequent updates.

✓ Great for tracking environmental and land-use changes.

♦ **Use Case**: Watching Amazon deforestation rates between 2010 and 2024.

C. Planet Labs

✓ Offers daily satellite imagery but requires a paid subscription.

✓ Best for real-time tracking of fast-moving events.

♦ **Use Case**: Observing temporary military camps appearing and disappearing.

D. Bing Maps (Bird's Eye View)

✓ Offers angled views that Google Maps doesn't provide.

✓ Useful for comparing changes in urban structures.

♦ **Use Case**: Identifying illegal construction projects by comparing before-and-after imagery.

E. OpenStreetMap (OSM) & Wayback Machine

✓ OSM contains crowdsourced map data, sometimes updated faster than satellite images.

✓ Wayback Machine archives older online maps and images.

◈ **Use Case**: Finding demolished buildings or renamed streets from past map versions.

3. Techniques for Analyzing Historical Imagery

A. Comparing Before-and-After Satellite Images

- Identify the exact coordinates of the location.
- Use Google Earth Pro's Time Slider to select different years.
- Compare details like building placements, roads, vegetation, and shadows.

◈ **Example**: Analysts tracked the expansion of China's artificial islands in the South China Sea by comparing satellite images from 2015 to 2023.

B. Detecting Pattern Changes Over Time

- Look for deforestation, flooding, or urban sprawl.
- Compare multiple sources (Google Earth, Sentinel Hub, Planet Labs) for accuracy.
- Overlay older maps with new satellite data to see mismatches.

◈ **Example**: Comparing images of North Korea's nuclear test sites to detect new underground tunnel construction.

C. Tracking Road & Infrastructure Development

- Compare road layouts from different years.
- Look for newly built bridges, highways, or airports.
- Cross-check with news reports and government data.

◈ **Example**: Analysts discovered secret roads leading to illegal mining sites in Africa by overlaying older maps with new satellite images.

D. Identifying Conflict-Related Damage

- Look for destroyed buildings, craters, or burned areas.
- Compare military installations before and after a conflict.
- Cross-reference with social media videos and news reports.

◆ **Example**: OSINT investigators confirmed war crimes in Syria by showing historical imagery of civilian buildings bombed over time.

4. Case Study: Tracking Illegal Deforestation in the Amazon

Step 1: Selecting the Investigation Area

- Analysts chose a suspected illegal logging site in Brazil.
- They used Google Earth Pro's Time Slider to compare images from 2010 to 2024.

Step 2: Identifying Changes Over Time

- In 2010, the area was dense rainforest.
- By 2015, patches of cleared land appeared.
- In 2020, a large logging road was visible.
- In 2024, the deforested land had expanded significantly.

Step 3: Cross-Verification

- Sentinel Hub confirmed tree loss through NDVI (vegetation index) analysis.
- Planet Labs' daily imagery showed loggers actively clearing land.
- Social media videos from locals matched the satellite evidence.

✓ **Result**: The investigation provided irrefutable evidence of illegal deforestation, leading to government action.

5. Key Takeaways

✓ Historical imagery is essential for tracking location changes over time.

✓ Google Earth Pro is the best free tool for accessing historical satellite images.

✓ Sentinel Hub and Planet Labs provide more frequent, high-resolution updates.

✓ Cross-referencing multiple sources enhances accuracy.

✔ Comparing before-and-after images can expose misinformation, illegal activities, and hidden developments.

By mastering historical imagery analysis, OSINT analysts can verify claims, monitor global events, and uncover critical intelligence in real-time.

7.5 Limitations of Satellite & Street View in OSINT Investigations

Satellite and street-view imagery are powerful tools in OSINT investigations, allowing analysts to verify locations, track changes over time, and gather intelligence from publicly available sources. However, these tools come with significant limitations that can impact accuracy, timeliness, and reliability. Understanding these challenges helps investigators avoid misinterpretation, identify gaps, and seek alternative data sources when necessary.

This chapter explores the key limitations of satellite and street-view imagery in OSINT, along with real-world case studies and workarounds to mitigate these challenges.

1. Incomplete or Outdated Imagery

A. Delayed Satellite Updates

✔ Most freely available satellite images (e.g., Google Earth, Bing Maps) are not live and may be months or years old.

✔ Some regions have frequent updates, while others may have stale images from years ago.

◆ **Example**: Investigators checking Google Earth for a newly built military base in a remote area found that the latest available image was from 2019, rendering the data useless.

✔ Workaround:

- Use commercial satellite services (e.g., Planet Labs, Sentinel Hub) for more frequent updates.

- Cross-check with social media, news reports, and user-generated content for recent evidence.

B. Street View Updates Are Inconsistent

✓ Google Street View updates depend on local regulations and company schedules.

✓ In many areas, Street View images may be several years old or missing entirely.

◆ **Example**: An OSINT analyst investigating a suspected human trafficking route found that the Street View imagery for a key highway hadn't been updated since 2016, making it unreliable for real-time analysis.

✓ **Workaround:**

- Use crowdsourced images from OpenStreetMap, Mapillary, or social media.
- Look for geotagged photos from local sources on Instagram, Twitter, or Flickr.

2. Limited Coverage & Restricted Areas

A. No Coverage in Certain Regions

✓ Some countries restrict or blur satellite and street-view images for security reasons.

✓ Military bases, government buildings, and sensitive infrastructure may be pixelated or removed.

◆ **Example**: Analysts tracking North Korea's missile sites found that commercial satellite images had blurred sections, making direct analysis impossible.

✓ **Workaround:**

- Use historical imagery (older images may be clearer).
- Look for leaked or declassified satellite data from intelligence sources.

B. Urban vs. Rural Disparity

✓ Satellite images of major cities are high resolution and frequently updated, while rural or conflict zones often lack detail.

✓ Street View may only cover major roads, leaving side streets, alleys, and remote areas undocumented.

◈ **Example**: Investigators tracking illegal deforestation in the Amazon struggled because Street View coverage was nonexistent in jungle areas.

✓ Workaround:

Use drone footage, on-the-ground social media reports, or crowd-sourced data.
Compare different mapping platforms (Google Earth, Bing, OpenStreetMap, etc.).

3. Image Manipulation & Misinformation Risks

A. Satellite Image Alteration

✓ Governments and companies intentionally modify satellite images to blur sensitive locations.

✓ Some platforms use AI-generated reconstructions, which can introduce artificial distortions.

◈ **Example**: A 2023 investigation found that a Chinese naval base appeared to have "moved" between two locations due to altered satellite imagery.

✓ Workaround:

- Compare multiple satellite providers (Google, Bing, Sentinel Hub, etc.).
- Use before-and-after analysis to detect inconsistencies.

B. Street View Image Alteration

✓ Faces, license plates, and sensitive locations are auto-blurred, making it harder to identify people or vehicles.

✔ Some locations remove Street View entirely, preventing OSINT analysts from accessing key details.

◆ **Example**: Investigators tracking a fugitive in Germany found that Street View was disabled in most areas, blocking potential leads.

✔ **Workaround:**

- Use user-generated content (Flickr, Instagram, YouTube, etc.).
- Search for dashcam footage or news reports from local sources.

4. Resolution & Detail Limitations

A. Low-Resolution Satellite Images

✔ Many free satellite images have low resolution, making it difficult to identify small details.

✔ High-resolution images (below 30 cm per pixel) are usually only available through paid services.

◆ **Example**: Analysts trying to identify military aircraft at an airbase found that the available satellite resolution was too low to distinguish plane models.

✔ **Workaround:**

- Use AI-based image enhancement tools to sharpen details.
- Subscribe to commercial providers like Maxar or Airbus for high-resolution imagery.

B. Street View Perspective Issues

✔ Street View provides limited angles and may not show rooftops, alleyways, or private properties.

✔ In some cases, objects like trees, parked cars, or construction can obscure key details.

♦ **Example**: A journalist investigating a suspect's residence found that Street View was blocked by tall hedges, preventing useful observations.

✓ **Workaround**:

- Use drone footage, news reports, or real-estate listings for better views.
- Check for 3D models in Google Earth Pro for a different perspective.

5. Weather, Shadows & Seasonal Limitations

A. Cloud Cover & Poor Visibility

✓ Satellite images may be obscured by clouds, reducing visibility.

✓ Nighttime imagery is often less detailed unless using specialized infrared sources.

♦ **Example**: A disaster relief team analyzing flooded areas in Bangladesh found that recent satellite images were covered by thick monsoon clouds, making assessment impossible.

✓ **Workaround**:

- Use SAR (Synthetic Aperture Radar) imagery from Sentinel Hub, which can see through clouds.
- Check historical imagery for better views.

B. Shadows & Seasonal Differences

✓ Shadows can distort object shapes, making analysis harder.

✓ Seasonal changes (snow cover, vegetation growth) alter landscape appearance.

♦ **Example**: An OSINT analyst trying to locate an arms smuggling route struggled because the desert trail disappeared under seasonal sand dunes in newer images.

✓ **Workaround**:

- Use Suncalc.org to predict shadow angles.
- Compare images from different seasons to see landscape changes.

6. Key Takeaways

✓ Satellite and street-view images are powerful tools, but they have major limitations regarding timeliness, coverage, and resolution.

✓ Governments may alter or restrict access to sensitive locations, requiring alternative verification methods.

✓ Weather, shadows, and seasonal changes can impact accuracy, making cross-referencing with historical data essential.

✓ Low-resolution images can make small object identification difficult, requiring higher-quality sources or AI enhancement.

✓ Always use multiple mapping platforms, social media sources, and OSINT tools to fill gaps and verify findings.

By understanding these limitations, OSINT analysts can avoid misinterpretations, spot potential misinformation, and improve the accuracy of their investigations.

7.6 Case Study: Analyzing Satellite Data to Confirm a Location

Satellite imagery has become a powerful tool in OSINT investigations, allowing analysts to verify locations, track movements, and uncover hidden intelligence. In this case study, we examine how satellite data was used to confirm the location of a secret military facility by cross-referencing satellite imagery, open-source intelligence, and social media clues.

Background: The Intelligence Lead

In early 2023, an OSINT investigator received a tip regarding a suspected military installation in a remote region of North Africa. The facility was rumored to house advanced weapons technology, but no official reports confirmed its existence.

The goal of this investigation was to:

✓ Identify the facility's exact location

✓ Determine its operational status

✓ Cross-verify the information using multiple OSINT techniques

Step 1: Initial Research & Open-Source Clues

The first step was gathering preliminary intelligence from public sources, including:

✓ News reports mentioning military expansions in the region

✓ Social media posts from locals about unusual activity

✓ Government procurement records hinting at new construction projects

🔍 Finding Clues:

A journalist's tweet included a blurry image of a military convoy heading toward an unknown base. The tweet mentioned a general location near the Libya-Algeria border. This provided a starting point for geolocation.

Step 2: Using Google Earth to Identify Suspected Locations

The analyst then turned to Google Earth Pro to examine the suspected area.

✓ **Step 1**: Scanned the Libya-Algeria border for large-scale construction sites

✓ **Step 2**: Focused on airstrips, road networks, and security perimeters, which are common indicators of military bases

✓ **Step 3**: Compared historical imagery to detect recent changes

🔍 Key Discovery:

An area that was empty in 2021 now had visible roads, buildings, and a cleared perimeter in a 2023 satellite image.

Step 3: Cross-Referencing Satellite Imagery with Other OSINT Sources

After identifying a potential location, the analyst cross-referenced data from different sources:

✓ Social Media Analysis:

- Searched for geotagged images near the area
- Found an Instagram post from a truck driver mentioning a new security checkpoint near the coordinates

✓ Weather & Sun Position Verification:

- Used Suncalc.org to compare shadow angles in social media images with satellite imagery
- Shadows matched, confirming the timeline of recent construction

✓ Flight Tracking Data:

- Checked ADS-B flight tracking websites for unusual aerial activity
- Noticed cargo planes landing near the suspected site, suggesting a military supply chain

Step 4: Enhancing Satellite Imagery for More Detail

To gain more clarity, the analyst used:

✓ Sentinel-2 (ESA) imagery for recent satellite captures

✓ Maxar high-resolution images (commercially available) to detect infrastructure details

🔍 Key Finding:

Higher-resolution images revealed security fencing, large hangars, and military vehicles, confirming it was an operational facility.

Step 5: Validating & Reporting the Findings

To ensure accuracy, the final step involved:

✓ Comparing before-and-after images to confirm recent activity

✓ Checking local news sources for additional verification

✓ Using mapping tools like OpenStreetMap to ensure correct geolocation

📌 **Final Conclusion:**

The site was confirmed as a new military base, likely operational since late 2022. The investigation demonstrated how satellite imagery, when combined with social media, flight tracking, and historical comparisons, can uncover hidden intelligence.

Key Takeaways

✓ Satellite imagery alone is not enough—cross-referencing with OSINT tools is essential

✓ Historical imagery analysis helps track changes over time

✓ Social media posts can provide real-world context to satellite findings

✓ Flight tracking & transport data can indicate a facility's operational status

This case study highlights the power of satellite OSINT in uncovering hidden locations and verifying intelligence in real-world investigations.

8. Open-Source Mapping: Google Earth & GIS Tools

In this chapter, we will dive into open-source mapping tools, with a focus on Google Earth and Geographic Information Systems (GIS), which are invaluable for OSINT analysts. Google Earth provides immersive, high-resolution imagery that allows users to explore locations, track changes, and measure distances with precision, while GIS tools offer advanced capabilities for layering data, analyzing spatial relationships, and creating custom maps. We will explore how these platforms can be used to extract intelligence from geospatial data, including how to integrate images, pinpoint locations, and analyze patterns in ways that enhance investigative workflows and provide critical insights into complex situations.

8.1 Introduction to GIS (Geographic Information Systems) in OSINT

Geographic Information Systems (GIS) are powerful tools that allow analysts to visualize, analyze, and interpret spatial data. In OSINT investigations, GIS helps uncover patterns, track locations, and verify information by overlaying various data sources onto a map. Whether identifying the movement of individuals, tracking events, or analyzing geographic changes over time, GIS enhances the accuracy and depth of geospatial intelligence.

How GIS Supports OSINT Investigations

GIS technology plays a crucial role in several OSINT applications, including:

✓ **Geolocation Verification**: Analysts use GIS to confirm whether an image, video, or report originates from the claimed location by comparing satellite imagery, terrain data, and publicly available maps.

✓ **Crime Mapping & Investigation**: Law enforcement agencies leverage GIS to analyze crime patterns and identify high-risk areas using geospatial heatmaps.

✓ **Disaster Response & Humanitarian Efforts**: GIS helps emergency responders and NGOs track natural disasters, conflicts, and humanitarian crises by visualizing real-time location-based data.

✓ **Tracking Digital Footprints**: Many OSINT investigations require mapping out connections between people, places, and events—GIS tools allow for data visualization that reveals hidden links.

Key Components of GIS in OSINT

GIS is composed of several essential elements that help analysts make sense of spatial data:

◆ **Spatial Data Layers**: GIS integrates multiple data layers (satellite imagery, social media geotags, weather conditions, etc.), allowing analysts to analyze patterns.

◆ **Georeferencing & Geocoding**: This process assigns geographic coordinates to locations, turning addresses, landmarks, and even images into mappable data points.

◆ **Remote Sensing**: GIS software can process aerial and satellite images to detect changes in land use, infrastructure, and activity over time.

◆ **Temporal Analysis**: Time-based GIS analysis enables OSINT professionals to track events, such as troop movements, natural disasters, or protests, by analyzing time-stamped geospatial data.

Popular GIS Tools for OSINT Analysts

Several GIS platforms provide open-source and commercial solutions for geospatial intelligence gathering:

✓ **Google Earth Pro**: A widely used tool for analyzing satellite imagery, terrain, and street views.

✓ **QGIS (Quantum GIS):** A free and open-source GIS tool that allows analysts to analyze complex spatial data with advanced geospatial functions.

✓ **ArcGIS**: A professional GIS platform used by governments and organizations for high-level geographic analysis.

✓ **OpenStreetMap (OSM):** A community-driven mapping tool with user-generated geographic data useful for tracking infrastructure changes.

✓ **Sentinel Hub**: Provides real-time access to satellite imagery from the European Space Agency's Sentinel-2 program, useful for tracking environmental and geopolitical changes.

Real-World OSINT Use Cases of GIS

📌 **Investigating Conflict Zones**: GIS has been used to track troop movements and infrastructure damage in conflict areas like Ukraine and Syria.

📌 **Monitoring Illegal Activities**: OSINT analysts have used GIS to uncover illegal mining operations, human trafficking routes, and deforestation by analyzing satellite imagery.

📌 **Tracking Protest Movements**: GIS tools help map out large-scale demonstrations and understand crowd movements through social media geotags and satellite images.

GIS is an essential tool for OSINT analysts, providing spatial awareness, verification capabilities, and predictive insights. By combining GIS with other OSINT techniques, analysts can enhance their ability to track, verify, and analyze geolocation data effectively.

8.2 How to Use Google Earth Pro for Advanced Mapping

Google Earth Pro is one of the most powerful tools available for OSINT analysts, providing high-resolution satellite imagery, historical data, and geospatial analysis capabilities. Whether verifying locations, tracking changes over time, or analyzing terrain features, Google Earth Pro is an essential tool for advanced mapping in OSINT investigations.

Step 1: Installing & Setting Up Google Earth Pro

Google Earth Pro is available as a free desktop application for Windows, macOS, and Linux. To get started:

- Download Google Earth Pro from the official Google website.

- Install and launch the application.
- Familiarize yourself with the interface, including navigation tools, search functions, and layer options.

Step 2: Navigating & Exploring Locations

Once Google Earth Pro is installed, users can start exploring geographic data.

✓ Search for Specific Locations:

- Use the Search Bar to enter coordinates, addresses, or place names.
- Click on results to zoom into the desired location.

✓ Navigation Controls:

- **Zoom In/Out**: Use the mouse scroll wheel or the zoom slider.
- **Pan & Rotate**: Click and drag the map to change perspectives.
- **Tilt View**: Press Shift + Left Click and drag to change the angle.

✓ Street View Mode:

- Drag the Pegman Icon (bottom right) onto a road or landmark for ground-level imagery.

Step 3: Using Historical Imagery for Timeline Analysis

Google Earth Pro provides historical satellite images, allowing analysts to track changes over time.

📌 How to Access Historical Imagery:

- Click on the Clock Icon in the top toolbar.
- A timeline slider appears, showing different image captures for the same location.
- Drag the slider to see how a place has evolved over time.

✓ Use Case: Tracking the construction of military bases, deforestation, urban expansion, or disaster recovery efforts.

Step 4: Measuring Distances & Areas

The Measure Tool in Google Earth Pro helps OSINT analysts estimate distances, areas, and perimeters.

📌 How to Measure Distances:

- Click the Ruler Icon in the toolbar.
- Select Line (for point-to-point measurement) or Polygon (for area measurement).
- Click on the map to place points and measure the distance between them.

✓ Use Case:

- Estimating the size of airstrips, borders, and secure zones.
- Measuring vehicle or troop movement routes.

Step 5: Overlaying and Analyzing Custom Data

Analysts can import KML/KMZ files, which contain geospatial data from other sources.

📌 How to Import Custom Data:

- Click File > Open and select a KML/KMZ file.
- The data will appear as an overlay on the map.

✓ Use Case:

- Overlaying crime heatmaps, migration routes, or protest locations.
- Importing flight paths, weather data, and infrastructure blueprints.

Step 6: Using Google Earth Pro with OSINT Techniques

◆ Cross-Referencing Satellite Imagery with Open-Source Data:

Compare Google Earth images with live satellite imagery from Sentinel Hub or historical maps from OpenStreetMap.

◆ Matching Locations from Social Media Clues:

Use Google Earth Pro's 3D terrain and landmark features to verify locations in photos or videos.

◆ **Exporting Maps for Reports:**

Take high-resolution screenshots and annotate images for intelligence reports.

Google Earth Pro is a critical OSINT tool for verifying geolocation data, tracking changes over time, and conducting in-depth geographic analysis. When combined with other OSINT techniques, it enables analysts to uncover valuable intelligence from satellite imagery and mapping data.

8.3 Extracting Coordinates & Terrain Data for Geolocation Investigations

Geolocation investigations rely on precise coordinates and terrain data to verify locations, analyze landscapes, and uncover hidden intelligence. OSINT analysts use satellite imagery, mapping tools, and elevation data to extract valuable insights from images and videos. This chapter explores methods for retrieving GPS coordinates, analyzing terrain features, and using geospatial tools to enhance OSINT investigations.

Step 1: Extracting Coordinates from Images & Videos

Many digital photos contain embedded GPS metadata (EXIF data) that can be extracted to determine where and when an image was taken.

🔍 **Method 1: Extracting GPS Data from Image Metadata**

✔ **Tools to Use:**

- ExifTool (Command-line & GUI)
- Jeffrey's Image Metadata Viewer (Online)
- OSINT Combine EXIF Data Viewer

📌 **How to Extract Coordinates:**

- Upload the image to ExifTool or an online EXIF viewer.

- Locate the GPS Latitude & Longitude values.
- Convert coordinates if needed (Decimal Degrees vs. Degrees, Minutes, Seconds).
- Enter the coordinates in Google Maps or OpenStreetMap to pinpoint the location.

✓ **Use Case:**

- Identifying where a social media image was originally taken.
- Geolocating leaked military photos to verify authenticity.

🔍 Method 2: Extracting Coordinates from Social Media Posts

Most social media platforms strip metadata, but some geolocation clues remain:

✓ Look for visible location tags in posts.

✓ Cross-check usernames or hashtags that might indicate a place.

✓ Use tools like Twitter API, GeoSocial Footprint, or Echosec to find geotagged content.

✓ **Use Case:**

- Finding the origin of a viral image posted on Twitter.
- Tracking disaster relief efforts through geotagged images.

Step 2: Extracting Coordinates from Satellite & Mapping Tools

If GPS metadata is unavailable, analysts must extract coordinates manually using mapping services.

🔍 Method 1: Using Google Earth Pro for Precise Coordinates

📌 **Steps:**

- Open Google Earth Pro and search for the suspected location.
- Enable the Grid Overlay (View > Grid) to display latitude/longitude lines.
- Click on the exact point of interest to retrieve precise coordinates.
- Save coordinates for cross-referencing with OSINT data.

✓ **Use Case:**

Identifying military bases, refugee camps, or secret facilities.

🔍 Method 2: Using OpenStreetMap (OSM) for Crowd-Sourced Data

OpenStreetMap provides community-driven mapping data that may be more detailed than commercial maps.

📌 Steps:

- Search for a location in OpenStreetMap (www.openstreetmap.org).
- Click on an area to reveal latitude/longitude coordinates.
- Use OSM-based tools like Overpass Turbo to extract additional place details.

✔ Use Case:

Verifying newly built infrastructure in unlisted locations.

Step 3: Analyzing Terrain & Elevation Data

Understanding the topography of an area helps analysts determine strategic advantages, environmental conditions, and possible obstructions.

🔍 Method 1: Using Google Earth Pro for Terrain Elevation

📌 Steps:

- Enable Terrain View in Google Earth Pro.
- Click on different points to view elevation data (displayed at the bottom).
- Compare with satellite images to determine hills, valleys, or flood zones.

✔ Use Case:

Assessing terrain before a crisis response operation.

🔍 Method 2: Using NASA SRTM & DEM Data for Elevation Analysis

For more advanced elevation analysis, OSINT analysts can use:

✓ NASA's Shuttle Radar Topography Mission (SRTM) Data

✓ Digital Elevation Models (DEM) from USGS Earth Explorer

📌 **How to Use:**

- Download SRTM or DEM data for the target area.
- Open in QGIS or Google Earth Pro for elevation visualization.
- Cross-reference with satellite imagery for land analysis.

✓ **Use Case:**

Mapping mountain routes for intelligence gathering.

Step 4: Cross-Referencing Data for Accuracy

To ensure the validity of extracted coordinates, analysts should:

✓ Compare multiple sources (Google Earth, Bing Maps, OSM).

✓ Use historical imagery to check for recent changes.

✓ Validate with social media or local reports when possible.

Extracting coordinates and terrain data is crucial for verifying geolocation in OSINT investigations. By combining image metadata, satellite mapping, and elevation tools, analysts can accurately identify locations, track changes over time, and support intelligence assessments with geospatial evidence.

8.4 Using Open-Source GIS Platforms for Enhanced OSINT Analysis

Geospatial Intelligence (GEOINT) plays a vital role in OSINT investigations, helping analysts visualize, verify, and interpret location-based data. Open-source Geographic Information System (GIS) platforms offer powerful tools for analyzing satellite imagery, mapping trends, and cross-referencing geolocation data. This chapter explores how OSINT professionals can leverage QGIS, OpenStreetMap, and other GIS tools to enhance geolocation investigations.

What is Open-Source GIS and Why is it Important?

GIS platforms allow analysts to:

✓ Map and analyze spatial data (satellite images, crime heatmaps, environmental data).

✓ Overlay multiple geospatial datasets for better cross-referencing.

✓ Track changes over time using historical satellite imagery.

✓ Identify patterns and relationships between places and events.

Unlike commercial GIS software (e.g., ArcGIS), open-source GIS tools provide free, customizable, and scalable solutions for OSINT professionals.

Key Open-Source GIS Platforms for OSINT

1. QGIS (Quantum GIS) – The Leading Open-Source GIS Tool

QGIS is a powerful, open-source GIS application widely used for geospatial analysis. It supports vector and raster data and allows analysts to process satellite imagery, GPS coordinates, and heatmaps.

📌 How to Use QGIS for OSINT Analysis:

- Download & Install QGIS from the official site (qgis.org).
- Import Geospatial Data (KML, KMZ, GeoJSON, or shapefiles).
- Add OpenStreetMap or Google Satellite Layers for real-world reference.
- Analyze Image Metadata (geotags, timestamps, camera models).
- Perform Spatial Analysis (distance measurement, heatmaps, elevation profiling).

✓ Use Case:

- Investigating crime patterns and movement tracking.
- Analyzing conflict zones using geospatial overlays.

2. OpenStreetMap (OSM) – The Crowdsourced Map for OSINT

OpenStreetMap (OSM) is a user-generated mapping platform that provides detailed geographic data, often more up-to-date than Google Maps in certain regions.

📌 How to Use OSM for OSINT:

- Search for a location using OSM's main website (www.openstreetmap.org).
- Extract GPS coordinates from locations by clicking on map points.
- Use Overpass Turbo (overpass-turbo.eu) to query map data (e.g., find specific buildings, roads, or businesses).
- Compare historical map changes to track infrastructure developments.

✔ Use Case:

- Monitoring urban expansion, refugee movements, or military infrastructure.
- Cross-referencing locations found in social media images.

3. Sentinel Hub – Real-Time Satellite Imagery for OSINT

Sentinel Hub provides free access to high-resolution satellite imagery from ESA's Sentinel-2 program. It is useful for tracking environmental changes, disaster response, and military activity.

📌 How to Use Sentinel Hub for OSINT:

- Go to www.sentinel-hub.com and access the EO Browser.
- Search for any location worldwide and select satellite imagery layers.
- Use historical imagery to detect changes over time.
- Export high-resolution images for further analysis in QGIS.

✔ Use Case:

- Detecting illegal deforestation, mining, or military movements.
- Tracking natural disasters and humanitarian crises.

4. GeoNames – A Global Geospatial Database

GeoNames is a publicly available geographic database containing over 12 million locations worldwide with associated metadata. It helps in place-name resolution and geolocation tracking.

📌 How to Use GeoNames for OSINT:

- Access www.geonames.org and search for a location name.
- Extract GPS coordinates, postal codes, and administrative boundaries.
- Use the GeoNames API for automating location-based searches.

✓ **Use Case:**

- Verifying location claims in OSINT investigations.
- Matching partial place names with actual geographic coordinates.

Step-by-Step Workflow: Using GIS for an OSINT Investigation

Scenario: You receive an image from social media showing an unknown military base. You need to geolocate the base using GIS tools.

Step 1: Extract Initial Clues

✓ Use ExifTool to check for GPS metadata in the image.

✓ If metadata is missing, look for landmarks, terrain features, and signs in the image.

Step 2: Use Satellite Imagery

✓ Open Google Earth Pro and compare features with the image.

✓ Use Sentinel Hub to check for recent satellite images of the area.

Step 3: Cross-Reference with GIS & Mapping Data

✓ Open QGIS and load OpenStreetMap layers.

✓ Use GeoNames to verify nearby locations.

✓ Query Overpass Turbo for infrastructure data like roads or buildings.

Step 4: Validate Findings & Report

✓ Compare with publicly available intelligence reports or social media posts.

✓ Export findings as a geospatial report with images and map overlays.

Open-source GIS platforms like QGIS, OpenStreetMap, and Sentinel Hub provide OSINT analysts with advanced geospatial tools for mapping, verification, and investigation. By integrating GIS analysis into OSINT workflows, analysts can uncover deeper intelligence, validate geolocation data, and track real-world events with high accuracy.

8.5 Tracking Geospatial Data from Open Data Sources

In OSINT investigations, geospatial data from open data sources plays a crucial role in verifying locations, monitoring events, and mapping trends. Governments, research institutions, and crowdsourced projects offer free and publicly available geospatial datasets, including satellite imagery, transportation networks, climate data, and urban infrastructure. This chapter explores how analysts can track and utilize these datasets for OSINT investigations.

Why Open Geospatial Data Matters in OSINT

Open geospatial data provides analysts with:

✓ Real-time location tracking (natural disasters, military movements, crisis response).

✓ Historical and live satellite imagery for comparative analysis.

✓ Crowdsourced mapping insights from volunteer and government organizations.

✓ Access to infrastructure, transportation, and environmental datasets.

By leveraging open data sources, OSINT analysts can validate geolocation findings, enhance mapping accuracy, and uncover hidden intelligence in global events.

Key Open Geospatial Data Sources for OSINT

1. OpenStreetMap (OSM) – A Crowdsourced Global Mapping Database

OpenStreetMap (OSM) is one of the most detailed and frequently updated open mapping platforms, maintained by volunteers worldwide.

📌 **How to Use OSM for OSINT:**

- Search for locations using www.openstreetmap.org.
- Extract latitude/longitude coordinates for further analysis.
- Use Overpass Turbo (overpass-turbo.eu) to query infrastructure data (roads, buildings, landmarks).
- Download OSM datasets and import them into QGIS for custom geospatial analysis.

✓ Use Case:

- Mapping protests, disaster zones, or military bases.
- Cross-referencing locations mentioned in social media posts.

2. NASA Earth Observatory & USGS Earth Explorer – Satellite Imagery & Terrain Data

NASA's Earth Observatory and the United States Geological Survey (USGS) Earth Explorer provide high-resolution satellite imagery and Digital Elevation Models (DEM) for global analysis.

📌 How to Use These Tools:

- Access earthdata.nasa.gov or earthexplorer.usgs.gov.
- Search for recent or historical satellite imagery by date and coordinates.
- Download DEM datasets to analyze terrain elevation.
- Cross-reference satellite imagery with ground-level photos from OSINT sources.

✓ Use Case:

- Tracking urban development or environmental changes.
- Verifying suspected missile sites, military movements, or illegal deforestation.

3. Sentinel Hub & Copernicus Open Data – Real-Time Satellite Monitoring

Sentinel Hub (Copernicus Programme) provides live and historical satellite imagery with multi-spectral analysis capabilities.

📌 How to Use Sentinel Hub for OSINT:

- Go to www.sentinel-hub.com and access the EO Browser.

- Search for a location using date filters to compare images over time.
- Use infrared and multi-spectral analysis to detect object movements (e.g., burned areas, military installations).
- Export high-resolution satellite images for further processing in GIS tools.

✓ Use Case:

- Monitoring war zones, natural disasters, and border changes.
- Tracking movements of ships, aircraft, or deforested regions.

4. GeoNames – A Global Geographical Database

GeoNames offers a comprehensive open-source geographical database, containing over 12 million locations with metadata like country codes, administrative regions, and time zones.

📌 How to Use GeoNames for OSINT:

- Access www.geonames.org.
- Search for a place name to retrieve geolocation details.
- Use the GeoNames API for automated searches in large datasets.

✓ Use Case:

- Cross-verifying obscure location names with actual coordinates.
- Finding remote locations mentioned in online forums or documents.

5. Humanitarian Data Exchange (HDX) – Crisis & Disaster Geospatial Data

The Humanitarian Data Exchange (HDX), maintained by the United Nations (UN OCHA), provides real-time crisis mapping and geospatial datasets for conflict zones, refugee movements, and natural disasters.

📌 How to Use HDX for OSINT:

- Go to data.humdata.org.
- Search for humanitarian datasets related to specific countries or disasters.
- Download and visualize the data in QGIS or Google Earth Pro.

✓ Use Case:

- Tracking refugee migration patterns and humanitarian crises.
- Verifying damage assessments in war-torn regions.

6. MarineTraffic & ADS-B Exchange – Real-Time Tracking of Ships & Aircraft

✓ **MarineTraffic (www.marinetraffic.com)** – Live tracking of global maritime activity, including cargo ships, oil tankers, and naval vessels.

✓ **ADS-B Exchange (www.adsbexchange.com)** – Open-source flight tracking for commercial and military aircraft movements.

📌 How to Use These Tools for OSINT:

- Search for specific vessels or aircraft by name or ID.
- Track historical movement patterns to detect anomalies.
- Correlate ship or aircraft sightings with satellite imagery for verification.

✓ Use Case:

- Monitoring illegal fishing, military drills, or covert naval operations.
- Tracking VIP aircraft flights to determine political movements.

Step-by-Step OSINT Workflow for Using Open Geospatial Data

Scenario: An analyst is investigating a suspected illegal military base and needs to confirm its location.

Step 1: Collect Initial Clues

✓ Use social media images, videos, or reports to determine an approximate location.

✓ Extract any available EXIF metadata from images.

Step 2: Cross-Reference with Open Geospatial Data

✓ Use OpenStreetMap (OSM) to check for roads or buildings in the suspected area.

✓ Use Sentinel Hub to compare historical vs. current satellite imagery for new structures.

Step 3: Validate Findings with GIS & Other Tools

✓ Use GeoNames to confirm place names and coordinates.

✓ Use QGIS to overlay multiple datasets for pattern analysis.

✓ If the location is near a coastline, check MarineTraffic for nearby ship activity.

Step 4: Verify & Report Findings

✓ Compare findings with independent OSINT sources (e.g., news reports, government data).

✓ Export data and create a geospatial intelligence report for further analysis.

Open geospatial data sources provide OSINT analysts with powerful tools for tracking, validating, and mapping location-based intelligence. By leveraging GIS platforms, satellite imagery, and real-time tracking services, investigators can enhance their ability to monitor global events, uncover hidden intelligence, and validate geolocation claims with high precision.

8.6 Case Study: Using GIS Tools to Map a Person's Movements

In OSINT investigations, GIS tools and geospatial data can be used to track and analyze a person's movements over time. Whether identifying a missing person, verifying a subject's location history, or investigating suspicious activity, mapping digital footprints through social media, satellite imagery, and open datasets can provide valuable intelligence.

In this case study, we will follow a step-by-step OSINT workflow to track the movements of a fictional individual, "John Doe," using open-source GIS tools, social media analysis, and satellite imagery.

Scenario: Tracking John Doe's Movements Through OSINT

A journalist has been investigating the movements of John Doe, a political activist who recently disappeared. His last known activity includes:

- A social media post with an image geotagged to Kyiv, Ukraine.
- A video uploaded to Twitter showing him in an unknown location.
- Reports of him traveling through Poland and Germany.

The goal is to map John Doe's movements using GIS platforms, social media images, and public datasets to determine his possible location.

Step 1: Extracting Geolocation Data from Social Media Posts

A. Reverse Image Search & Metadata Extraction

✓ First, check the image posted on John Doe's social media for metadata.

✓ Use EXIF tools (ExifTool, Jeffrey's Image Metadata Viewer) to check for GPS coordinates, timestamps, and camera details.

🔎 **Finding:**

The EXIF metadata confirms that the image was taken in Kyiv, Ukraine (exact coordinates: 50.4501° N, 30.5234° E).

B. Cross-Referencing Image Landmarks with Google Earth & OSM

✓ Import the extracted GPS coordinates into Google Earth Pro or QGIS.

✓ Use Google Street View and OpenStreetMap to compare landmarks in the image.

🔎 **Finding:**

The photo was taken near Independence Square, Kyiv.

Step 2: Analyzing Videos for Background Clues

A video of John Doe was uploaded to Twitter, but the location was not specified.

✓ Extract key frames using FFmpeg or VLC Player.

✓ Look for recognizable landmarks, signs, or environmental features (e.g., street signs, billboards, cars).

✓ Use Google Lens & TinEye to compare the background to known locations.

𝒫 Finding:

- The video background shows a train station with signs in Polish.
- Cross-referencing with OpenStreetMap and Google Earth Pro suggests it was filmed near Warszawa Centralna railway station, Poland.

Step 3: Tracking Movement via Flight & Train Data

Since John Doe was last seen in Poland, we check for potential travel routes.

✓ Use ADS-B Exchange (www.adsbexchange.com) to track private and commercial flights.

✓ Check railway schedules from Poland to Germany using open transit data.

✓ Use MarineTraffic if sea travel is suspected.

𝒫 Finding:

- Train records from open databases indicate that a train departed from Warsaw to Berlin on the day of the video upload.
- Social media analysis shows John Doe "liked" a tweet mentioning Berlin Central Station.

Step 4: Verifying Berlin Sightings with GIS & Satellite Imagery

✓ Use Sentinel Hub & Google Earth Pro to check recent satellite imagery of Berlin Central Station.

✓ Analyze crowdsourced OpenStreetMap (OSM) edits for any new data on movement patterns.

✓ Search Twitter & Instagram for public photos near Berlin's train station that match John Doe's last known outfit.

🔎 Finding:

- A recent photo posted by a tourist near Berlin Central Station shows a person matching John Doe's description.
- The timestamp aligns with the estimated arrival time from Poland.

Step 5: Creating a GIS-Based Movement Map

✓ Import the extracted locations into QGIS to generate a movement timeline.

✓ Overlay satellite imagery and transportation routes to verify travel paths.

✓ Cross-reference timestamps to confirm a possible final destination.

🔎 Final Analysis:

- John Doe's movements suggest he traveled from Kyiv → Warsaw → Berlin.
- His last known presence in Berlin Central Station suggests he may have continued westward.

Key OSINT Techniques Used in This Case Study

✓ **EXIF Metadata Extraction** – Confirmed the first location (Kyiv).

✓ **Reverse Image & Video Analysis** – Identified key landmarks (Warsaw, Berlin).

✓ **GIS Mapping (Google Earth, QGIS, OpenStreetMap)** – Mapped movement patterns.

✓ **Flight & Train Tracking (ADS-B Exchange, Open Data)** – Verified travel routes.

✓ **Social Media Correlation** – Cross-referenced images, timestamps, and locations.

Conclusion: The Power of GIS in OSINT Investigations

This case study highlights how GIS tools and OSINT techniques can effectively track a person's movements across multiple countries using open data, social media, and geospatial intelligence.

By integrating metadata analysis, satellite imagery, and transport records, investigators can reconstruct a timeline of movement and identify potential locations with high accuracy.

GIS-based OSINT is invaluable for:

- Missing person investigations.
- Tracking fugitives or persons of interest.
- Monitoring activist movements in conflict zones.

By leveraging open-source tools like QGIS, Sentinel Hub, and OpenStreetMap, OSINT analysts can generate accurate movement maps and enhance geolocation tracking capabilities.

9. Tracking Live Events Through Geotagged Media

In this chapter, we will explore how geotagged media—photos, videos, and social media posts with embedded location data—can be leveraged to track live events in real-time. Geotags provide precise geographic coordinates, enabling OSINT analysts to pinpoint the origin of media, track the movement of events, and verify the authenticity of content as it unfolds. We will discuss tools and techniques for collecting, analyzing, and cross-referencing geotagged media from various platforms, as well as strategies for monitoring live events and identifying emerging trends. Understanding how to track and contextualize geotagged media empowers analysts to stay ahead of the curve and gather actionable intelligence in rapidly changing situations.

9.1 How Live Social Media Posts Can Be Used for OSINT

The rise of real-time social media updates has transformed Open-Source Intelligence (OSINT) investigations, allowing analysts to track live events, breaking news, and on-the-ground movements in near real-time. Platforms like Twitter (X), Facebook, Instagram, TikTok, and Telegram provide a wealth of user-generated content that can reveal locations, identities, timestamps, and contextual details.

This section explores how live social media posts can be leveraged for OSINT, the tools used to extract relevant intelligence, and best practices for monitoring digital activity.

1. Why Live Social Media is Critical for OSINT

Live social media content offers:

✓ **Real-time situational awareness** – Monitor ongoing conflicts, protests, natural disasters, or criminal activities as they unfold.

✓ **Geolocation insights** – Many social media posts contain embedded metadata, geotags, or recognizable landmarks.

✓ **Crowdsourced intelligence** – Users on the ground provide first-hand information, images, and videos.

✓ **Trend analysis** – Identifying popular hashtags, viral content, and coordinated disinformation campaigns.

Example:

During protests or conflict zones, Twitter and Telegram often feature on-the-ground reports, photos, and livestreams from individuals present at the event. Analysts can extract key data points, verify their authenticity, and cross-reference with satellite imagery, geotagged media, and official reports.

2. Extracting OSINT from Live Social Media Posts

A. Searching Social Media for Real-Time Events

✓ **Twitter Advanced Search & Boolean Operators** – Identify specific topics, locations, and timeframes.

✓ **Hashtag & Keyword Monitoring** – Use trending hashtags and keywords to track discussions.

✓ **Geo-Search Queries** – Twitter allows location-based searches like:

near:"Kyiv, Ukraine" within:50km

✓ **Telegram Channel Monitoring** – Many OSINT Telegram groups provide real-time updates on global events.

B. Extracting Metadata & Geolocation

✓ **Check for geotags** – Some social media platforms embed GPS coordinates.

✓ **Identify background elements** – Billboards, signs, and architecture can help determine location.

✓ **Use EXIF metadata tools** – If the original image is available, use ExifTool or Jeffrey's Image Metadata Viewer to extract hidden details.

C. Livestream & Video Analysis

✓ **Extract keyframes** – Use FFmpeg or InVID to capture still images from live videos.

✓ **Audio fingerprinting** – Background sounds can provide clues (e.g., languages spoken, emergency sirens).

✓ **Reverse search images** – Use Google Lens, TinEye, and Yandex to check if the footage is old or misleading.

3. Case Example: Tracking a Protest in Real-Time

A journalist receives a tip that a protest is taking place in São Paulo, Brazil. They want to verify the event's authenticity and track its developments.

Step 1: Identifying Relevant Hashtags & Keywords

🔍 Search #ProtestoSP, "São Paulo protests," "demonstration in São Paulo" on Twitter & Facebook.

Step 2: Verifying Images & Videos

🔍 Use Google Lens to check if shared images are old or manipulated.
🔍 Extract video frames and match landmarks with Google Earth or OpenStreetMap.

Step 3: Locating Livestreams & On-the-Ground Reports

🔍 Monitor Facebook Live, Instagram Stories, TikTok, and Periscope for real-time footage.
🔍 Join local Telegram groups discussing the event.

Step 4: Cross-Referencing with News & Official Reports

🔍 Compare social media reports with local news channels, government updates, and OSINT Twitter accounts.

Result:

The protest is confirmed as authentic, with timestamped live videos, verified images, and real-time news reports. Analysts can now track its escalation or potential security risks.

4. OSINT Tools for Live Social Media Monitoring

✓ **TweetDeck** – Monitor multiple Twitter searches and hashtags in real-time.

✓ **Hoaxy & Botometer** – Detect bot-driven disinformation campaigns.

✓ **Echosec & Dataminr** – Advanced social media monitoring for crisis events.

✓ **OSINTCombine's Geo-Location Tool** – Helps identify locations in images.

✓ **Hunchly** – Archives social media posts for evidentiary purposes.

5. Ethical & Legal Considerations

✓ **Avoid personal data breaches** – Do not dox individuals or expose private data.

✓ **Verify authenticity before sharing** – Ensure posts are not misinformation or deepfakes.

✓ **Respect terms of service** – Many platforms have policies on data collection and monitoring.

Live social media posts are a powerful resource for OSINT analysts, providing real-time insights into global events, crises, and investigations. By leveraging the right tools and methodologies, analysts can extract valuable intelligence while maintaining ethical and legal standards.

9.2 Finding Geotagged Content on Twitter, Instagram & TikTok

Geotagged content from social media platforms like Twitter (X), Instagram, and TikTok is a valuable resource in OSINT investigations. Users often upload photos, videos, and status updates with location data embedded, which can be used to track movements, confirm events, or verify the authenticity of media.

This section explores how to find and extract geotagged content, the tools required, and best practices for using geolocation data in OSINT.

1. How Geotagging Works on Social Media

✓ **Explicit Geotagging** – Users manually add a location to posts (e.g., tagging "Central Park, NYC").

✓ **Implicit Geotagging** – Platforms automatically add metadata based on GPS, IP addresses, or device data.

✓ **Visual Clues** – Even without geotags, images may contain landmarks, street signs, or weather conditions that reveal location details.

Key Consideration:

Some platforms strip metadata (EXIF data) for privacy reasons, but OSINT techniques can still extract location clues.

2. Finding Geotagged Content on Twitter (X)

A. Using Twitter Advanced Search

Twitter allows users to search for posts within a specific location radius using the geocode filter.

Example: Searching tweets from Kyiv, Ukraine (within 50km):

geocode:50.4501,30.5234,50km

🔍 **Steps:**

✓ Go to Twitter Advanced Search or use manual Boolean queries.

✓ Filter by date range to track recent geotagged posts.

✓ Use near: and within: operators for location-based searches.

Example:

"explosion" OR "blast" OR "fire" near:"Beirut, Lebanon" within:10km

✓ Use TweetDeck to monitor multiple searches in real-time.

B. Finding Location-Tagged Media on Twitter

✓ Search for "📍" (location pin emoji) to find tweets where users manually tagged locations.

✓ Look for attached images/videos and use reverse image search to verify authenticity.

✓ If GPS coordinates are available, cross-reference with Google Maps, OpenStreetMap, or Google Earth.

3. Extracting Geotagged Posts from Instagram

Instagram heavily relies on location-based content, and while it removes EXIF metadata, users frequently tag locations in their posts.

A. Searching Instagram Locations Manually

✓ Go to Instagram's search bar and enter a location (e.g., "Times Square").

✓ Select Places to view posts tagged with that location.

✓ Scroll through images and note landmarks, street signs, and timestamps.

B. Using Google Search for Instagram OSINT

Instagram's internal search is limited, but you can use Google Dorks:

Find posts tagged at a specific location:

site:instagram.com "Eiffel Tower"

Find posts from a specific user that might include geotags:

site:instagram.com/influencer_name "New York"

✓ Use third-party Instagram scrapers like Picuki, ImgInn, or OSINTGram for deeper searches.

4. Tracking Geotagged TikTok Videos

TikTok is rich in location-based content, especially for viral events, natural disasters, or protests. While TikTok removes EXIF metadata, users often include hashtags, captions, or visual clues that reveal locations.

A. Searching for Location-Based Content on TikTok

✓ Use the TikTok Search Bar and enter a location keyword (e.g., "Miami Beach").

✓ Look for hashtags like #ParisViews, #NYCStreet, #UkraineWar to find related videos.

B. Extracting Location Clues from TikTok Videos

✓ Analyze backgrounds for street signs, billboards, and store names.

✓ Use Google Lens to reverse search landmarks.

✓ If a user mentions a location in the comments or caption, cross-check with other posts.

Example:

A user posts a TikTok with the caption:

"Hiking in Yosemite today!"

✓ Search "Yosemite" in TikTok to find other videos from the same location.

✓ Check timestamps to verify if it was recently recorded.

5. Tools for Finding Geotagged Content

✓ **Echosec** – Finds geotagged social media posts on Twitter, Instagram & Telegram.

✓ **TweetDeck** – Live Twitter monitoring for location-based posts.

✓ **Google Lens & TinEye** – Reverse search Instagram & TikTok images.

✓ **Picuki, ImgInn, OSINTGram** – Extract Instagram location data.

✓ **YouTube DataViewer** – Analyze video metadata and timestamps.

6. Ethical & Legal Considerations

✓ **Respect privacy laws** – Do not dox individuals or misuse location data.

✓ **Verify authenticity** – Cross-check geotagged posts with satellite imagery or official reports.

✓ **Understand platform policies** – Some sites prohibit scraping geolocation data.

Geotagged content from Twitter, Instagram, and TikTok is a powerful resource for OSINT investigations. By searching location-based posts, extracting visual clues, and cross-referencing with mapping tools, analysts can track events, verify claims, and identify individuals in real-time.

9.3 Using Crowdsourced Images & Videos for Crisis Intelligence

In crisis situations such as natural disasters, armed conflicts, protests, or humanitarian emergencies, crowdsourced images and videos from social media provide real-time intelligence that can assist OSINT analysts, journalists, and response teams. These user-generated visuals help verify ground conditions, track unfolding events, and assess damage or threats.

This section explores how to collect, verify, and analyze crowdsourced media while maintaining ethical standards and ensuring data integrity.

1. Why Crowdsourced Media is Valuable in Crisis Intelligence

✓ **Real-time updates** – First-hand footage from people on the ground can provide faster insights than official reports.

✓ **Situational awareness** – Helps analysts assess damages, movements, and humanitarian needs.

✓ **Verifiable evidence** – Social media content can confirm attacks, protests, or environmental disasters.

✓ **Cross-referencing with official sources** – Comparing user reports with satellite imagery, live news, and government statements helps validate information.

Example:

During the 2020 Beirut explosion, eyewitness videos from social media showed the blast wave, location, and damage radius before official news agencies reported on it. OSINT analysts used these videos to confirm coordinates, analyze the explosion pattern, and track emergency responses.

2. Collecting Crowdsourced Images & Videos for OSINT

A. Finding Relevant Social Media Posts

✓ **Twitter (X) Advanced Search** – Use hashtags, keywords, and location-based searches.

✓ **Instagram & TikTok Hashtags** – Look for #HurricaneDamage, #Earthquake, #UkraineWar to find crisis-related content.

✓ **Telegram & WhatsApp Groups** – Many crisis reporters and activists share exclusive photos/videos in closed groups.

✓ **Reddit & Discord Communities** – Subreddits like r/UkraineWarVideoReport contain user-submitted intelligence.

🔍 **Example Query for a Crisis in California:**

site:twitter.com "wildfire" OR "fire damage" near:"Los Angeles, CA" within:50km

✓ Use Google Dorks to find location-specific videos (e.g., "California flood site:instagram.com").

B. Extracting Metadata & Location Clues from Media

Most social media platforms strip EXIF metadata, but analysts can still find hidden location clues:

✓ **Reverse search images** – Use Google Lens, Yandex, or TinEye to check if an image was previously published.

✓ **Identify landmarks & terrain** – Compare buildings, road signs, or landscapes with Google Earth, OpenStreetMap, or Wikimapia.

✓ **Analyze weather & shadows** – Check local weather reports to verify if the scene matches real conditions.

✓ **Check reflections & mirrors** – Storefront glass, vehicle windows, or water surfaces may reveal hidden details in an image.

3. Verifying Crowdsourced Media for Authenticity

Misinformation and fake crisis photos/videos often spread rapidly during emergencies. OSINT analysts must verify content before using it for intelligence gathering.

A. Confirming Timestamp & Source

✓ **Check post timestamps** – Compare upload time with reported event time.

✓ **Use InVID Toolkit** – Extract video metadata and frame-by-frame analysis.

✓ **Look for eyewitness comments** – Are other users confirming the event?

B. Cross-Referencing with Other OSINT Sources

✓ **Compare with live news reports** – Are journalists reporting the same event?

✓ **Use satellite imagery** – Platforms like Sentinel-2, Google Earth, and Maxar can verify location details.

✓ **Check official government sources** – Are emergency agencies responding in that area?

C. Spotting Fake & Misleading Media

✓ **Reverse search old images** – Many viral crisis photos are recycled from past events.

✓ **Check AI-generated media** – Use tools like Deepware Scanner to detect deepfakes.

✓ **Look for inconsistencies** – Is the clothing, technology, or environment era-appropriate?

4. Case Example: Verifying a Warzone Video

An OSINT analyst receives a video of an airstrike in Syria circulating on Telegram. The goal is to verify its authenticity.

Step 1: Extract Key Details from the Video

🔍 Look for landmarks, street signs, and weather conditions.
🔍 Extract frames using FFmpeg or InVID for reverse searching.

Step 2: Cross-Check with Satellite Imagery

🔍 Compare the bombed buildings with recent satellite images of Syria.

Step 3: Verify Time & Weather Conditions

🔍 Check historical weather data – If the video shows a clear sky but weather reports confirm rain, it's likely fake.

Step 4: Confirm with Local Sources

🔍 Search local Telegram & Twitter accounts for independent confirmations.

✓ **Final Conclusion** – If the video matches location data, weather reports, and independent sources, it can be considered credible.

5. OSINT Tools for Crisis Image & Video Verification

✓ **Google Lens & TinEye** – Reverse search images to detect duplicates.

✓ **InVID & FFmpeg** – Analyze and extract frames from videos.

✓ **Wolfram Alpha & Timeanddate**.com – Check historical weather patterns.

✓ **Google Earth Pro & Sentinel-2** – Compare images with real-time satellite data.

✓ **TweetDeck & Telegram Search** – Monitor crisis-related hashtags & posts.

6. Ethical & Legal Considerations in Crisis OSINT

✓ **Avoid exposing personal details** – Blur faces or remove identifying info when sharing analysis.

✓ **Do not spread unverified content** – False crisis reports can endanger lives.

✓ **Respect platform policies** – Some social media sites have restrictions on media extraction.

Crowdsourced images and videos are powerful tools for OSINT investigations in crisis situations. By collecting, verifying, and analyzing real-time social media content, analysts can provide valuable intelligence for security, humanitarian efforts, and media fact-checking.

9.4 Verifying Timestamp & Location Consistency in Live Content

Live content—such as real-time social media posts, live-streamed videos, and on-the-ground images—plays a critical role in OSINT investigations. However, misinformation, outdated media, and manipulated content can make it difficult to determine the authenticity of such content. To ensure reliability, analysts must verify timestamps, location consistency, and contextual clues before considering live content as factual intelligence.

This section explores the methods, tools, and best practices for verifying live content by checking for timestamp accuracy, geolocation consistency, and cross-referencing with other sources.

1. Why Verifying Timestamp & Location Consistency is Crucial

✓ **Prevents misinformation** – Many false reports come from old videos being reshared as current events.

✓ **Confirms authenticity** – Ensures that an image or video was actually captured at the stated time and place.

✓ **Supports geospatial intelligence** – Verifies that footage aligns with the claimed location.

✓ **Assists in crisis response** – Helps emergency responders and journalists get accurate situational awareness.

Example:

During the 2022 Russian invasion of Ukraine, many old explosion videos were circulated as "new attacks." OSINT analysts debunked several of them by checking timestamps and matching geolocation markers against satellite imagery.

2. Verifying Timestamps of Live Content

A. Checking Social Media Post Timestamps

✓ Most platforms display local timezones based on the viewer's settings.

✓ Some posts may show delayed timestamps due to scheduled posts or slow uploads.

✓ Cross-check the time with external sources, such as news reports or official agencies.

B. Using Metadata & EXIF Data for Timestamps

📌 If an image or video contains EXIF metadata, chck for:

✓ **Creation date & time** – Was it recently taken, or is it an old photo?

✓ **Time zone settings** – Is the metadata consistent with the uploader's claimed location?

✓ **Camera clock accuracy** – Some devices may have incorrect system time, so verification is needed.

🔍 **Tools for Extracting Metadata:**

✓ **ExifTool** – Extracts metadata from photos & videos.

✓ **Metadata2Go** – Online tool for checking timestamps in images.

✓ **Jeffrey's Image Metadata Viewer** – Provides detailed EXIF data, including timestamp & GPS.

Example:

An image from a protest claims to be from February 2024, but the metadata shows "July 2019." This suggests it was reused to mislead the audience.

3. Confirming Location Consistency in Live Content

A. Matching Landmarks & Background Features

✓ Identify buildings, street signs, mountains, or natural features in the image/video.

✓ Compare with Google Earth, Street View, OpenStreetMap, and Wikimapia.

✓ Use Google Lens or TinEye to check if the image appears in older sources.

Example:

A viral video claims to show a flood in New York City, but analysis shows that the buildings match Jakarta, Indonesia instead.

B. Checking Weather & Environmental Conditions

✓ Use Timeanddate.com or Wolfram Alpha to verify if the weather in the footage matches the actual conditions at the claimed time.

✓ Compare sunlight, cloud cover, and shadows in the image with historical weather reports.

🔍 Example:

A social media video claims to be from a hurricane in Florida on January 15th, but weather records show sunny and clear skies at that time. This suggests the video is fake or from another date.

C. Cross-Referencing Satellite & Traffic Data

✓ Use Google Earth Pro & Sentinel-2 to check if recent satellite images match the video's environment.

✓ Check Google Maps traffic layers or Waze to see if reported road conditions align with the claim.

🔍 Example:

A video claims a bridge collapsed in London, but satellite images and live traffic reports show that the bridge is still intact. This suggests fabricated content.

4. Case Study: Verifying a Viral Warzone Video

A video claims to show an airstrike in Gaza from March 2024. OSINT analysts verify it using the following steps:

✓ **Step 1: Extract Metadata**

The video lacks EXIF data (common for social media uploads), so analysts extract keyframes instead.

✓ **Step 2: Reverse Image Search**

Using Google Lens & Yandex, analysts find an identical video uploaded in 2017.

✓ **Step 3: Weather & Shadows Analysis**

The video shows heavy rain, but weather reports confirm clear skies on March 2024 in Gaza.

✓ **Step 4: Location Verification**

Analysts compare building structures in the video to Google Earth and find a match in Syria, not Gaza.

Conclusion: The video was misattributed and recycled from an older event.

5. OSINT Tools for Timestamp & Location Verification

Q Timestamps & Metadata Extraction:

✓ **ExifTool** – Extracts date/time data from images.

✓ **Metadata2Go** – Checks metadata online.

✓ **Jeffrey's Image Viewer** – Analyzes timestamps & camera info.

Q Geolocation Verification:

✓ **Google Earth Pro** – Compare buildings & terrain with satellite imagery.

✓ **Google Street View & OpenStreetMap** – Cross-check landmarks.

✓ **Sentinel-2 & Maxar Satellite Data** – Confirm changes over time.

Q Weather & Environmental Checks:

✓ **Timeanddate.com** – Check historical weather conditions.

✓ **Wolfram Alpha** – Compare sunlight & cloud cover data.

✓ **Shadows Calculator** – Verify time of day based on shadows.

6. Ethical & Legal Considerations

✓ **Avoid spreading unverified content** – False timestamps can lead to misinformation.

✓ **Respect privacy laws** – Do not expose personal information when verifying images.

✓ **Follow platform policies** – Some social media sites prohibit automated metadata scraping.

Verifying timestamp and location consistency in live content is a critical step in OSINT investigations. By using metadata extraction, reverse image search, weather analysis, and geolocation tools, analysts can determine whether an image or video is authentic or misleading.

9.5 Detecting Disinformation Through Image & Video Analysis

Disinformation spreads rapidly through manipulated images, edited videos, and misleading captions. In OSINT investigations, verifying the authenticity, source, and context of visual media is crucial to counter false narratives. This section covers techniques, tools, and best practices for detecting disinformation using image and video analysis.

1. Understanding How Disinformation Spreads

Disinformation campaigns often manipulate images and videos to create false narratives, influence public opinion, or cause panic. These manipulations typically fall into the following categories:

✓ **Reused Old Media** – A real image/video is repurposed with a false context (e.g., an explosion from 2014 being reshared as a recent attack).

✓ **Digitally Edited Media** – Elements are added, removed, or altered using software like Photoshop or AI tools.

✓ **AI-Generated & Deepfake Content** – Synthetic images or videos are created using AI to impersonate real events or people.

✓ **Misleading Captions** – An authentic image/video is used, but with a deceptive title that changes its meaning.

✓ **Staged or Manipulated Footage** – Videos may be intentionally scripted or altered to mislead viewers.

Example:

During the 2022 Ukraine conflict, old explosion videos from Syria were reshared with captions claiming they were from Kyiv bombings. OSINT analysts debunked them by reverse image searching keyframes.

2. Key Methods for Detecting Disinformation in Images & Videos

A. Reverse Image Search & Keyframe Analysis

✓ Use tools like Google Lens, TinEye, Yandex, or Bing Image Search to check if the image appears in older sources.

✓ Extract keyframes from videos using tools like FFmpeg or InVID-WeVerify, then reverse search those frames.

Example:

A viral image claims to show a natural disaster in California, but a reverse search reveals it was from an earthquake in Nepal (2015).

B. Analyzing Metadata & EXIF Data

✓ Extract metadata using ExifTool, Metadata2Go, or Jeffrey's Image Metadata Viewer.

✓ Look for inconsistencies in timestamps, camera model, or GPS data.

✓ Be cautious—many platforms strip EXIF data upon upload, so metadata may not always be available.

Example:

A social media image claims to be taken in March 2024, but metadata shows it was actually captured in 2018.

C. Detecting Photo Manipulation & Edits

✓ Use Error Level Analysis (ELA) to detect digital alterations (tools: FotoForensics, Forensically).
✓ Check for inconsistent lighting, shadows, and perspective in the image.
✓ Zoom in to look for pixelation, blurring, or unnatural textures around edited areas.

Example:

A political campaign image shows a crowd of thousands, but ELA reveals that people were digitally cloned to exaggerate the size.

D. Identifying AI-Generated & Deepfake Content

✓ Check for distorted facial features, asymmetric eyes, or unnatural backgrounds in AI-generated images.
✓ Use deepfake detection tools like Deepware Scanner, Reality Defender, and Sensity AI.
✓ Run GAN-detection tests to determine if an image was AI-generated.

Example:

A supposed "leaked" photo of a celebrity turns out to be AI-generated, with unnatural hair and mismatched earrings.

E. Contextual & Geolocation Verification

✓ Compare buildings, landmarks, and terrain in an image with Google Earth, Street View, and OpenStreetMap.

✓ Use timeanddate.com to verify whether weather and lighting conditions match the claimed time of the image.

✓ Check social media cross-posting to see if the same content appears under different claims elsewhere.

Example:

A viral protest image claims to be from New York (2024), but analysis of street signs reveals it was actually from Berlin (2019).

3. Tools for Detecting Image & Video Disinformation

✓ **Reverse Image Search** – Google Lens, TinEye, Yandex, Bing

✓ **Keyframe Extraction for Video** – InVID-WeVerify, FFmpeg

✓ **Metadata & EXIF Analysis** – ExifTool, Metadata2Go, Jeffrey's EXIF Viewer

✓ **Photo Manipulation Detection** – FotoForensics, Forensically, Image Edited?

✓ **AI & Deepfake Detection** – Deepware Scanner, Reality Defender, Sensity AI

✓ **Geolocation Verification** – Google Earth, Street View, OpenStreetMap

4. Case Study: Debunking a Fake War Video

A video claims to show a fighter jet bombing a city in 2023, spreading panic. OSINT analysts verify its authenticity using these steps:

✓ **Step 1: Keyframe Extraction & Reverse Image Search**

- Analysts extract keyframes and run them through Google Lens & Yandex.
- The exact same video appears in a 2018 news report from Syria—it is NOT recent.

✓ **Step 2: Metadata Analysis**

- The video's metadata has no EXIF data (expected for social media).
- Checking the uploader's previous posts reveals a pattern of disinformation.

✓ Step 3: Geolocation Verification

- The skyline in the video does not match the claimed location.
- Using Google Earth, analysts confirm the buildings belong to a different country.

✓ Step 4: Weather & Lighting Check

- The video shows clear skies, but weather records show a storm on that day—another inconsistency.

Conclusion:

The video was recycled from a past event and falsely labeled to spread disinformation.

5. Best Practices for OSINT Analysts

✓ Always cross-check images/videos with multiple verification methods.

✓ Be skeptical of viral media—especially from unverified accounts.

✓ Use metadata, geolocation tools, and weather data to confirm accuracy.

✓ Educate others on disinformation tactics to reduce the spread of false content.

Detecting disinformation in images and videos requires a multi-layered approach combining reverse searching, metadata analysis, AI detection, and contextual verification. OSINT analysts must be critical, methodical, and persistent in verifying visual content before drawing conclusions.

9.6 Case Study: Verifying a Protest Location Using Geotagged Photos

In OSINT investigations, geotagged photos can provide critical evidence for verifying the location of events such as protests, conflicts, and political demonstrations. This case study walks through the step-by-step process of verifying the location of a protest using open-source intelligence (OSINT) techniques.

1. Scenario: A Viral Protest Photo with an Unverified Claim

A photo circulates on social media showing a large protest, claiming to be from a recent demonstration in Buenos Aires, Argentina (2024). The image has sparked discussions and news reports, but some users question its authenticity.

An OSINT analyst sets out to verify whether the protest actually took place in Buenos Aires or if the claim is misleading.

2. Step-by-Step OSINT Investigation

Step 1: Reverse Image Search to Identify Previous Uses

✓ The analyst uses Google Lens, TinEye, and Yandex to check if the image has been posted before.

✓ **Results**: The same image appears in a 2021 protest report from Santiago, Chile. This suggests it is an old image being misused.

✓ However, to confirm, the analyst continues the investigation.

Step 2: Extracting Metadata & Checking Geotags

✓ The analyst downloads the highest-quality version of the image and extracts EXIF metadata using ExifTool and Metadata2Go.

✓ Findings:

- GPS coordinates are embedded in the metadata.
- The coordinates point to Plaza Baquedano, Santiago, Chile, not Buenos Aires.
- The image's timestamp also shows 2021, contradicting the claim.

💡 **Conclusion**: The metadata strongly indicates the image is not recent and not from Buenos Aires. However, the analyst verifies further to ensure the metadata is reliable.

Step 3: Geolocation Analysis Using Landmarks & Street Features

✓ To confirm the photo's true location, the analyst examines buildings, signs, and objects visible in the image.

✓ Using Google Earth, Street View, and OpenStreetMap, they compare:

- Statues and monuments
- Billboards and storefronts
- Street signs and road markings

✓ Findings:

- The statue in the background matches the one in Plaza Baquedano, Chile.
- A billboard advertisement in the image was only displayed in 2021.
- Street layouts and road markings confirm an exact match with Plaza Baquedano.

💡 Conclusion: The physical environment in the image matches Santiago, Chile, further disproving the Buenos Aires claim.

Step 4: Cross-Referencing Social Media Posts from the Claimed Event

✓ The analyst searches Twitter, Instagram, and Facebook for posts using hashtags related to the Buenos Aires protest.

✓ They use TweetDeck and GeoSocialFootprint to find geotagged images and videos from the actual event.

✓ Findings:

- Authentic Buenos Aires protest images show different locations, banners, and crowd formations.
- No other verified sources posted the viral protest image from Buenos Aires.

💡 Conclusion: Social media evidence confirms that the viral image is not from the recent protest in Buenos Aires.

3. Final Verdict: Image is Misleading

After verifying the metadata, landmarks, and social media evidence, the analyst debunks the claim that the protest photo is from Buenos Aires in 2024. It was actually taken in Santiago, Chile, in 2021, and was misused to mislead audiences.

✓ Key Lessons:

- Always reverse search images before trusting claims.
- Check metadata for geotags and timestamps.
- Use landmarks and geolocation tools to verify locations.
- Cross-reference social media posts to confirm real-time events.

By using OSINT techniques, analysts can fact-check viral misinformation and prevent false narratives from spreading.

10. Video Analysis & Frame Extraction for OSINT

In this chapter, we will focus on the critical techniques of video analysis and frame extraction for OSINT purposes. Videos often contain a wealth of information that can be overlooked at first glance, including key visual, auditory, and metadata clues that can provide insights into events, locations, and people. By extracting individual frames and analyzing them for hidden details—such as landmarks, movements, or timestamps—analysts can uncover valuable intelligence. We will explore the tools and methods for frame extraction, as well as techniques for analyzing video content, identifying inconsistencies, and verifying the authenticity of videos in order to enhance investigative efforts.

10.1 How Video OSINT Differs from Image-Based Investigations

While both images and videos serve as valuable sources in OSINT investigations, videos present unique challenges and opportunities that differ from still-image analysis. A single video contains thousands of frames, audio, metadata, motion patterns, and contextual clues that can provide deeper intelligence than a single image. This section explores the key differences between video and image-based OSINT, the advantages of video analysis, and the specialized techniques required for extracting actionable intelligence from videos.

1. Key Differences Between Image and Video OSINT

A. Volume of Information

- Images provide a single frame of visual data, while videos capture multiple frames per second, offering more context and movement.
- **Example**: A protest image may show a moment in time, but a video can reveal crowd size, movement patterns, and changes over time.

B. Metadata & Compression

- Videos store more metadata than images, including frame timestamps, codec information, and GPS coordinates (if enabled).

- However, many social media platforms strip or alter metadata, making retrieval harder.

C. Motion & Audio Analysis

- Videos capture movement, speech, and environmental sounds, which provide more investigative leads than static images.
- Audio can be transcribed, translated, and analyzed for speaker identification and keyword recognition.

D. Source Identification

- Reverse image searching works well for individual images, but video reverse searching is more complex.
- Analysts must extract keyframes and check them against Google Lens, TinEye, or Yandex to trace video origins.

E. Manipulation Detection

- Videos are harder to manipulate compared to images, but deepfake and AI-generated videos are increasingly sophisticated.
- Detecting frame inconsistencies, unnatural face movements, and audio mismatches is essential for spotting fake videos.

2. Advantages of Video Analysis in OSINT

A. Provides More Context

- Videos capture the before and after of an event, revealing additional context that a single image may lack.
- **Example**: A video of a crime scene may show suspects entering and leaving, while a photo only shows a still moment.

B. Enables Lip-Reading & Speaker Analysis

- Investigators can identify spoken words even in muted or low-quality videos using lip-reading software.
- Speaker recognition AI can compare voices to known databases.

C. Tracks Object & Person Movements

- Video analysis allows for tracking vehicle movements, identifying repeat offenders, and monitoring patterns over time.
- **Example**: In protests, video analysis can detect individuals changing clothes to avoid detection.

D. Verifies Location & Time Consistency

- Videos contain multiple angles of the same location, making geolocation easier.
- The lighting, shadows, and sun position across multiple frames help estimate time of recording.

3. Essential Techniques for Video OSINT

A. Keyframe Extraction for Reverse Searching

Videos contain thousands of frames—analysts extract keyframes to perform reverse image searches.

Tools: InVID-WeVerify, FFmpeg, VLC Media Player

Process:

- Extract frames from different timestamps in the video.
- Search them using Google Lens, Yandex, or TinEye to find previous uploads.

B. Metadata & EXIF Data Analysis

Video metadata can include:

✓ Timestamps – When the video was recorded

✓ GPS Coordinates – If location tracking was enabled

✓ Device Information – Camera model, resolution, compression settings

Tools: ExifTool, MediaInfo

C. Audio & Speech Analysis

- Extract background noises, speaker conversations, or hidden voices.

- Convert speech to text for keyword analysis.

Tools: Audacity, Deepgram, Whisper AI

D. Frame-by-Frame Analysis for Manipulation Detection

- Identify deepfake videos or edited footage using frame-by-frame inspection.
- Detect unnatural facial expressions, lighting inconsistencies, and abrupt cuts.

Tools: Deepware Scanner, Forensically, FakeCatcher

E. Geolocation & Object Recognition

- Identify landmarks, street signs, license plates, and weather patterns.
- Cross-reference with Google Earth, OpenStreetMap, and weather archives.

Example: A video claims to be from New York, but street signs reveal it was actually filmed in London.

4. Challenges in Video-Based OSINT

A. Platform Compression & Metadata Stripping

- Most social media platforms compress videos and remove metadata, making source verification harder.
- **Solution**: Download the original video (if possible) instead of a reposted, compressed version.

B. Video Deepfakes & AI Manipulation

- AI-generated videos are becoming harder to detect with the naked eye.
- **Solution**: Use AI-based deepfake detection tools to scan facial anomalies, unnatural blinking, and mouth movements.

C. Analyzing Large Video Files

- Videos can be several GBs in size, making processing difficult.
- **Solution**: Use tools like FFmpeg to extract relevant segments and analyze them separately.

5. Case Study: Verifying a Protest Video

A viral video claims to show a recent protest in Paris (2024). An OSINT analyst verifies its authenticity using:

✓ **Step 1: Keyframe Extraction & Reverse Search**

- Extracts frames at different timestamps and reverse searches them.
- **Findings**: A frame matches a protest from 2018, proving the claim is false.

✓ **Step 2: Metadata & Timestamp Verification**

- Extracts video metadata and finds the file's creation date is 2018, contradicting the claim.

✓ **Step 3: Geolocation & Landmark Analysis**

- Cross-checks street signs, shop names, and landmarks with Google Street View.
- Confirms the location is accurate, but the date is misleading.

✓ **Step 4: Crowd & Object Movement Analysis**

- Analyzes movement patterns in the video.
- Detects inconsistencies between claimed protest routes and actual city layouts.

Conclusion:

The video is real but is being misrepresented as a 2024 event—debunking the claim.

6. Best Practices for Video OSINT Analysts

✓ Always extract keyframes for reverse searching.

✓ Analyze metadata for timestamps, GPS, and device information.

✓ Use frame-by-frame analysis to detect edits and deepfakes.

✓ Verify context using geolocation, audio, and environmental clues.

✓ Cross-check social media sources to confirm real-time events.

By applying these OSINT techniques, investigators can verify the authenticity of videos, identify misinformation, and uncover hidden intelligence from video content.

10.2 Extracting Key Frames & Enhancing Image Quality

In OSINT investigations, videos contain vast amounts of information, but analyzing them efficiently requires extracting key frames—still images that represent crucial moments in the footage. Extracted frames can then be enhanced and analyzed for geolocation, object recognition, metadata retrieval, and manipulation detection. This chapter explores key frame extraction techniques, tools for enhancing image quality, and best practices for maximizing investigative value from video evidence.

1. Why Extract Key Frames from Videos?

Unlike images, videos consist of thousands of frames. Instead of analyzing an entire video, extracting key frames allows OSINT analysts to:

✓ Identify crucial moments without watching the whole video.

✓ Perform reverse image searches to trace the video's origins.

✓ Analyze visual clues like landmarks, timestamps, and objects.

✓ Detect manipulation by comparing frames for inconsistencies.

✓ Improve image quality for clearer analysis.

2. Extracting Key Frames from Videos

A. What Are Key Frames?

- Key frames are significant frames in a video that capture distinct events or scene changes.
- Instead of extracting every frame, key frames help focus on important visual details.

B. Methods for Extracting Key Frames

1. Manual Extraction (Basic Method)

- ◆ **Best for**: Small video clips, quick analysis
- ◆ **Tools**: VLC Media Player, Windows Snipping Tool, Mac Screenshot

Steps in VLC:

- Open the video in VLC Media Player.
- Pause at an important moment.
- Press Shift + S (Windows/Linux) or Cmd + Shift + S (Mac) to take a screenshot.
- The image is saved in the default screenshots folder.

2. Automated Extraction (Advanced Method)

- ◆ **Best for**: Large videos, forensic analysis, high accuracy
- ◆ **Tools**: FFmpeg, InVID-WeVerify, SceneDetect

Using FFmpeg (Command Line-Based Extraction)

FFmpeg is a powerful tool that can extract frames automatically.

Extract a frame every second:

ffmpeg -i video.mp4 -vf "fps=1" frames/output%d.png

Extract key frames based on scene changes:

ffmpeg -i video.mp4 -vf "select=eq(pict_type\,I)" -vsync vfr frames/output%d.png

- ◆ This method captures only I-frames (key moments) instead of every frame.

Using InVID-WeVerify (Browser-Based Analysis)

- InVID is a video verification tool used by OSINT analysts.
- Extracts thumbnails from YouTube, Twitter, and Facebook videos.
- Automatically detects video edits and inconsistencies.

Using SceneDetect (AI-Based Frame Selection)

- Uses machine learning to detect scene transitions.
- Automatically extracts high-quality key frames without duplicates.

💡 **Key Takeaway**: Automated extraction saves time and ensures accuracy in selecting only relevant frames.

3. Enhancing Extracted Images for OSINT

Once key frames are extracted, enhancing their quality improves visibility, clarity, and analysis.

A. Why Enhance Images?

✓ Make blurry images readable (useful for text on signs, license plates).

✓ Improve lighting to see details in dark or overexposed areas.

✓ Reduce noise and sharpen edges for better pattern recognition.

✓ Increase resolution to aid in AI-based analysis.

B. Techniques for Image Enhancement

1. Brightness & Contrast Adjustment

◆ **Best for**: Dark, low-contrast images
◆ **Tools**: Photoshop, GIMP, OpenCV

- Increase brightness and contrast to improve visibility.
- Avoid overexposing, which may wash out details.

2. Sharpening & Noise Reduction

◆ **Best for**: Blurry or grainy images
◆ **Tools**: Forensically, Waifu2x, Topaz Gigapixel AI

- AI-based tools reduce noise while sharpening edges.
- Useful for license plates, blurry faces, and street signs.

3. Upscaling Low-Resolution Images

◆ **Best for**: Pixelated, low-quality video frames

◆ **Tools**: Waifu2x, Remini, Let's Enhance

- AI upscaling increases image resolution while preserving details.
- **Example**: A 240p video frame can be enhanced to 720p or higher.

4. Reverse Image Search on Enhanced Frames

- After enhancement, run the frame through Google Lens, Yandex, or TinEye.
- Higher-quality images improve match accuracy.

💡 **Pro Tip**: Be cautious—over-enhancement can introduce artifacts that distort real details.

4. Case Study: Extracting Key Frames to Identify a Location

Scenario

A low-resolution video shows an unknown location, with a claim that it was filmed in Kyiv, Ukraine. The OSINT analyst must verify its location.

Step 1: Extracting Key Frames

✓ Used FFmpeg to extract frames every 2 seconds.

✓ Selected the clearest frames showing landmarks and signs.

Step 2: Enhancing the Best Frame

✓ Used Waifu2x AI to increase resolution.

✓ Applied sharpening and noise reduction to improve clarity.

Step 3: Reverse Image Search & Geolocation

✓ Ran the enhanced frame through Google Lens and Yandex.

✓ Found a matching street in Warsaw, Poland—not Kyiv.

✓ Cross-referenced with Google Earth to confirm location.

Conclusion

- ◆ The claim was false—the video was misattributed.
- ◆ Image enhancement + reverse searching exposed the truth.

5. Best Practices for Extracting & Enhancing Video Frames

✓ Extract multiple frames from different timestamps for accuracy.

✓ Use AI-based upscaling only when necessary (avoid over-enhancement).

✓ Verify results with reverse image searches to confirm authenticity.

✓ Check video metadata—it may contain timestamps and location data.

✓ Cross-reference with street views, satellite imagery, and OSINT tools.

By combining key frame extraction, image enhancement, and geolocation, OSINT analysts can extract maximum intelligence from video footage.

10.3 Identifying Landmarks, Objects & People in Video Footage

Video footage is a powerful resource in OSINT investigations, often revealing critical clues about a location, individuals, or objects present in the scene. By breaking down a video into analyzable frames, investigators can identify landmarks, objects, and even people to verify claims, trace movements, and confirm locations. This section explores the techniques, tools, and best practices for extracting intelligence from video footage.

1. Why Identifying Landmarks, Objects & People Matters in OSINT

✓ Verifies locations by matching landmarks with known places.

✓ Identifies individuals to confirm their presence in a specific area.

✓ Detects objects such as weapons, vehicles, or signs that provide contextual evidence.

✓ Cross-references visual clues with online data to track movements or events.

2. Identifying Landmarks in Video Footage

Landmarks—such as buildings, statues, mountains, and street signs—can help geolocate where a video was filmed.

A. Key Techniques for Landmark Identification

1. Reverse Image Search on Extracted Frames

◆ **Best for**: Finding online matches of landmarks.
◆ **Tools**: Google Lens, Yandex Image Search, TinEye.

- Extract a clear frame with a recognizable structure.
- Upload it to a reverse image search engine.
- Compare results with online images to determine the location.

2. Using AI-Based Landmark Recognition

◆ **Best for**: Automated landmark identification.
◆ **Tools**: Google Vision AI, Microsoft Azure Computer Vision, Mapillary.

- AI can analyze images and suggest possible locations.
- Works best with well-known landmarks and urban environments.

3. Cross-Referencing with Google Earth & Street View

◆ **Best for**: Confirming locations with real-world imagery.
◆ **Tools**: Google Earth, Google Street View, Bing Maps, Yandex Maps.

- Match building structures, road signs, and terrain with video frames.
- Compare timestamps to see if a location has changed over time.

B. Case Example: Locating a Protest Site

A video claims to show a protest in Paris. By analyzing a frame, investigators spot:

✓ A monument in the background.

✓ A road sign in French confirming a location in France.

✓ A building with a distinctive facade found in Google Street View.

💡 **Conclusion**: The protest did occur in Paris, but the video was filmed months earlier—proving it was misleadingly reposted.

3. Recognizing Objects for OSINT Investigations

Objects in a video can provide critical context about location, time, and activity.

A. Common Objects Used for Geolocation & Verification

🔎 **Vehicles & License Plates:**

- Car models and license plate formats can confirm country of origin.
- Some regions have unique taxi colors or emergency vehicle designs.

🔎 **Street Signs & Billboards:**

- Language, font, and style help identify a country or city.
- Adverts may contain company names, phone numbers, or locations.

🔎 **Weather & Clothing:**

- Snow, palm trees, or dry landscapes help narrow down climates.
- Local fashion trends may indicate cultural and seasonal context.

🔎 **Currency & Documents:**

- Money exchanged in a video may indicate a specific country.
- Visible IDs or passports can reveal nationality or identity.

B. Tools for Object Recognition in Videos

- **Google Lens / Yandex Vision** – Identifies objects & text.
- **Clarifai** – AI-powered object detection.
- **YOLO (You Only Look Once)** – Open-source AI for object recognition.

💡 **Example: A video claims to show a war zone. Analysts spot:**

✓ Vehicles with European license plates.

✓ Green road signs in Cyrillic script.

✓ Billboard with a recognizable phone number.

💡 **Conclusion**: The video is actually from Ukraine, not the claimed Middle Eastern conflict.

4. Identifying People in Video Footage

Facial recognition and object tracking in videos can help identify individuals, detect deepfakes, or confirm someone's presence at an event.

A. Techniques for Identifying Individuals

1. Reverse Image Search on Faces

◆ **Best for**: Finding publicly available images of a person.
◆ **Tools**: PimEyes, Yandex Image Search, Betaface API.

- Extract a clear face shot from the video.
- Run it through a facial search engine to find matches.

2. Analyzing Clothing & Accessories

◆ **Best for**: Matching individuals based on unique attire.

- Logos, tattoos, or distinctive clothing help verify identities.
- **Example**: A journalist spotted a protester's unique backpack in multiple videos, confirming their presence.

3. Gait & Body Shape Recognition

◆ **Best for**: Cases where facial recognition is unreliable.

- AI tools analyze walking style & body proportions.
- Used by law enforcement for suspect tracking.

B. Challenges in Identifying People

⚠ Blurred or low-resolution video reduces accuracy.
⚠ Disguises (hats, masks) make recognition difficult.

⚠ Legal & ethical concerns in facial recognition.

C. Case Study: Identifying a Wanted Criminal

A video shows an unidentified suspect at an event. Analysts:

✓ Extract frames of the person's face & clothing.

✓ Use PimEyes to find matching online profiles.

✓ Identify a social media account linking the suspect to a crime.

💡 **Conclusion**: The suspect's identity was confirmed via open-source analysis.

5. Best Practices for Identifying Landmarks, Objects & People in Videos

✓ Extract high-quality frames before analyzing.

✓ Use multiple techniques—reverse search, AI tools, and geolocation.

✓ Cross-reference data from public records and social media.

✓ Verify results with multiple sources to avoid false positives.

✓ Consider legal & ethical implications before using facial recognition.

By combining landmark analysis, object detection, and person identification, OSINT investigators can validate videos, trace locations, and expose false claims effectively.

10.4 Analyzing Shadows, Weather & Background Noise for Verification

Video verification is a crucial part of OSINT investigations, especially when determining the authenticity of a claim. Shadows, weather conditions, and background noise provide hidden but valuable clues that can help verify when and where a video was recorded. By analyzing these environmental factors, investigators can cross-check timestamps, locations, and context to detect misinformation or confirm an event's legitimacy.

1. The Importance of Environmental Factors in Video OSINT

✓ Shadows help determine time of day and direction in a video.

✓ Weather conditions help verify if the environment matches the claimed location/date.

✓ Background noise (such as voices, sirens, or nature sounds) can provide contextual clues about the surroundings.

These elements act as forensic evidence, allowing analysts to confirm whether a video is genuine or manipulated.

2. Using Shadows for Time & Location Verification

A. How Shadows Indicate Time & Direction

Shadows in a video can help estimate:

🔎 **Time of day** – Longer shadows suggest early morning or late afternoon.
🔎 **Sun position** – Shadows cast in a specific direction can indicate cardinal directions (North, South, East, West).
🔎 **Seasonal clues** – Sun angles differ depending on the time of year.

B. Tools for Shadow Analysis

- **SunCalc** – Estimates sun position & shadow length at any location/date.
- **Google Earth Pro** – Historical imagery helps verify shadow movement over time.
- **Shadow Calculator (Sun Position Tools)** – Calculates sun azimuth & altitude based on shadows.

💡 **Example**: A video claims to show a morning protest in London, but shadows indicate the sun is positioned westward.

✓ **Conclusion**: The video was filmed in the afternoon, contradicting the claim.

3. Weather Analysis for Video Verification

A. Checking Weather Conditions in a Video

Weather inconsistencies often expose staged or misrepresented videos. Key elements to verify:

✓ **Cloud patterns & rain** – Does the video show rain when the official weather records show clear skies?

✓ **Temperature indicators** – Are people dressed in heavy jackets when the claimed date suggests summer?

✓ **Snow, fog, or wind** – Is there snow on the ground when it wasn't recorded on that date?

B. Tools for Weather Verification

- **Wunderground Historical Weather** – Provides past weather reports for any location.
- **Ventusky & Windy** – Live & historical wind and storm data.
- **NASA Worldview** – Satellite imagery of past weather conditions.

💡 **Example**: A video claims to show a hurricane hitting Miami on August 3, 2023. Checking historical weather data reveals no storm on that date.

✓ **Conclusion**: The video is misleading—likely from a different event or date.

4. Background Noise as an OSINT Clue

A. What Sounds Can Reveal

Audio in a video can confirm or disprove location claims by analyzing:

🔊 **Languages & accents** – Do people speak the local language? Does their accent match the region?

🔊 **Public announcements** – Background speech (e.g., subway announcements, radio news) can hint at a location.

🔊 **Sirens & emergency vehicles** – Different countries have distinct siren sounds (e.g., U.S. vs. European ambulances).

🔊 **Wildlife & environment sounds** – Birdsong, insects, or city traffic can indicate urban or rural areas.

B. Tools for Background Noise Analysis

- **Audacity** – Audio editing & spectrogram analysis.

- **AIsoundID** – Identifies common sounds in a recording.
- **Google Audio Search** – Can detect spoken phrases and match them to known locations.

💡 **Example**: A video claims to be filmed in Tokyo, but background noise includes European-style sirens and announcements in German.

✓ **Conclusion**: The video was not filmed in Tokyo, exposing misinformation.

5. Case Study: Debunking a Viral Video with Environmental Clues

Claim:

A video shared widely online claims to show a nighttime military strike in Kyiv, Ukraine, in February 2023.

Analysis:

✓ **Shadows & lighting** – The moonlight positioning doesn't match the expected astronomical data for Kyiv that night.

✓ **Weather check** – The video shows clear skies, but Kyiv had recorded heavy snowfall that day.

✓ **Background sounds** – The police sirens don't match Ukrainian siren sounds—instead, they match emergency sounds from Syria.

Conclusion:

📌 The video was actually from Syria in 2016, but was falsely repurposed as footage from Ukraine in 2023. The shadows, weather, and audio all contradicted the claim, proving it was misinformation.

6. Best Practices for Using Shadows, Weather & Background Noise in OSINT

✓ Extract high-quality frames from videos for shadow & lighting analysis.

✓ Compare video weather with historical weather records for consistency.

✓ Listen to background noise carefully—accents, sirens, and announcements can reveal hidden clues.

✓ Cross-check multiple sources (e.g., satellite imagery, weather data, maps) before drawing conclusions.

✓ Consider time zones & seasonal variations to detect discrepancies.

By applying environmental verification techniques, OSINT analysts can debunk false claims, verify locations, and confirm real-world events with higher accuracy.

10.5 Using AI & Machine Learning for Automated Video Analysis

With the increasing volume of digital video content available online, AI and machine learning (ML) have become essential tools for OSINT analysts. Automated video analysis helps detect objects, recognize faces, extract metadata, and verify content efficiently. AI-driven tools can analyze thousands of frames within minutes, making it possible to identify locations, track movements, and detect manipulated footage that would be nearly impossible to verify manually.

1. The Role of AI in Video OSINT

AI-powered tools help automate and enhance the process of analyzing video content by performing tasks such as:

✓ **Object Detection** – Identifies vehicles, weapons, buildings, and other relevant objects.

✓ **Facial Recognition** – Matches faces in videos with publicly available databases.

✓ **Text & Symbol Recognition (OCR)** – Extracts text from license plates, signs, and documents.

✓ **Audio Analysis** – Detects spoken language, background noise, and unique sound patterns.

✓ **Deepfake Detection** – Identifies AI-generated or altered videos.

By integrating AI with OSINT workflows, investigators can process large datasets quickly, extract useful information, and verify the authenticity of video content.

2. Object Detection & Scene Recognition

AI-powered video analysis tools use computer vision to detect objects and categorize scenes automatically.

A. How Object Detection Works

🔍 AI models, trained on massive datasets, recognize objects in video frames.
🔍 They assign labels to detected objects (e.g., "car," "firearm," "protester").
🔍 AI can track an object across multiple frames, identifying movement patterns.

B. Scene Recognition for Contextual Analysis

AI can classify entire scenes based on environmental features, such as:

🔎 Urban vs. rural areas
🔎 Indoor vs. outdoor settings
🔎 Military zones vs. civilian spaces
🔎 Natural disasters (e.g., flooding, wildfires)

💡 **Example**: A viral video claims to show a protest in Berlin, but AI analysis detects palm trees and desert terrain—indicating the video is actually from a Middle Eastern country.

AI Tools for Object Detection & Scene Analysis

- **Google Cloud Vision** – Recognizes objects, text, and faces in video frames.
- **Amazon Rekognition** – Detects objects, faces, and unsafe content in videos.
- **YOLO (You Only Look Once)** – Open-source object detection AI for real-time analysis.

3. Facial Recognition & Person Tracking

AI-based facial recognition helps OSINT investigators identify people appearing in videos, even across different platforms.

A. How AI Matches Faces in Videos

✓ AI extracts unique facial features (eyes, nose shape, jawline) from video frames.

✓ It compares these features against publicly available images (social media, databases).

✓ If a match is found, it reveals potential identities and associated profiles.

💡 **Example**: A journalist is investigating a criminal suspect seen in a leaked video. AI facial recognition finds a match on social media, linking the suspect to previous illegal activities.

B. AI for Gait & Movement Analysis

Even if a person's face is obscured, AI can track walking patterns and body posture to identify individuals based on their movement.

AI Tools for Facial & Movement Recognition

- **Clearview AI** – Searches public internet sources to find matching faces.
- **Face++** – Analyzes facial landmarks and expressions.
- **OpenPose** – Tracks body movements and walking patterns.

4. Text & Symbol Recognition (OCR) for Video OSINT

AI-powered Optical Character Recognition (OCR) extracts text from video frames to identify locations, businesses, license plates, and signs.

A. How OCR Helps OSINT Investigators

✓ Identifies license plates to track vehicle movements.

✓ Reads street signs, billboards, or store names to geolocate videos.

✓ Extracts document text shown in a video.

💡 **Example**: A terrorist recruitment video features a hidden document in the background. AI-based OCR reveals classified text, helping analysts trace the source.

AI Tools for OCR & Text Extraction

- **Tesseract OCR** – Open-source text recognition tool.
- **Google Cloud Vision OCR** – Extracts text from images & videos.

- **Plate Recognizer** – Identifies license plates from video footage.

5. Audio & Speech Analysis for Verification

AI-driven speech recognition and audio analysis help OSINT professionals verify video authenticity by detecting:

✓ **Accents & Dialects** – Identifies regional speech patterns.

✓ **Background Sounds** – Detects sirens, gunshots, city noises, or wildlife.

✓ **Fake Audio** – Detects AI-generated or manipulated voice recordings.

A. Example: Verifying a Propaganda Video

A militant group releases a threatening video, claiming to be recorded in Afghanistan.

✓ AI audio analysis detects Spanish-language radio chatter in the background.

✓ Cross-referencing reveals that the video was actually filmed in South America.

AI Tools for Audio & Speech Analysis

- **Deepgram** – AI-based speech-to-text and audio classification.
- **Auphonic** – Enhances and cleans up distorted audio.
- **Sonix AI** – Automatically transcribes and analyzes speech patterns.

6. AI & Deepfake Detection

AI-generated deepfake videos are becoming more realistic and harder to detect. OSINT analysts need AI-powered tools to recognize subtle manipulations.

A. Common Deepfake Indicators

✓ **Inconsistent facial expressions** – AI often struggles with natural eye blinking or lip movement.

✓ **Unnatural lighting & reflections** – Shadows or reflections might be misaligned.

✓ **Audio-visual mismatches** – Lip movements may not perfectly sync with speech.

💡 **Example**: A fake video of a world leader making a controversial statement spreads online. AI-based deepfake detection analyzes facial movements and confirms the video is AI-generated.

AI Tools for Deepfake Detection

- **Microsoft Video Authenticator** – Detects manipulated videos using AI.
- **Deepware Scanner** – Identifies deepfake content in online videos.
- **Sensity AI** – Analyzes videos for deepfake characteristics.

7. Case Study: Unmasking a Fake Military Video with AI Analysis

Claim:

A video claims to show a Russian military airstrike in Ukraine in January 2024.

AI Analysis Findings:

✓ **Object Detection**: AI identifies tanks from an outdated Soviet-era model not in current use.

✓ **Weather Check**: The video shows lush green trees, but satellite data confirms Ukraine was covered in snow that day.

✓ **Audio Analysis**: Background noise reveals Arabic speech, indicating the video is from a Middle Eastern conflict zone.

Conclusion:

📌 The video was actually from Syria in 2017 and was misleadingly re-uploaded as recent footage from Ukraine. AI tools debunked the misinformation within minutes.

8. Best Practices for Using AI in Video OSINT

✓ **Combine multiple AI tools** – Object detection, facial recognition, OCR, and deepfake detection should be used together for maximum accuracy.

✓ **Always verify AI results manually** – AI can produce false positives; cross-check findings with open-source intelligence methods.

✓ **Stay updated on deepfake advancements** – AI-generated videos are evolving, and detection techniques must adapt to new manipulation methods.

AI-driven video analysis is revolutionizing OSINT investigations, enabling analysts to process vast amounts of data quickly, detect false narratives, and verify real-world events with high accuracy.

10.6 Case Study: Identifying a Suspect from Surveillance Footage

In early 2023, a high-profile burglary took place at an electronics store in Berlin, Germany. The store's CCTV cameras captured footage of a masked individual breaking in and stealing valuable equipment. While the suspect's face was partially covered, investigators believed that advanced OSINT techniques using AI-powered video analysis could help uncover their identity.

1. Collecting & Enhancing the Surveillance Footage

Step 1: Extracting Key Frames from the Video

✓ Investigators extracted high-quality frames where the suspect's face, clothing, and any identifiable features were visible.

✓ Frame-by-frame analysis helped isolate clear shots of tattoos, shoe patterns, and hand movements.

Step 2: Enhancing Image Quality

✓ AI-based video enhancement tools were used to sharpen blurry frames, clarify low-light areas, and improve resolution.

✓ Adobe Enhance Video AI & Topaz Video Enhance AI helped in denoising the footage and improving facial details.

💡 **Key Discovery**: The suspect had a partially visible tattoo on their wrist.

2. Facial Recognition & Person Tracking

Step 3: Running AI-Based Facial Recognition

✓ Despite the mask, AI tools like Clearview AI and PimEyes were used to analyze visible facial features, ear structure, and eye spacing.

✓ The system compared frames against millions of publicly available social media images.

💡 **Key Discovery**: The software found a possible match—a social media photo of a man with the same eye structure and tattoo design.

Step 4: Cross-Referencing with Social Media OSINT

✓ Investigators searched the suspect's username, friends, and tagged locations to build a digital footprint.

✓ Analyzing posts, stories, and geotagged locations revealed a recent photo in Berlin near the crime scene.

💡 **Key Discovery**: The suspect had posted a video wearing the same unique sneakers seen in the surveillance footage.

3. Object & Clothing Recognition

Step 5: Identifying Clothing & Accessories

✓ AI-based object recognition tools like Amazon Rekognition and IBM Watson identified brand logos, shoe designs, and unique clothing patterns.

✓ Investigators searched for online stores selling the exact hoodie & shoes to track purchase history.

💡 **Key Discovery**: The suspect purchased the hoodie online using a traceable account.

Step 6: License Plate Recognition (LPR)

✓ The CCTV footage showed a partial view of the suspect's getaway car.

✓ AI-powered license plate recognition (LPR) tools like OpenALPR analyzed blurry digits and cross-referenced local traffic cameras.

💡 **Key Discovery**: The full license plate was reconstructed, leading to a registered vehicle linked to the suspect's address.

4. Audio & Environmental Analysis

Step 7: Enhancing Background Audio

✓ AI-based speech-to-text analysis extracted faint audio from the footage.

✓ Enhanced audio revealed the suspect whispering a name, which was analyzed for possible accomplices.

💡 **Key Discovery**: The name matched a known associate in the suspect's social media network.

Step 8: Using Street View & Satellite Data for Geolocation

✓ Investigators used Google Earth & OpenStreetMap to verify the route taken based on CCTV timestamps & landmarks.

✓ Surrounding buildings, traffic lights, and graffiti patterns matched previous social media check-ins by the suspect.

💡 **Key Discovery**: The suspect had visited the crime scene a day earlier, possibly scouting the location.

5. Arrest & Legal Action

Step 9: Presenting Digital Evidence

✓ OSINT investigators compiled a digital timeline, showing:

◆ Surveillance video analysis matching facial features & clothing.
◆ Social media footprints confirming location & attire.
◆ License plate data linking the suspect to a getaway vehicle.
◆ Enhanced background audio revealing accomplice information.

🔍 Final Outcome:

📌 Law enforcement arrested the suspect based on overwhelming digital evidence.
📌 The suspect's social media activity, clothing match, and getaway vehicle played a crucial role in the conviction process.

6. Key Takeaways from This Case Study

✓ AI-powered facial & object recognition can identify partially concealed suspects.

✓ Social media OSINT plays a vital role in verifying identities & locations.

✓ Audio analysis can reveal overlooked clues in surveillance videos.

✓ AI-based LPR can reconstruct blurred license plates for vehicle tracking.

✓ Cross-referencing satellite, street view, and OSINT techniques improves verification accuracy.

📌 **Conclusion**: This case highlights how modern OSINT combines AI, geolocation, and video forensics to successfully track suspects using digital footprints.

11. Case Study: Solving Crimes with Image OSINT

In this chapter, we will examine a real-world case study that demonstrates the power of image-based OSINT in solving crimes. Through detailed analysis of visual evidence—such as photographs, videos, and geotagged media—analysts can piece together crucial information that helps identify suspects, verify alibis, and uncover hidden connections. We will walk through the step-by-step process of how image OSINT techniques were applied in a specific criminal investigation, highlighting the tools and strategies used to track down key evidence. This case study will illustrate the practical applications of image analysis, providing a deeper understanding of how visual intelligence can be pivotal in criminal justice and security operations.

11.1 Using Image Analysis to Track Down Criminals & Missing Persons

In the digital age, images play a critical role in tracking down criminals and locating missing persons. Investigators, law enforcement agencies, and OSINT analysts rely on advanced image analysis techniques to extract clues, verify locations, and identify individuals based on publicly available data. Whether it's identifying a suspect from security footage, tracing a missing person through social media posts, or verifying the authenticity of an image, OSINT techniques provide valuable insights. This chapter explores how image-based investigations are conducted, the tools used, and real-world case applications.

1. Leveraging Reverse Image Search in Investigations

One of the fundamental methods in image-based OSINT is reverse image searching, which allows analysts to find the origin of a photograph, track reposts, and identify patterns.

✓ **Tracking Down Criminals**: Law enforcement agencies use reverse image search engines like Google Lens, TinEye, and Yandex to check if a suspect's image appears in different locations online. A simple mugshot or a social media profile photo can reveal past activity, aliases, and connections.

✓ **Finding Missing Persons**: Families and search organizations use reverse image search to locate missing persons by tracking their last known social media photos or finding similar images posted elsewhere. This technique has been instrumental in cases where traffickers manipulate victims' identities and re-upload their pictures with altered details.

💡 **Case Example**: A missing teenager was found after an investigator used Yandex reverse image search to locate an altered version of her social media profile picture on a classified ads website.

2. Identifying Clues from Social Media Images

Social media platforms provide a wealth of information through user-posted images. OSINT investigators can extract critical location data, timestamps, and user interactions to track a person's movements.

What Clues Can Be Extracted?

🔍 **Geotags & Metadata**: While many platforms strip EXIF metadata from uploaded images, some platforms still retain location data, which can be extracted with tools like ExifTool, FOCA, and FotoForensics.

🔍 **Background Objects & Landmarks**: Even if an image doesn't contain direct location data, background details—such as billboards, unique buildings, street signs, and natural landscapes—can help pinpoint a specific area.

🔍 **Reflections & Shadows**: Mirrors, windows, and even sunglasses can reveal information about the surroundings, including the photographer or other individuals present in the scene.

💡 **Case Example**: A fugitive on the run was identified after investigators analyzed the reflection in his sunglasses in a selfie he posted online, which revealed the location of a distinct hotel sign in the background.

3. Analyzing Surveillance Footage & CCTV Images

Security cameras provide crucial footage for tracking criminals and identifying suspicious behavior. However, analyzing low-quality video frames requires specialized techniques.

Enhancing Image Quality from Footage

✓ **AI-Based Image Enhancement**: Tools like Topaz Gigapixel AI, ClearID, and Adobe Enhance can clarify blurry images, increase sharpness, and improve facial recognition accuracy.

✓ **Object & License Plate Recognition**: Using tools like OpenALPR, investigators can extract license plate numbers from surveillance footage, even in low-resolution or night-time images.

✓ **Behavioral Analysis & Pattern Recognition**: AI-driven video analytics can track a suspect's movement patterns, identify recurring visits to locations, and detect suspicious activities.

💡 **Case Example**: Investigators used AI-enhanced CCTV footage to extract a partial license plate number, which was cross-referenced with local traffic databases to identify a getaway car.

4. Identifying Criminals Using Facial Recognition & AI

AI-powered facial recognition has transformed OSINT investigations by allowing authorities to compare facial features across massive databases.

How Facial Recognition Assists OSINT Investigations

✓ **Comparing Faces Against Databases**: Platforms like Clearview AI, PimEyes, and Amazon Rekognition scan faces against publicly available images to find matches.

✓ **Cross-Matching Social Media Profiles**: Even if a suspect uses different names and accounts, AI can detect similar facial structures across multiple platforms.

✓ **Age Progression & Missing Persons Identification**: AI tools help predict how a missing person might look after months or years of disappearance, aiding long-term search efforts.

💡 **Case Example**: A criminal who had been in hiding for years was discovered after a facial recognition match found his image in a newly created online dating profile.

5. Tracking Missing Persons Using OSINT & Geolocation

When someone goes missing, every image posted online can provide a breadcrumb trail leading to their whereabouts. OSINT analysts use a combination of image clues, social media activity, and geolocation techniques to track movements.

Methods for Tracking Missing Persons

✓ **Checking Recent Social Media Uploads**: Even if metadata is removed, the type of environment, weather, and background objects in a photo can provide insights into where the person might be.

✓ **Crowdsourced Image & Video Analysis**: Platforms like Bellingcat use community-driven efforts to verify missing person cases by analyzing user-submitted media.

✓ **Satellite & Street View Comparison**: Google Earth and Bing Maps can help match landscapes, buildings, or intersections seen in a missing person's last known image.

💡 **Case Example**: A missing backpacker was located after investigators compared recent social media photos with Google Street View images, leading to a remote hiking trail where they had last been seen.

6. Ethical & Privacy Considerations in Image-Based Investigations

While OSINT tools provide powerful capabilities, ethical concerns must always be addressed:

⚠️ **Respecting Privacy**: Just because an image is publicly available does not always mean it should be used in an investigation.
⚠️ **Avoiding False Accusations**: OSINT analysts must verify findings through multiple sources before drawing conclusions.
⚠️ **Legal Boundaries**: Investigating private individuals without legal permission may violate data protection laws like GDPR and CCPA.

7. Key Takeaways

✓ Reverse image searching helps track down criminals & missing persons by identifying reposted or altered images.

✓ Social media images contain valuable clues like geotags, background landmarks, and timestamps.

✓ AI-powered facial recognition can identify individuals across multiple online platforms.

✓ CCTV footage & surveillance images can be enhanced to extract key details for investigations.

✓ Ethical considerations must always be taken into account when using OSINT techniques.

📌 **Conclusion**: Image analysis is an indispensable tool in modern investigations, helping law enforcement, journalists, and OSINT analysts uncover critical details in criminal cases and missing person searches.

11.2 How Investigators Use Open-Source Images in Crime Solving

Open-source images—photos and videos publicly available online—have become a crucial asset for investigators solving crimes. From social media posts to satellite imagery, these resources provide valuable clues about suspects, victims, and crime scenes. Law enforcement agencies, journalists, and OSINT analysts leverage open-source images to identify locations, verify alibis, track movements, and even uncover hidden connections. In this section, we'll explore the various ways investigators use open-source imagery, the tools they rely on, and real-world case examples.

1. What Are Open-Source Images?

Open-source images are any publicly accessible images found online, including:

✓ Social media photos (Instagram, Twitter, Facebook, TikTok)

✓ User-uploaded videos (YouTube, live-streaming platforms)

✓ Publicly shared satellite imagery (Google Earth, Sentinel Hub)

✓ News articles & press photos

✓ Government & corporate databases (CCTV footage, city cameras)

These images often contain hidden clues that can be extracted using OSINT techniques.

2. Identifying Crime Scenes Using Online Photos

One of the first steps in an OSINT image-based investigation is determining the location of a crime scene. Investigators analyze details in photos or videos to pinpoint an exact location.

Techniques Used to Identify Crime Scenes

🔍 **Landmarks & Background Objects**: Unique buildings, billboards, street signs, and natural features help identify a region or city. Tools like Google Lens, Mapillary, and OpenStreetMap assist in cross-referencing objects with known locations.

🔍 **Geotagging & Metadata**: Some images retain EXIF metadata, which includes GPS coordinates, timestamps, and camera details. Analysts use tools like ExifTool and FotoForensics to extract and verify metadata.

🔍 **Comparing Images with Street View**: Google Earth, Bing Maps, and Yandex Maps help match background elements, such as road layouts, skyline features, and storefronts, with real-world locations.

💡 **Case Example**: Investigators identified a human trafficking operation by analyzing the background of a TikTok live stream, which contained a partially visible sign and a distinct highway exit that was matched to a specific location.

3. Tracking Suspects Through Social Media Images

Criminals frequently leave digital breadcrumbs in their online photos. OSINT investigators analyze their social media posts to determine where they are, who they associate with, and what activities they engage in.

How Social Media Images Help Investigations

✓ **Reverse Image Search**: Helps identify if a suspect's photo has been used on multiple accounts or linked to past crimes. Tools like Google Reverse Image Search, TinEye, and PimEyes assist in finding matches.

✓ **Reflections & Background Analysis**: Mirrors, car windows, and sunglasses often capture unexpected details that reveal more than what the suspect intended.

✓ **Tracking Locations Over Time**: By analyzing multiple posts, investigators can map out a pattern of movement and predict where a suspect might be heading.

💡 **Case Example**: A fugitive was caught after posting a picture at a fast-food restaurant. Investigators identified the restaurant through its unique furniture design, cross-referenced it with Google Maps, and alerted local authorities.

4. Verifying Alibis & Uncovering Deception

Open-source images are also used to confirm or debunk suspect alibis. If a suspect claims to have been in one place at a certain time, investigators can analyze images from that time frame to verify the claim.

Methods for Verifying Alibis

✓ **Analyzing Weather & Shadows**: The sun's position and weather conditions in an image can be checked against historical weather records to confirm if a suspect's claim is accurate.

✓ **Cross-Checking Surveillance Footage**: CCTV cameras, dashcams, and smart doorbells provide time-stamped footage that can confirm or contradict a suspect's statements.

✓ **Timestamp Analysis**: Even if an image's metadata is altered, analysts can verify authenticity by cross-referencing with other sources, such as news footage or social media check-ins.

💡 **Case Example**: A suspect in a burglary claimed to be at home during the crime, but an image of him at a shopping mall ATM, taken minutes before the incident, disproved his alibi.

5. Using AI & Facial Recognition in Image Analysis

Advancements in AI have significantly improved image-based OSINT investigations. Facial recognition, object detection, and deep learning algorithms help identify suspects, weapons, and vehicles from blurry or low-resolution images.

Key AI Tools Used in Crime Investigations

✓ **Clearview AI & PimEyes**: Facial recognition software compares suspect images with millions of online photos.

✓ **Amazon Rekognition & Microsoft Azure AI**: Identifies objects, text, and emotions in crime scene photos.

✓ **OpenALPR**: Extracts license plate numbers from surveillance images.

💡 **Case Example**: A stolen car linked to an armed robbery was identified by running traffic cam footage through OpenALPR, which matched the license plate to a suspect's vehicle.

6. Case Studies: Real-World Examples of Image-Based Crime Solving

💡 Case #1: Catching a Serial Fraudster Using Reverse Image Search

A scammer was caught after using the same stolen profile picture across multiple fraudulent online shops. Investigators ran a reverse image search and discovered the image had been taken from a real business owner's website.

💡 Case #2: Identifying a Terrorist Safe House Using Google Earth

A terrorist group posted propaganda videos with unusual roof shapes and mountain ranges in the background. Analysts matched these features using Google Earth and pinpointed the group's hideout in a remote location.

💡 Case #3: Locating a Kidnapper Through Instagram Photos

A kidnapper's Instagram selfies contained reflections of unique city buildings. OSINT analysts used Google Street View to match the structures and helped authorities rescue the victim within 24 hours.

7. Ethical & Legal Considerations in Using Open-Source Images

While open-source images provide powerful investigative tools, ethical and legal concerns must always be considered:

⚠️ **Privacy Laws & Regulations**: Some jurisdictions have strict data protection laws (e.g., GDPR, CCPA) that limit how images can be used in investigations.
⚠️ **Avoiding False Positives**: Misidentifying a suspect due to AI errors or faulty image analysis can have serious consequences. Always verify through multiple sources.
⚠️ **Responsible Use of Facial Recognition**: Many facial recognition databases contain unverified data, which can lead to incorrect matches and privacy violations.

8. Key Takeaways

✓ Open-source images provide crucial clues in crime investigations, helping locate suspects, verify alibis, and analyze crime scenes.

✓ Reverse image searching, geolocation analysis, and metadata extraction are essential tools for investigators.

✓ Social media images can reveal hidden details, including reflections, timestamps, and background landmarks.

✓ AI-powered facial recognition and license plate analysis improve crime-solving accuracy.

✓ Ethical considerations must always be taken into account when using open-source images in investigations.

📌 **Conclusion**: Open-source image analysis has revolutionized modern crime investigations. With the right tools and techniques, OSINT investigators can extract valuable intelligence from publicly available photos, leading to faster crime resolution and stronger evidence gathering.

11.3 Combining Image & Geolocation OSINT with Other Data Sources

Image and geolocation intelligence (GEOINT) are powerful tools in OSINT investigations, but their full potential is realized when combined with other data sources. Cross-referencing images with social media activity, public records, satellite imagery, and financial data can provide a more comprehensive understanding of a subject's movements, connections, and activities. This chapter explores how OSINT analysts merge multiple data streams to enhance investigative accuracy and efficiency.

1. The Power of Multi-Source OSINT Analysis

Using images and geolocation data in isolation has limitations. A photo may provide clues about a location, but without additional context, it can be difficult to determine the date, the people involved, or the events surrounding it. By integrating other data sources, investigators can verify findings, uncover new leads, and reduce the risk of misinformation.

Key Benefits of Multi-Source OSINT Analysis

✓ **Improved Accuracy**: Cross-referencing image details with metadata, satellite views, and public databases ensures findings are credible and verifiable.

✓ **Contextual Understanding**: A single image can be misleading without additional data. Combining sources helps establish who, what, when, and where.

✓ **Detecting Anomalies & Deception**: If an image is manipulated or staged, additional sources (like social media posts, weather reports, and timestamps) can reveal inconsistencies.

✓ **Faster Investigations**: Automated tools and databases help analysts quickly filter out false leads and focus on high-value intelligence.

2. Cross-Referencing Images with Social Media Data

Social media platforms contain a wealth of images, videos, and location-based posts that can be used to verify geolocation intelligence. Investigators analyze profiles, timestamps, hashtags, and engagement patterns to establish connections.

Methods for Cross-Referencing Social Media Data

🔍 **Reverse Image Search**: Checking if an image appears across multiple platforms helps verify authenticity and track reposting trends. Tools like Google Lens, TinEye, and PimEyes assist in finding original sources.

📍 **Geotagged Posts**: Many social media users tag locations in their photos. Investigators use Twitter's advanced search, Instagram's location tags, and TikTok's metadata to map a subject's movements.

☐ **Timestamp Verification**: Comparing an image's timestamp with social media check-ins, live-streams, or local news reports ensures chronological accuracy.

💡 **Case Example**: Investigators tracked a fugitive by analyzing Instagram posts with recognizable city landmarks. Cross-referencing the images with local street cams and Google Street View helped pinpoint his real-time location.

3. Verifying Image Locations with Public & Private Databases

To confirm the authenticity of geolocated images, analysts compare them with publicly available datasets and private intelligence sources.

Data Sources for Verifying Locations

✓ **Public Mapping Databases**: Google Earth, OpenStreetMap, Bing Maps, and Sentinel Hub provide historical and current satellite images for location verification.

✓ **Government Records & Licenses**: Land registry databases, building permits, and business directories can confirm whether a structure or facility exists at a given location.

✓ **Security Camera Footage**: Many cities have publicly accessible CCTV and traffic camera feeds that can confirm events captured in photos.

✓ **Weather Data Archives**: Websites like Time and Date or NOAA provide historical weather records to check if an image's conditions match reality.

💡 **Case Example**: A suspect claimed to have been in Paris on a specific date, but OSINT analysts discovered his image's background showed a sunny sky when official weather reports confirmed heavy rainfall that day—proving his alibi was false.

4. Combining GEOINT with Financial & Transaction Data

Financial transactions, credit card purchases, and blockchain analysis can be combined with image intelligence to establish a subject's movement patterns and activities.

Methods for Using Financial Data in Image & GEOINT Investigations

✓ **Matching Receipts & Transactions with Locations**: If a suspect uploads a photo of a restaurant meal or hotel stay, cross-checking bank records or business receipts can confirm or contradict the timeline.

✓ **Cryptocurrency & Dark Web Analysis**: Many criminals use Bitcoin or other cryptocurrencies, and OSINT analysts use blockchain explorers to trace transactions linked to specific locations or purchases.

✓ **ATM & Retail Security Footage**: If an image is taken near a financial institution, investigators can request withdrawal logs and security camera footage.

💡 **Case Example**: Investigators uncovered a fraud operation after a suspect posted an image of a luxury watch. Cross-referencing the purchase timestamp with credit card records revealed that the transaction was linked to a stolen identity.

5. Integrating Mobile Data & Telecommunications in Image-Based OSINT

Cell phone data, call logs, and Wi-Fi geolocation can supplement image-based intelligence. OSINT analysts use mobile forensics to correlate photos, location pings, and digital footprints.

Key Techniques for Mobile Data Integration

✓ **Wi-Fi & Bluetooth Tracking**: If an image includes a visible router name or Bluetooth device, it can be cross-referenced with public databases to determine location.

✓ **Call & Message Logs**: Investigators use metadata from cell towers to track a subject's phone movement in relation to the images they post.

✓ **IMEI & Device Fingerprinting**: If an image is captured on a specific phone model, tracking its IMEI number can reveal past locations.

💡 **Case Example**: A missing person was found when OSINT analysts identified a Wi-Fi hotspot in the background of a social media photo. Using public Wi-Fi mapping tools, they traced the hotspot to a remote café, leading to a successful rescue.

6. AI & Machine Learning for Multi-Source Image OSINT

Artificial intelligence and machine learning enhance OSINT investigations by automating image comparisons, facial recognition, and anomaly detection.

How AI Enhances Image-Based Investigations

☐ **Facial Recognition Software**: Identifies suspects and missing persons from databases of publicly available images.
☐ **Automated Geospatial Analysis**: AI-driven tools like PlanetScope and DeepGlobe analyze satellite imagery for environmental changes, movement patterns, and structural modifications.
🏙 **Behavioral Pattern Detection**: AI can analyze thousands of images and predict where a person is likely to go next based on past movements.

💡 **Case Example**: AI-powered satellite imagery detected a pattern of vehicle movements near an abandoned warehouse, which led to the discovery of an illegal weapons storage facility.

7. Case Study: Identifying a Human Trafficking Network Using Multi-Source OSINT

A global human trafficking network was exposed using a combination of:

✔ Reverse Image Searches to find matching photos of victims across multiple escort websites.

✔ Social Media Analysis to track posts of traffickers luring victims.

✔ Satellite Imagery & Geolocation Tools to map frequent travel routes and safe houses.

✔ Financial Data to trace suspicious transactions and crypto payments.

✔ AI Facial Recognition to match missing persons with known traffickers.

Through multi-source OSINT integration, law enforcement agencies rescued several victims and dismantled an international trafficking ring.

8. Key Takeaways

✓ Combining image intelligence with other OSINT sources increases accuracy and efficiency.

✓ Social media data, public databases, and financial records help verify locations and identities.

✓ AI and machine learning automate facial recognition, geospatial tracking, and behavioral predictions.

✓ Multi-source analysis is crucial in crime investigations, fraud detection, and national security efforts.

✓ Ethical considerations and privacy laws must be respected when merging different OSINT datasets.

✦ **Conclusion**: Successful OSINT investigations depend on combining multiple intelligence sources to cross-verify data, detect deception, and generate actionable insights. Whether solving crimes, tracking threats, or identifying fraud, image & geolocation OSINT is most powerful when integrated with broader digital intelligence techniques.

11.4 Real-World Cases Where Image Intelligence Helped Solve Crimes

Image intelligence has played a crucial role in solving crimes worldwide, from identifying criminals through facial recognition to geolocating victims based on photo backgrounds. OSINT analysts, law enforcement agencies, and investigative journalists have used open-source images, metadata, and geospatial data to track down fugitives, expose fraud, and dismantle criminal networks. In this section, we examine notable real-world cases where image intelligence was the key to cracking an investigation.

1. Identifying a War Criminal Using Reverse Image Search

In 2018, an independent group of OSINT researchers uncovered the identity of a war criminal responsible for human rights violations in the Middle East. A single image of a uniformed soldier appeared on social media, but no one knew his identity.

How Image OSINT Helped Solve the Case

✓ **Reverse Image Search**: Analysts used Google Lens and TinEye to trace the image to an older, low-quality version on an obscure military forum.

✓ **Facial Recognition**: The subject's face was compared to publicly available photos using open-source tools like PimEyes.

✓ **Uniform & Insignia Analysis**: Experts identified military patches and rank insignia unique to a specific faction.

✓ **Geolocation of the Background**: The landscape in the image was cross-referenced with Google Earth Pro and Sentinel-2 satellite imagery to confirm the location.

🔎 **Outcome**: OSINT analysts provided law enforcement with strong evidence, which led to the identification, arrest, and trial of the suspect for war crimes.

2. Finding a Missing Child Through Social Media Photo Clues

In 2020, a missing child case gained traction after a concerned citizen spotted a photo of a young girl on a private Facebook group. The case had been cold for months, but investigators leveraged image intelligence to track her down.

How Image OSINT Helped Solve the Case

✓ **EXIF Metadata Analysis**: Analysts extracted GPS coordinates from the image using tools like ExifTool, revealing a possible location in Eastern Europe.

✓ **Background Details & Geolocation**: The image included a playground with unique structures. Researchers compared it with Google Street View to pinpoint the park.

✓ **Social Media Cross-Referencing**: By analyzing post timestamps and social media activity, investigators determined who uploaded the photo and their connection to the missing child.

🔎 **Outcome**: Law enforcement raided the suspect's residence and rescued the child. The traffickers were arrested, and OSINT techniques played a pivotal role in closing the case.

3. Tracking Down a Fraudster Using Instagram Travel Photos

A financial fraudster had scammed multiple victims through an elaborate Ponzi scheme and fled the country. He continued posting vacation photos on Instagram, believing they wouldn't reveal his whereabouts. However, OSINT analysts were able to track him down using image intelligence techniques.

How Image OSINT Helped Solve the Case

✓ **Landmark Identification**: Analysts used Google Image Search and Yandex to match backgrounds with famous tourist locations.

✓ **Cross-Referencing Social Media Posts**: Each image was compared to public Snapchat and TikTok location-based stories, revealing real-time movements.

✓ **Analyzing Shadows & Weather Conditions**: Investigators determined the exact time of day using solar position calculators, verifying his presence at specific locations.

✓ **Tracking Hotel Windows & City Views**: By examining the hotel balcony view in his images, analysts found a match in booking sites and travel forums.

🔎 **Outcome**: Authorities issued an international arrest warrant, leading to his capture in Thailand, thanks to OSINT image analysis.

4. Solving a Homicide Case Using Security Camera Footage & Image Enhancement

In a 2019 unsolved homicide case, law enforcement had grainy CCTV footage of a suspect leaving the crime scene, but the face was unclear. Investigators turned to OSINT and forensic image analysis to identify the killer.

How Image OSINT Helped Solve the Case

✓ **Video Frame Extraction & Enhancement**: Investigators extracted high-quality still frames from the video and enhanced them using AI-based image restoration tools.

✓ **Clothing & Shoe Recognition**: The suspect's unique sneakers and jacket were matched to a brand and model, narrowing the suspect pool.

✓ **Social Media Matching**: Analysts found a similar outfit in a suspect's old Instagram post, leading to further verification.

✓ **Street View Correlation**: The building's reflections in glass windows were used to cross-reference the exact camera position using Google Street View.

🔎 **Outcome**: The suspect was arrested after fingerprints and witness testimonies confirmed the findings from the OSINT image analysis.

5. Verifying a Terrorist's Location Through Open-Source Photos

A known terrorist leader was hiding in an unknown location but continued to release propaganda photos and videos online. Intelligence agencies used OSINT methods to pinpoint his hiding spot.

How Image OSINT Helped Solve the Case

✓ **Background Object Analysis**: Investigators noticed a specific type of electrical pole and road markings, which were matched to a region in North Africa.

✓ **Weather & Seasonal Clues**: The foliage and sun angles suggested a specific time of year, helping narrow the timeframe.

✓ **Satellite Imagery Comparison**: Structures in the background were compared with historical satellite images, revealing a likely compound.

✓ **Sound Analysis in Video Files**: Audio forensics identified a distinct call to prayer, which was compared with mosque recordings in different cities.

🔎 **Outcome**: The suspect's location was confirmed, leading to a coordinated military operation that neutralized the threat.

Key Takeaways from These Real-World Cases

✓ **Reverse Image Search Helps Uncover Identities** – Criminals often reuse images across platforms, making them traceable with Google Lens, TinEye, and Yandex.

✓ **Metadata (EXIF Data) Can Reveal Hidden Information** – GPS coordinates, timestamps, and camera models provide clues about an image's authenticity and origin.

✓ **Social Media Images Can Be Cross-Referenced** – People unknowingly reveal clues about their locations, habits, and associates in publicly posted images.

✓ **AI & Machine Learning Enhance Image Analysis** – Advanced algorithms improve facial recognition, object detection, and image restoration for law enforcement.

✓ **Satellite & Street View Data Are Crucial for Geolocation** – Comparing images with Google Earth, OpenStreetMap, and Sentinel-2 helps pinpoint exact locations.

✓ **Criminals Can Be Identified by Their Backgrounds** – Even minor details like street signs, weather conditions, and shadows can expose a suspect's whereabouts.

✦ **Conclusion**: Image intelligence is one of the most powerful tools in OSINT investigations. Whether tracking down fugitives, solving fraud cases, or exposing war criminals, the ability to analyze, verify, and geolocate images has led to countless breakthroughs in crime-solving efforts.

With the advancement of AI, OSINT tools, and geospatial intelligence, investigators can now solve crimes with greater accuracy and speed—proving that even the smallest image detail can lead to big revelations.

11.5 Applying OSINT Image Techniques to Cyber & Financial Crimes

As financial crimes and cyber fraud continue to evolve, OSINT (Open-Source Intelligence) image analysis techniques have become essential in uncovering fraudulent schemes, tracking illicit financial activities, and exposing cybercriminal networks. From tracing stolen assets to identifying scammers hiding behind fake profiles, image intelligence plays a crucial role in investigations involving money laundering, identity fraud, online scams, and dark web operations. This section explores how OSINT professionals apply image analysis techniques to solve cyber and financial crimes.

1. Identifying Fake Profiles & Online Scams Through Reverse Image Search

Cybercriminals often create fake profiles using stolen or AI-generated images to conduct fraud, romance scams, phishing attacks, or business impersonation schemes. By applying reverse image search techniques, OSINT analysts can detect these fraudulent activities and link scammers to multiple online identities.

How OSINT Image Techniques Help Detect Fake Profiles:

✓ **Reverse Image Searching**: Using Google Lens, TinEye, and Yandex, investigators can check if a profile picture appears elsewhere, often revealing stolen identities.

✓ **AI-Generated Image Detection**: Tools like GAN image detectors help distinguish between real and deepfake-generated profile images used in financial fraud.

✓ **Cross-Platform Profile Matching**: By searching for the same photo on LinkedIn, Instagram, and dating apps, investigators can uncover multiple fraudulent accounts linked to a scammer.

✓ **Background Analysis**: Inconsistencies in photo backgrounds, lighting, and reflections often indicate manipulated or AI-generated images.

🔎 **Real-World Example:**

Investigators used reverse image search to expose a fraudster who created multiple fake LinkedIn accounts impersonating high-ranking executives. The scammer used these profiles to conduct business email compromise (BEC) attacks, tricking employees into transferring money.

2. Tracking Down Fraudulent E-Commerce & Investment Scams

Cybercriminals often use stolen or manipulated images to promote fake e-commerce stores, Ponzi schemes, or cryptocurrency frauds. OSINT image analysis can verify the authenticity of product listings, investment opportunities, and business claims.

How Image OSINT Uncovers Fraudulent Businesses:

✓ **Verifying Business Location Photos**: Comparing images of offices, warehouses, or headquarters with Google Street View helps confirm whether a company actually exists.
✓ **Detecting Stock Photo Misuse**: Scammers frequently use stock images or AI-generated visuals on fake websites. Reverse searching product images can expose deception.
✓ **Tracking Stolen Product Photos**: Fraudulent sellers steal images from legitimate e-commerce sites. Reverse image search can link scam websites to their source.
✓ **Analyzing Cryptocurrency & NFT Images**: Investigating NFT or crypto investment frauds involves checking metadata and watermarks to verify authenticity.

🔎 **Real-World Example:**

A global Ponzi scheme used fake luxury real estate images to lure investors. OSINT researchers discovered that the photos were stolen from property listing websites, leading to the exposure of the fraudulent operation.

3. Using Image Metadata & Geolocation in Money Laundering Investigations

Financial criminals use fake invoices, real estate purchases, and luxury goods transactions to launder illicit funds. OSINT analysts can extract EXIF metadata from photos to uncover critical details such as GPS coordinates, timestamps, and camera models used in money laundering operations.

How OSINT Image Analysis Helps in Money Laundering Cases:

✓ **EXIF Metadata Extraction**: Investigators extract hidden GPS data from images of real estate, vehicles, or jewelry purchases to track money laundering routes.

✓ **Analyzing Social Media Luxury Displays**: Criminals flaunt their wealth on Instagram and TikTok, revealing locations, assets, and associates.

✓ **Matching Real Estate Photos with Property Registries**: Image analysis can help verify whether a listed property actually exists or is a front for illicit transactions.

✓ **Identifying Patterns in Luxury Item Purchases**: OSINT tools help analyze watches, cars, and yachts featured in social media images to track money laundering operations.

🔍 **Real-World Example:**

A notorious drug cartel's money laundering scheme was exposed when investigators matched the GPS coordinates from a luxury car photo on Instagram with a known cartel member's property. The evidence helped authorities seize millions in assets.

4. Detecting Cybercrime Networks Using Dark Web Image Analysis

Cybercriminals operating on the dark web often share stolen data, fraudulent documents, and illicit goods through image-based advertisements. OSINT experts use image recognition tools to track these illicit activities across forums, marketplaces, and Telegram groups.

How OSINT Image Analysis Helps Uncover Cybercrime Operations:

✓ **Detecting Watermarks & Logos**: Many darknet marketplaces add unique watermarks or digital fingerprints to images, which can be traced back to specific sellers.

✓ **Analyzing Stolen ID Photos**: Fraudulent identity documents sold on the dark web often contain traces of editing or inconsistencies in fonts, lighting, and backgrounds.

✓ **Cross-Referencing Dark Web & Surface Web Images**: Images of stolen credit cards, fake passports, or counterfeit goods are often tested in open-source marketplaces before full distribution.

✓ **AI-Powered Facial Recognition**: OSINT analysts use facial recognition tools to identify criminals appearing in darknet forums or cryptocurrency scam videos.

🔎 **Real-World Example:**

A major cyber fraud ring selling fake passports was dismantled after OSINT investigators matched ID document images from a dark web forum with leaked data from a previous security breach.

5. Identifying Fake Invoices & Document Forgeries Through Image Analysis

Financial criminals create fake invoices, bank statements, and forged identification documents for fraud and tax evasion. OSINT tools can detect anomalies in these images to uncover deception.

How OSINT Image Techniques Help Detect Forged Documents:

✓ **Image Enhancement for Forensic Analysis**: AI tools enhance low-quality scans to detect manipulated text and stamp alterations.

✓ **Checking Document Templates Against Public Records**: Comparing official templates of passports, IDs, and bank statements with submitted documents can expose forgeries.

✓ **Verifying Official Seals & QR Codes**: Many forged documents lack correct security features, which can be identified through image magnification.

✓ **Analyzing Digital Artifacts in Scanned Images**: Detecting pixel inconsistencies, compression artifacts, and cloning patterns helps reveal document tampering.

🔎 **Real-World Example:**

A multi-million dollar tax fraud case was exposed when OSINT analysts found discrepancies in invoice images. The criminals had digitally altered dates and serial numbers, leading to their conviction.

Key Takeaways from OSINT Image Techniques in Cyber & Financial Crimes

✓ **Reverse Image Search Uncovers Fake Identities** – Scammers and fraudsters use stolen images, which can be detected using Google Lens, TinEye, and Yandex.

✓ **Metadata Extraction Helps in Money Laundering Cases** – Hidden GPS data, timestamps, and camera details can trace illicit transactions and assets.

✓ **Social Media Images Reveal Luxury Purchases Linked to Crime** – Criminals unknowingly expose themselves through Instagram posts, TikTok videos, and LinkedIn updates.

✓ **Dark Web Image Analysis Links Cybercriminals to Illegal Activities** – Investigators track stolen documents, counterfeit goods, and fraud schemes through darknet image analysis.

✓ **AI-Powered Image Analysis Enhances Fraud Detection** – Advanced tools help identify manipulated documents, detect forgeries, and analyze financial records.

📌 **Conclusion**: OSINT image intelligence is a game-changer in cyber and financial crime investigations. By leveraging reverse image search, metadata extraction, geolocation tools, and forensic document analysis, investigators can track scammers, expose fraud, and dismantle criminal networks. As financial crimes become more sophisticated, mastering OSINT image techniques is essential for modern investigators, analysts, and law enforcement agencies.

11.6 Final Challenge: Conducting a Complete OSINT Image Investigation

In this final challenge, we bring together all the techniques and methodologies covered in this book to conduct a full-scale OSINT image investigation. This exercise is designed to simulate a real-world case where analysts must use a combination of reverse image searching, metadata extraction, geolocation analysis, and social media tracking to uncover crucial intelligence.

The Case Scenario: Unmasking an Online Scammer

A financial fraud investigator has received a tip about an investment scam operating under different aliases on social media. The scammer, posing as a cryptocurrency expert, lures victims into sending money with promises of high returns. Victims report that they interacted with this individual primarily through Instagram and Telegram, where he shared images of luxury cars, exotic vacations, and cryptocurrency trading setups.

Your mission is to:

- Identify the person behind the fraudulent accounts
- Verify if the images used on social media are authentic or stolen
- Determine the scammer's location using image-based OSINT techniques
- Uncover additional social media accounts and connections

Step 1: Reverse Image Search – Tracing Stolen or Reused Images

Objective:

Find out whether the images used on the scammer's social media profiles are unique or have been copied from other sources.

Action Plan:

✓ **Use Reverse Image Search Tools** – Conduct searches using Google Lens, TinEye, and Yandex on the scammer's profile pictures, background images, and any posted photos.

✓ **Check for Image Manipulation** – Investigate whether the images have been cropped, mirrored, or edited to evade detection.

✓ **Look for Multiple Usage Instances** – If the same image appears on different websites, stock photo libraries, or unrelated profiles, it suggests the scammer is using stolen images.

Findings:

- The "luxury car" image appears in an old Instagram post from a Dubai-based influencer, meaning the scammer likely stole it.
- The "crypto trading setup" image is a stock photo from Shutterstock, proving it is fake.
- The profile picture is found on a LinkedIn profile of a legitimate businessman, suggesting identity theft.

Step 2: EXIF Metadata Extraction – Analyzing Hidden Image Data

Objective:

Determine whether any of the posted images contain hidden metadata revealing the scammer's actual location or camera details.

Action Plan:

✓ **Extract EXIF Data** – Use tools like ExifTool, Jeffrey's Image Metadata Viewer, and FotoForensics to analyze image files.

✓ **Check for GPS Coordinates** – If any photos retain location data, they could reveal where the scammer took them.

✓ **Compare Timestamps** – Look at when the images were taken and whether they align with the scammer's claims.

✓ **Analyze Camera Details** – Determine if multiple images share the same device metadata, suggesting they were taken by the same person.

Findings:

- Some images have no EXIF metadata, indicating they were stripped (common among scammers).
- A single vacation image contains GPS coordinates pointing to a resort in Thailand, potentially revealing the scammer's real location.
- The device information from a few images suggests they were taken with an iPhone 13 Pro, which can help verify future uploads.

Step 3: Geolocation Analysis – Pinpointing Locations Using Photo Clues

Objective:

Analyze visual details within images to determine where they were taken.

Action Plan:

✓ **Analyze Landmarks & Backgrounds** – Use Google Lens and Mapillary to compare visible buildings, mountains, and structures.

✓ **Read Street Signs & Billboards** – Look for language, company names, or phone numbers in the images.

✓ **Match Architecture & Vehicles** – Identify unique architectural styles or license plate formats to narrow down a country.

✓ **Compare With Satellite & Street View** – Use Google Earth, Yandex Maps, or Bing Maps to match locations.

Findings:

- A photo of a skyline closely matches Bangkok, Thailand.
- A reflection in sunglasses reveals a storefront name, which when searched, confirms a location near Sukhumvit Road, Bangkok.
- A beach resort photo contains a unique umbrella design, which is linked to a known luxury hotel in Phuket.

Step 4: Social Media Tracking – Uncovering Other Profiles & Connections

Objective:

Expand the investigation by finding additional social media profiles, aliases, and connections.

Action Plan:

✓ **Cross-Search Usernames & Email IDs** – Use tools like WhatsMyName, Social Searcher, and Namechk to check if the scammer uses the same username elsewhere.

✓ **Check Followers & Friends** – Identify mutual friends, frequent commenters, or tagged individuals in posts.

✓ **Monitor Telegram & Dark Web Mentions** – Use OSINT Telegram tools and dark web search engines to check for scam-related discussions.

Findings:

- The scammer has multiple profiles on Instagram and Twitter under different names but with similar images.
- His Telegram username matches a known scammer group, suggesting a connection to a larger fraud network.
- One of his followers appears to be a collaborator, reposting similar scam content.

Final Report & Conclusion

After conducting a full OSINT image investigation, the following conclusions can be drawn:

Key Findings:

✓ The scammer's images were stolen from influencers, stock photo websites, and unrelated social media accounts.

✓ EXIF metadata from one photo contained GPS coordinates pointing to Thailand, indicating a possible real location.

✓ Visual analysis of background details, street signs, and architecture suggests he operates in Bangkok & Phuket, Thailand.

✓ Cross-referencing usernames and social media accounts linked the scammer to multiple fraudulent profiles and Telegram groups.

Recommended Next Steps:

- Report the findings to relevant financial fraud agencies, social media platforms, and law enforcement.
- Monitor the scammer's activities for new posts, checking for fresh image metadata or clues.
- Continue cross-referencing images in case new connections or locations emerge.
- Engage with cryptocurrency fraud watch groups to warn potential victims.

📌 **Conclusion**: This challenge illustrates how OSINT professionals can conduct end-to-end image investigations using reverse image search, metadata extraction, geolocation analysis, and social media tracking. By applying these techniques, investigators can expose online scammers, uncover hidden details, and ultimately help prevent financial crimes.

Your Turn: Conduct an OSINT Investigation!

Now that you've seen how a full OSINT image investigation works, try it yourself:

🔍 Find an image online and analyze it using reverse search tools.
□□ Attempt to geolocate an image using visible landmarks.
□□♂□ Search for the same image across different platforms to track its history.

By practicing these skills, you'll refine your ability to investigate digital images and uncover critical intelligence in real-world scenarios.

12. Ethical Considerations in Geolocation OSINT

In this chapter, we will explore the ethical considerations involved in geolocation OSINT, emphasizing the importance of balancing investigative goals with privacy rights and legal frameworks. While geospatial data offers powerful tools for analysis, it also raises significant concerns regarding surveillance, consent, and potential misuse of personal information. We will discuss best practices for respecting privacy, navigating ethical dilemmas, and ensuring that geolocation data is used responsibly in investigations. Additionally, we will cover the role of regulations and laws, such as GDPR and other privacy standards, in guiding ethical OSINT practices, ensuring analysts stay within legal boundaries while maximizing the value of geospatial intelligence.

12.1 The Legal Boundaries of Image & Geolocation Investigations

The use of image and geolocation intelligence (OSINT) in investigations must always align with legal frameworks and ethical principles. While open-source intelligence techniques provide powerful tools for tracking individuals, verifying locations, and uncovering hidden information, they also come with privacy risks, potential legal violations, and ethical dilemmas. Understanding the legal boundaries is essential for conducting responsible and lawful investigations.

Understanding the Legal Landscape

Laws governing image and geolocation investigations vary significantly by country and jurisdiction. However, common legal principles regulate the collection, use, and distribution of publicly available images and location data.

1. Privacy Laws & Data Protection Regulations

Many regions have strict privacy laws that limit how images and geolocation data can be collected and analyzed:

- **General Data Protection Regulation (GDPR) [EU]** – Prohibits the unauthorized collection, processing, or sharing of personal data, including geolocation information tied to an individual.

- **California Consumer Privacy Act (CCPA) [US]** – Gives individuals the right to know what personal data is being collected, including any geolocation data used for tracking.
- **UK Data Protection Act (DPA)** – Governs the use of images and location-based tracking under strict consent requirements.
- **Other Jurisdictions** – Countries such as Canada, Australia, and Brazil have data protection laws that restrict how personal images and location data can be used without consent.

2. Legal Use of Publicly Available Images

Many OSINT investigations rely on publicly accessible images found on:

✓ Social media platforms (Twitter, Instagram, Facebook, TikTok)

✓ News websites and blogs

✓ Publicly available street view and satellite imagery

✓ Open government datasets

Key Legal Considerations:

✔ **Public vs. Private Content** – If an image is publicly posted, it may be legally analyzed. However, using photos from private accounts or restricted platforms may violate terms of service and privacy laws.

✔ **Fair Use & Copyright Issues** – Images found online are often protected by copyright. Using them for investigative purposes (without republishing them) is generally legal, but reposting or modifying them could lead to copyright infringement claims.

✔ **Terms of Service Violations** – Platforms like Facebook, Instagram, and LinkedIn prohibit automated data scraping, which means OSINT analysts must navigate legal gray areas when collecting large datasets.

3. Geolocation & Surveillance Laws

The use of geolocation intelligence raises additional legal concerns, especially when tracking individuals:

- **GPS Tracking & Stalking Laws** – Many countries prohibit unauthorized tracking of individuals using GPS-based technologies.

- **Facial Recognition & Biometric Data** – Some jurisdictions, like the EU and Illinois (BIPA law in the U.S.), restrict the use of facial recognition for identification without consent.
- **Drones & Aerial Surveillance** – Laws vary on whether OSINT investigators can use drones to capture images for geolocation purposes. Many regions require permits or prohibit drone-based surveillance altogether.

4. Ethical & Legal Risks in OSINT Investigations

Investigators must balance intelligence gathering with legal and ethical obligations:

● **Risk of Misidentification** – Incorrectly identifying a person or location could lead to defamation, harassment, or legal action.

● **Unlawful Data Collection** – Extracting metadata from images shared in private messages or restricted forums may violate hacking laws (e.g., the U.S. Computer Fraud and Abuse Act).

● **Secondary Harm & Doxxing** – Sharing geolocation intelligence about a person without consent could lead to harassment, stalking, or physical harm.

Best Practices for Legal & Ethical OSINT Investigations

To ensure compliance with legal and ethical standards, investigators should follow these best practices:

✓ **Use Only Publicly Available Data** – Ensure images and location data come from public sources, avoiding private accounts or restricted platforms.

✓ **Verify Data Before Publishing** – Double-check findings to prevent false identifications or misinformation.

✓ **Understand Platform Terms of Service** – Avoid automated scraping or violating site policies when gathering intelligence.

✓ **Respect Privacy & Anonymity** – If an investigation does not require identifying an individual, keep findings anonymous.

✓ **Document Investigative Steps** – Maintain records of how data was collected, verified, and analyzed to ensure legal compliance.

By understanding the legal boundaries of image and geolocation intelligence, OSINT investigators can conduct lawful, responsible, and ethical digital investigations while minimizing legal risks.

12.2 Understanding Privacy Risks & Responsible Data Collection

The use of image and geolocation intelligence in OSINT investigations presents significant privacy risks that must be carefully managed. While collecting publicly available data is often legal, investigators must balance information gathering with ethical responsibility to avoid misuse, unauthorized surveillance, or harm to individuals. This section explores the privacy risks associated with OSINT investigations and outlines best practices for responsible data collection.

Key Privacy Risks in Image & Geolocation OSINT

1. Unintended Exposure of Personal Data

Images often contain hidden metadata (EXIF data), GPS coordinates, and timestamps, which can unintentionally expose an individual's real-time location, home address, or personal details.

⬥ **Example**: A social media photo with embedded GPS data could reveal the exact location where it was taken, making the person vulnerable to doxxing or stalking.

2. Identifying & Targeting Vulnerable Individuals

Tracking people using images can put activists, journalists, whistleblowers, and victims of abuse at risk.

⬥ **Example**: Reverse image searching a protestor's photo could expose their identity and location, leading to harassment or legal consequences in authoritarian regions.

3. Misuse of Publicly Available Data

Even if an image is publicly accessible, using it for surveillance, tracking, or harmful purposes can be ethically questionable and, in some cases, illegal.

⬥ **Example**: Collecting and cross-referencing social media images to track someone's movements without their knowledge or consent could violate privacy laws.

4. Data Retention & Storage Risks

Investigators often store collected images, metadata, and location data in databases. Improper handling of this data can lead to:

✗ Unauthorized access and data breaches

✗ Sharing sensitive findings without proper security measures

✗ Unintentional legal liability if the data is used for harmful purposes

5. Facial Recognition & Biometric Privacy Concerns

AI-powered facial recognition tools raise serious privacy issues, as they can be used to identify individuals without consent. Some jurisdictions have already banned or restricted their use.

◆ **Example**: Scraping images from social media to build a private facial recognition database could violate data protection laws (e.g., GDPR, CCPA).

Principles of Responsible Data Collection in OSINT

To conduct ethical OSINT investigations while minimizing privacy risks, investigators should follow these core principles:

1. Collect Only Necessary & Relevant Data

✓ Avoid mass data collection—only gather images and geolocation data that are directly relevant to the investigation.

✓ If personal information isn't required, do not collect or store it.

2. Follow Platform Terms of Service & Legal Guidelines

✓ Understand platform policies before extracting images from Twitter, Instagram, Facebook, or TikTok.

✓ Do not scrape or automate data collection on platforms where it's prohibited.

3. Respect Anonymity & Minimize Harm

✓ If an investigation does not require identifying a person, blur or anonymize images.

✓ Avoid publishing sensitive geolocation data unless it serves a clear public interest and is legally permissible.

4. Verify Data Before Sharing or Acting on It

✓ Cross-check findings using multiple OSINT techniques to avoid false positives or misidentification.

✓ Do not assume an image's geolocation or context without verification—many images are miscaptioned or taken at different times.

5. Secure & Encrypt Stored Data

✓ Use secure databases and encrypted storage when handling collected images or metadata.

✓ Delete unnecessary data once an investigation is completed to reduce privacy risks.

Ethical Use of OSINT Data in Investigations

Responsible OSINT practitioners balance intelligence gathering with ethical responsibility. Before using images or geolocation data, ask:

◆ Is this data publicly available, and do I have the right to use it?
◆ Does this investigation serve a legitimate public interest?
◆ Could publishing this data put someone at risk?
◆ Have I followed legal, ethical, and security guidelines?

By maintaining ethical standards and prioritizing privacy protection, OSINT investigators can minimize risks and prevent misuse while leveraging image and geolocation intelligence responsibly.

12.3 How OSINT Investigators Can Prevent Misinformation Spread

Misinformation is a significant challenge in OSINT investigations, especially when dealing with images and geolocation data. False or misleading images can easily go viral, fueling disinformation campaigns, hoaxes, and propaganda. OSINT investigators play a crucial role in identifying, verifying, and preventing the spread of misinformation. This section explores strategies, tools, and ethical responsibilities for ensuring accurate intelligence.

Understanding How Misinformation Spreads Through Images & Geolocation

Misinformation often spreads through misattributed, manipulated, or contextually misleading images and videos. Some common tactics include:

1. Reusing Old Images in a False Context

◆ **Example**: An image from a 2011 natural disaster is shared as proof of a current event, misleading the public.

2. Manipulating Image Content (Editing, Cropping, Deepfakes)

◆ **Example**: A political rally image is digitally altered to add or remove individuals, changing the perceived narrative.

3. Misrepresenting Locations & Geotags

◆ **Example**: A warzone photo from Syria is falsely claimed to be from Ukraine, spreading false reports about the conflict.

4. Staged or Fabricated Content

◆ **Example**: A viral video of a supposed riot turns out to be staged footage created for propaganda purposes.

5. Using AI-Generated Deepfakes & Synthetic Media

◆ **Example**: A fake news report with an AI-generated anchor is shared to push a false narrative.

Methods to Prevent Misinformation in Image & Geolocation OSINT

1. Reverse Image Searching to Verify Authenticity

✓ Use Google Lens, TinEye, Yandex, and Bing Image Search to check if an image has been used before in a different context.

✓ Identify older versions of the image to see if it has been misattributed or repurposed.

2. Extracting & Analyzing Metadata

✓ Use tools like ExifTool, Jeffrey's Image Metadata Viewer, and ExifPilot to examine timestamp, GPS location, and device info.

✓ Cross-check metadata with the claimed source and event details to detect inconsistencies.

3. Geolocation Verification

✓ Compare the background of an image with Google Earth, Bing Maps, OpenStreetMap, and Wikimapia.

✓ Look for landmarks, street signs, weather conditions, and shadows to verify if an image was taken at the claimed location.

✓ Use SunCalc to confirm if the lighting and shadows match the reported time of day.

4. Video Frame Extraction & Forensic Analysis

✓ Extract keyframes from videos using ffmpeg or InVID to analyze them individually.

✓ Check for inconsistencies in background details, timestamps, and resolution changes that indicate manipulation.

5. Cross-Referencing Claims with Trusted Sources

✓ Compare reported events with official news sources, eyewitness reports, and fact-checking organizations (e.g., Snopes, Bellingcat, BBC Reality Check).

✓ Use archived versions of web pages to detect edits or removed information.

6. Detecting AI-Generated & Deepfake Images

✓ Use AI-detection tools like Deepware Scanner, Reality Defender, and Microsoft's Video Authenticator to spot deepfake images.

✓ Look for unnatural facial features, inconsistent lighting, or distorted backgrounds—common signs of AI-generated media.

Ethical Considerations When Debunking Misinformation

✓ **Verify Before Sharing** – OSINT investigators must avoid amplifying false content, even when trying to debunk it.

✓ **Provide Clear Evidence** – Use screenshots, metadata analysis, and comparisons to transparently explain why an image is false.

✓ **Avoid Political Bias** – Stay neutral and focus on facts, avoiding confirmation bias when analyzing information.

✓ **Educate & Inform** – Instead of just dismissing misinformation, provide context on how disinformation tactics work.

By applying rigorous verification techniques, OSINT investigators can combat misinformation, expose false narratives, and ensure accurate intelligence gathering.

12.4 Avoiding False Accusations & Image Misinterpretation

In OSINT investigations, the misinterpretation of images and geolocation data can lead to false accusations, reputational damage, and legal consequences. While image intelligence is a powerful tool, it must be applied with rigorous verification, critical thinking, and ethical responsibility to avoid misidentifications and incorrect conclusions.

This section explores common pitfalls, best practices, and real-world examples of how OSINT investigators can prevent false accusations based on image analysis.

How False Accusations Happen in Image & Geolocation OSINT

1. Misidentifying People in Photos & Videos

◆ **Example**: An OSINT investigator wrongly identifies an innocent person as a criminal suspect based on a blurry image from security footage.

◆ **Risk**: This can lead to harassment, legal issues, or real-world harm to the wrongly accused person.

2. Incorrectly Geolocating an Image

◆ **Example**: A viral photo claims to show a protest in one country, but it was actually taken in a different location years ago.

◆ **Risk**: Spreading misinformation and fueling false narratives.

3. Misinterpreting Image Context

◆ **Example**: A photo of people holding weapons is shared as "proof" of terrorist activity, but the image is actually from a military training exercise.

◆ **Risk**: This can lead to false accusations, panic, or even diplomatic conflicts.

4. Relying Solely on Reverse Image Search

◆ **Example**: A reverse image search finds an old version of an image online, but fails to recognize that the image has been edited, cropped, or repurposed.

◆ **Risk**: This can lead to wrong conclusions about its origin, intent, or authenticity.

5. Trusting AI-Based Image Recognition Without Human Verification

◆ **Example**: A facial recognition tool falsely matches an individual's face with a criminal in a database.

◆ **Risk**: Automated tools are not always accurate, and without human review, they can misidentify individuals, leading to wrongful accusations.

Best Practices to Avoid False Accusations in OSINT

1. Cross-Verify Images Using Multiple OSINT Methods

✓ Never rely on a single tool or technique—use reverse image search, metadata analysis, and geolocation tools together.

✓ Compare findings with trusted news sources, official reports, and eyewitness accounts.

2. Check Image Metadata & Source Before Drawing Conclusions

✓ Use ExifTool, Jeffrey's Image Metadata Viewer, or FotoForensics to check for GPS data, timestamps, and editing history.

✓ Confirm that the image has not been altered or taken out of context.

3. Analyze Background Details for Geolocation & Time Verification

✓ Use Google Earth, Bing Maps, OpenStreetMap, and Wikimapia to match landmarks, streets, and terrain.

✓ Check weather conditions, shadows, and lighting with tools like SunCalc to confirm the time and date.

4. Be Cautious with Facial Recognition & AI Tools

✓ AI-based image analysis is prone to false positives, so always verify with human review.

✓ If identifying a person, use additional OSINT techniques like social media cross-referencing rather than relying on AI alone.

5. Use Cautious Language & Disclaimers When Reporting Findings

✓ Instead of stating, "This person is definitely involved," use "This individual resembles the subject, but further verification is needed."

✓ Label findings as preliminary until multiple sources confirm them.

6. Avoid Publishing Unverified Claims

✓ Before sharing an OSINT discovery, ensure it is factually correct and responsibly framed.

✓ If an image investigation is inconclusive, do not speculate—acknowledge the uncertainty instead.

Real-World Example: A False Accusation Due to Image Misinterpretation

◆ **Case**: In 2013, during the Boston Marathon bombing investigation, an innocent college student was wrongly accused of being a suspect based on an image shared online.
◆ **Mistake**: OSINT users on Reddit and other forums used visual analysis and crowd-sourced investigations but misidentified the individual.
◆ **Consequence**: The false accusation led to harassment, distress for the family, and police involvement.

◆ **Lesson**: OSINT investigators must avoid jumping to conclusions based on incomplete or misleading image analysis. Verification and responsibility are crucial.

Final Thoughts: Ethical Responsibility in Image-Based OSINT

◆ **Err on the Side of Caution** – It is better to withhold an unverified claim than to risk damaging an innocent person's reputation.
◆ **Recognize the Limits of OSINT** – Image-based investigations cannot always provide definitive proof, and must be supplemented with other evidence.
◆ **Follow Legal & Ethical Standards** – Misinterpretation of images can lead to defamation, lawsuits, or ethical violations.

By applying careful verification, avoiding speculation, and using responsible reporting, OSINT investigators can prevent false accusations and uphold ethical intelligence practices.

12.5 The Future of AI, Deepfakes & Image Manipulation in OSINT

As artificial intelligence (AI) continues to evolve, deepfake technology, AI-generated images, and advanced image manipulation are becoming more sophisticated, posing both challenges and opportunities for OSINT (Open-Source Intelligence) investigators. While AI tools can enhance image verification and analysis, they also create new risks—especially with realistic deepfakes, synthetic media, and AI-assisted misinformation.

This section explores the impact of AI on image-based OSINT, the dangers of deepfakes, and how investigators can adapt to new technologies to maintain the integrity of digital intelligence.

The Role of AI in OSINT Image Analysis

AI-powered tools are transforming image and video OSINT by automating tasks that were once manual and time-consuming. Some key advancements include:

1. AI-Assisted Reverse Image Search

◆ AI-driven reverse image search engines (Google Lens, Yandex, Pimeyes) can now recognize faces, objects, and backgrounds with increasing accuracy.
◆ Enhanced pattern recognition helps in finding modified or cropped versions of an image across the web.

2. Automated Image Recognition & Object Detection

◆ AI-powered tools like Amazon Rekognition, Microsoft Azure Vision, and Google Vision AI can identify faces, landmarks, vehicles, weapons, and logos in images.
◆ These tools help OSINT analysts quickly filter large datasets to find key visual elements in investigations.

3. AI-Based Geolocation Assistance

◆ AI tools can analyze landscapes, street signs, and architectural styles to estimate an image's location.
◆ Google Earth, Sentinel Hub, and AI-powered GIS systems improve satellite and aerial image analysis.

4. Deepfake Detection & Synthetic Image Analysis

◆ AI is being used to detect deepfakes and altered images, with tools like:

✓ **Deepware Scanner** – Detects AI-generated deepfake videos.

✓ **Reality Defender** – Identifies synthetic media manipulation.

✓ **Microsoft's Video Authenticator** – Assesses deepfake credibility.

The Threat of Deepfakes & AI-Generated Misinformation

While AI offers benefits, malicious actors are using deepfake and image manipulation techniques to spread misinformation, commit fraud, and create fake personas for espionage or cybercrime.

1. Deepfake Videos & Synthetic Face Generation

◆ AI can generate hyper-realistic fake videos of political leaders, celebrities, or journalists saying things they never said.
◆ Deepfake voice synthesis makes misinformation even more convincing.
◆ **Example**: In 2022, deepfake videos of Ukrainian President Volodymyr Zelenskyy surfaced, falsely showing him surrendering to Russia.

2. AI-Created Fake Social Media Profiles

◆ AI-generated faces from ThisPersonDoesNotExist.com are being used to create fake social media accounts for disinformation campaigns.
◆ Malicious actors use AI-generated influencers and bots to manipulate online discourse and spread propaganda.

3. Image Manipulation for False Evidence

◆ AI tools can alter images to remove, add, or change objects, making fake news more convincing.
◆ **Example**: A deepfake image of an explosion at the Pentagon went viral in 2023, briefly causing a dip in the stock market before being debunked.

How OSINT Investigators Can Combat AI-Generated Misinformation

1. Deepfake & AI Image Detection Tools

✓ Use AI-driven forensic tools like Forensicly, Deepware Scanner, and Pindrop to detect manipulated media.

✓ Look for inconsistencies in lighting, shadows, and reflections, which AI often struggles to perfect.

2. Cross-Referencing with Verified Sources

✓ Compare images with historical versions, official media, and trusted databases.

✓ If an image or video lacks an authentic source, it should be treated with caution.

3. Examining Metadata & Image Fingerprints

✓ Extract metadata using ExifTool, FotoForensics, or Jeffrey's Image Metadata Viewer to check for inconsistencies in timestamps and GPS data.

✓ Reverse search images on multiple platforms (Google, Bing, Yandex, TinEye) to detect prior usage.

4. Monitoring AI-Generated Content Trends

✓ Stay updated on new AI models capable of producing fake content, such as StyleGAN, DALL·E, and Stable Diffusion.

✓ Recognize how synthetic media is being weaponized in misinformation campaigns.

5. Training & Awareness for OSINT Investigators

✓ Regularly train on emerging AI threats and use AI to enhance investigative capabilities.

✓ Educate journalists, researchers, and the public on how to spot AI-generated misinformation.

The Future: AI as Both a Threat & a Tool for OSINT

◆ The arms race between deepfake creators and detection tools will continue to evolve.

◆ AI-powered OSINT tools will become more automated, improving investigative speed and accuracy.

◆ OSINT investigators must adapt, cross-verify, and stay ahead of AI-driven deception tactics.

By understanding the capabilities and limitations of AI, OSINT analysts can leverage technology for truth-seeking while safeguarding against deception.

12.6 Case Study: A Legal & Ethical Controversy in Image OSINT

The rapid growth of OSINT (Open-Source Intelligence) has led to ethical dilemmas and legal controversies, particularly in image and geolocation investigations. One high-profile case that highlights the complex intersection of ethics, legality, and investigative techniques is the 2020 controversy surrounding the use of facial recognition in OSINT investigations.

The Controversy: Clearview AI & OSINT Investigations

In early 2020, the facial recognition startup Clearview AI was revealed to have scraped billions of publicly available images from social media platforms, news sites, and other online sources. The company then created a reverse image search tool that allowed law enforcement, private investigators, and intelligence agencies to identify individuals simply by uploading a photo.

This revelation sparked global controversy, raising questions about:

✓ **Privacy violations** – Were people's publicly posted images fair game for law enforcement?

✓ **Ethical concerns** – Should OSINT professionals have unrestricted access to facial recognition tools?

✓ **Legal boundaries** – Did Clearview AI violate data protection laws like GDPR (Europe) or CCPA (California)?

The OSINT Debate: Public vs. Private Data in Investigations

Arguments in Favor of Using Clearview AI

✓ **Publicly available data** – Proponents argued that any image posted publicly is fair game for OSINT investigations.

✓ **Crime prevention** – Law enforcement used Clearview AI to identify suspects, missing persons, and victims of human trafficking.

✓ **Efficiency** – OSINT analysts could identify anonymous individuals in images much faster than traditional investigative methods.

Arguments Against Clearview AI's Methods

✗ **Lack of consent** – Individuals never agreed to have their faces included in a massive facial recognition database.

✗ **Privacy invasion** – Unlike traditional OSINT techniques, this tool made it nearly impossible to remain anonymous online.

✗ **Legal violations** – Several countries, including Canada, Australia, and parts of the EU, ruled that Clearview AI's data collection violated privacy laws.

Legal Consequences & Global Response

United States

✓ Some law enforcement agencies defended the use of Clearview AI, citing public safety and counterterrorism efforts.

✓ However, major tech companies, including Facebook, Twitter, and Google, sent cease-and-desist letters to Clearview AI, demanding they stop scraping their platforms.

European Union (EU)

✗ The General Data Protection Regulation (GDPR) ruled that Clearview AI's data collection was illegal, leading to fines and bans in multiple EU countries.

✗ In 2022, Italy fined Clearview AI €20 million for violating privacy laws.

Australia & Canada

✗ National privacy watchdogs ruled that Clearview AI must delete all images of their citizens and cease operations in these countries.

Ethical Lessons for OSINT Analysts

This case study highlights the need for responsible OSINT practices. Ethical OSINT investigators should:

✓ **Understand legal frameworks** – Be aware of local and international data privacy laws before using facial recognition tools.

✓ **Seek consent when appropriate** – Avoid using intrusive technologies that violate privacy rights.

✓ **Prioritize verification & responsible reporting** – Ensure collected data is accurate, ethical, and does not cause harm.

✓ **Balance public interest vs. personal privacy** – Just because data is public does not mean it should be used without ethical consideration.

As OSINT continues to evolve, the debate between security, privacy, and ethical responsibility will remain a central challenge for analysts worldwide.

A single image can tell a story, reveal hidden details, and unlock crucial intelligence—if you know how to analyze it properly. In the world of Open-Source Intelligence (OSINT), image and geolocation analysis is a powerful investigative tool used by journalists, law enforcement, cybersecurity professionals, and researchers to verify information, track subjects, and solve real-world cases.

Image & Geolocation Intelligence: Reverse Searching and Mapping is a deep dive into the techniques and tools used to extract valuable insights from photos, videos, and satellite imagery. Whether you're tracking down the origin of a photo, verifying a location, or conducting a geospatial analysis, this book provides the step-by-step guidance needed to sharpen your OSINT skills.

What You'll Learn in This Book

- **Reverse Image Searching**: Master the use of Google Images, Yandex, Bing, and specialized OSINT tools to trace image origins.
- **EXIF & Metadata Extraction**: Learn how to retrieve hidden data embedded in photos, such as GPS coordinates, camera settings, and timestamps.
- **Satellite & Aerial Imagery Analysis**: Use Google Earth, Sentinel Hub, and other mapping tools to verify locations and track geographical changes.
- **Geolocation Verification**: Learn how to confirm locations using architectural details, weather conditions, and topographical features.
- **Social Media Image Investigations**: Discover how to analyze photos from Instagram, Twitter, and Facebook for intelligence gathering.
- **Facial Recognition & Object Detection**: Explore ethical ways to match faces and identify objects in images using AI-powered tools.
- **Geospatial OSINT Techniques**: Leverage open maps, crowd-sourced geodata, and street views to analyze locations and movements.
- **Deepfake & Image Manipulation Detection**: Learn how to spot altered images and fake media in disinformation campaigns.
- **Privacy & Ethical Considerations**: Understand the ethical and legal boundaries of image and geolocation investigations.

With real-world case studies, hands-on exercises, and expert tips, Image & Geolocation Intelligence gives you the investigative edge to extract valuable intelligence from visual data. Whether you're verifying news, tracking threats, or solving criminal cases, this book provides the essential knowledge to master visual OSINT.

Thank you for exploring Image & Geolocation Intelligence: Reverse Searching and Mapping. The ability to analyze images and verify locations is a crucial skill in today's digital landscape, where misinformation and deception are rampant. By learning these techniques, you are equipping yourself with powerful tools to uncover the truth and contribute to more informed investigations.

Every image tells a story, and we hope this book has helped you decode and interpret the hidden details within visual data. As always, ethical and responsible use of OSINT techniques is paramount—these skills should be used for verification, fact-checking, and legitimate investigations, not for invasion of privacy or malicious intent.

Your curiosity and dedication to learning are what make the OSINT community thrive. We appreciate your time and effort in studying this field, and we encourage you to continue expanding your skills. If you found this book valuable, we'd love to hear from you—your feedback helps us improve and develop more advanced resources for intelligence professionals and researchers.

Stay observant, stay ethical, and keep searching for the truth.

Continue Your OSINT Journey

Expand your skills with the rest of **The OSINT Analyst Series**:

- **OSINT Foundations**: The Beginner's Guide to Open-Source Intelligence
- **The OSINT Search Mastery**: Hacking Search Engines for Intelligence
- **OSINT People Finder**: Advanced Techniques for Online Investigations
- **Social Media OSINT**: Tracking Digital Footprints
- **Domain, Website & Cyber Investigations with OSINT**
- **Email & Dark Web Investigations**: Tracking Leaks & Breaches
- **OSINT Threat Intel**: Investigating Hackers, Breaches, and Cyber Risks
- **Corporate OSINT**: Business Intelligence & Competitive Analysis
- **Investigating Disinformation & Fake News with OSINT**
- **OSINT for Deep & Dark Web**: Techniques for Cybercrime Investigations
- **OSINT Automation**: Python & APIs for Intelligence Gathering
- **OSINT Detective**: Digital Tools & Techniques for Criminal Investigations
- **Advanced OSINT Case Studies**: Real-World Investigations
- **The Ethical OSINT Investigator**: Privacy, Legal Risks & Best Practices

We look forward to seeing you in the next book!

Happy investigating!